D1134998

A FIELD GUIDE TO AUSTRALIAN WILDFLOWERS
VOLUME TWO

A FIELD GUIDE TO

AUSTRALIAN WILDFLOWERS

VOLUME TWO

illustrated by
MARGARET HODGSON

text by
ROLAND PAINE

RIGBY

RIGBY PUBLISHERS • ADELAIDE
SYDNEY • MELBOURNE • BRISBANE • PERTH
NEW YORK • LONDON • AUCKLAND
First published 1977
Reprinted 1982
Copyright © 1977 M. Hodgson and R. Paine
ISBN 0 7270 0203 1
All rights reserved
Wholly designed and typeset in Australia
Printed in Hong Kong
by South China Printing Co.

CONTENTS

PREFACE

Day by day new names are being given to plants which we have learned to know and recognise quite familiarly. No sooner do we learn the new name than it is changed again. Firstly, the species name may be changed and, secondly, the genus. Botanists and research workers have added to their duties the demands of the evergrowing interest of the nature lover and the 'expert' amateur naturalist who presents his local herbarium with seemingly endless numbers of specimens for positive identification.

Many of these specimens are quickly and immediately identified; morphology, habitat and location (area) are all important for identification. However, a few specimens are not so easily identified. Because of some slight variation, the specimen may be identified as far as genus, species, variety, or it may be found that the specimen is known by botanists in one state by one name but by a different name in another state. Several reasons exist for this.

One example of this is *Cheiranthera cyanea* Brongn. being placed in synonymy with *C. linearis* A. Cum. ex Lindley by Putterlick in 1839, and he then being followed by subsequent authors. This has resulted in the name of the type species of the genus, *C. cyanea*, disappearing gradually from modern literature. Researchers studying Brongniart's illustration find sufficient evidence to assume that Putterlick's opinion of *C. cyanea* and *C. linearis* being conspecific is correct. Therefore M. Eichler (1965) accepts the earlier name as the correct name for the plant. (The type locality for *C. cyanea* Brongn. was not indicated with the original description, but it was described in Duperrey's *Voyage de le Coquille*, and from this it is assumed the plant was collected at Sydney in 1824 during the only anchorage in Australia.)

The type species name of *Sollya angustifolia* Lindley (1831) provides another example. It is incorrect because Lindley should have named this species *Sollya fusiformis* as it was based on *Billardiera fusiformis* Labill. (1805). In 1857 Payer described in detail a specimen which probably flowered in the garden of the Museum of National History in Paris as *Sollya fusiformis* without any reference to *Billardiera fusiformis* Labill. which was a published Tasmanian type, but probably came from King George Sound, Western Australia. Finally it was resolved that *Sollya heterophylla* Lindley (1831) is the correct name, being the oldest legitimate synonym, despite *S. fusiformis* Payer most probably being conspecific.

Not only in authors' descriptions and acceptance of names is there a possibility of error or confusion, but in areas of distribution.

Until 1972, there had been no record of *Correa lawrenciana* in northern New South Wales. Previously, var. *glandulifera* had been recorded from Macpherson Range at Springbrook in Queensland. It is interesting to note that Robert Brown, in his manuscript notes, recorded a glandular species of *Correa* from Newcastle, N.S.W. Mr Paul Wilson from Western Australia who recently revised the genus *Correa* for Australia had not seen a specimen of any *Correa lawrenciana* variety from Newcastle, but believed that var. *glandulifera* did once extend southwards into New South Wales, although he felt that it would be unlikely that it would be present as far south as Newcastle. It now seems that Mr Wilson was correct and that var. *glandulifera* does extend into New South Wales. In 1972 large stands of *Correa lawrenciana* var. *glandulifera* were discovered in the Gibraltar Ranges of north New South Wales.

Again we find that, for various reasons during their taxonomic work, authors tend to interpret family limits differently.

In J. C. Willis's '*Dictionary of the Flowering Plants and Ferns*' ed. VIII (1973) we find: *Calectasia* spp. members of *Xanthorrhoeaceae* family. In the National Herbarium of Victoria we find *Calectasia* is placed in its own family, the *Calectasiaceae*. In South Australia we find *Calectasia* in the *Liliaceae* family; in Western Australia, *Xanthorrhoeaceae* is a subfamily of *Liliaceae*; and in New South Wales *Xanthorrhoeaceae* is a family! And this cites only one example of many where the genus is classified in different families and subfamilies, or where different authors have classified subfamilies as families.

How often have replies from herbaria in answer to questions for identification read: 'We have only three previous collections of this species; further specimens would be appreciated . . .', or '. . . apparently a rare species; as we have only three previous collections, further specimens would be welcome', or 'we would like to retain this rare specimen . . .'

In the last few centuries, many botanists, research workers and assistants have observed, collected and documented a tremendous amount of knowledge.

The aboriginals of each country, from experience, were first to gain an intimate knowledge of nature. This was necessary for their survival. With more organised education and the application of existing knowledge, professional researchers and their helpers, together with amateur nature lovers the world over, have now tabulated data which, when fed into computers, could compile a complete dossier of many of the world's plants and their distribution.

Yet another aspect now enters the field of research. Men like Professor John Swan and others from CSIRO in their search for alkaloids are in close collaboration with men like D. E. Symon who supply draft keys to species for collectors in the field.

All this ensures that botany is entering a new and exciting phase. A new awareness has awakened in the scientist, botanist and nature lover alike, each in his own sphere, resulting in an immense corpus of information and knowledge.

The information about each specimen illustrated in this volume, like the first volume, has been compiled from personal observation, and information supplied by herbaria, universities, CSIRO, botanists, and research workers. Many published works have also been consulted and freely used, together with unpublished draft keys by research workers, copies of which have been forwarded to me. I wish to thank Professor John Swan, Vice Chancellor of Monash University; D. E. Symon of Adelaide for the loan of certain unpublished draft keys which were of great help in final identification of critical taxonomic groups; John Williams, Senior Lecturer in Botany at the University of New England; James

Armstrong, Royal Herbarium Sydney; Margery McKenna, Hawthorn, Victoria; and many, many others. My special thanks to Valma Woolley for her patience and understanding while typing this manuscript. I wish to recommend the following as excellent books of reference:

Flora of South Australia, J. M. Black; *Guide to Native Australian Plants*, A. M. Blombery; *Handbook of the Vascular Plants of the Sydney District and the Blue Mountains*, N. C. W. Beadle, O. D. Evans, and R. C. Carolin; *How to know Western Australian Wildflowers*, W. E. Blackall and B. J. Grieve; *Orchids of Australia*, W. Nicholls; *Orchids of New South Wales*, H. M. R. Rupp; *West Australian Plants*, J. S. Beard; *Wild Flowers of Australia*, T. Y. Harris; *Wildflowers of Victoria*, J. Galbraith and others; *Queensland Flora*, F. M. Bailey; *A Dictionary of Botany*, George Usher; *The Language of Botany*, C. Debenham, and many other similar works.

As you traverse this continent of Australia you too will find, as we have found, an unbelievable variation in species from state to state as well as within a state—a testimony to the infinite handiwork of the World's Creator.

May I suggest that should you be serious enough to find yourself collecting specimens for positive identification, you collect the following data at the same time and record it in a special field book.

Name: (to the best of your ability) e.g., *Dendrobium* sp.

Location: e.g., Gwydir Highway 16.5 km from Inverell

Altitude: e.g., approx. 325 metres A.S.L.

Niche: e.g., beside old log

Habitat: e.g., tall woodlands, or rainforest

Abundance: e.g., common, rare, only one seen

Habit: e.g., erect shrub slender plant, climber-creeper

Aspect: e.g., north-east slope ,

Collector: e.g., Roly Paine

Preserved: e.g., 5% ethyl alcohol

Date: e.g., 28/2/75

Specimen number: e.g., E 00. 137 (for your own file)

Herbaria will need a copy of such information. In both Vol. I and II the areas stated, and flowering seasons given, are a generalisation. It would not be impossible to find some plant outside of the area given, and outside the stated flowering time.

This volume is also a guide to help create a greater interest and desire to expand the reader's knowledge and to seek books and works of greater detail. If we have done this, then our work has been worthwhile.

Roland L. Paine

INTRODUCTION

It is not surprising that such a large and unique continent as Australia would be the home for many thousands of species of wildflowers.

Our earlier *A Field Guide to Australian Wildflowers* Volume 1 was limited in size and the number of flowers it could describe. But from the many requests that resulted from it, and with the reprints of the first edition, it became apparent that the first volume would need to be supplemented with a second. Even so, these two volumes could not contain a tenth of Australia's wildflowers; one has only to remember that Gibraltar Range National Park alone has recorded over 525 species of wildflowers. And there are many national parks in Australia, each with its own indigenous species.

Much of Australia's native flora is becoming scarce, if not rare, as more rainforest and forest are felled to make way for man's progress. Many of our wildflowers are rarely seen. Some orchids are known to have flowering cycles of five and seven years with the blooms lasting only a few days, while others are to be found growing in trees thirty to thirty-five metres above the ground.

We have endeavoured to include those flowers which will be seen along highways and byways, in the adjacent hills and fields, and along creeks and rivers of the coastal strips and inland areas. A little rare material has been included for the observer with a keen eye. This book also contains material that was gathered for Volume I, and new specimens which we have since gathered during our travels.

Margaret Hodgson

ABBREVIATIONS

Aff. = akin to, allied to.

Nov. = new.

sp. = species. (singular)

spp. = species. (plural)

ssp. = subspecies.

syn. = synonym = name equivalent to or same as.

var. = variety.

LEAF DESCRIPTIONS

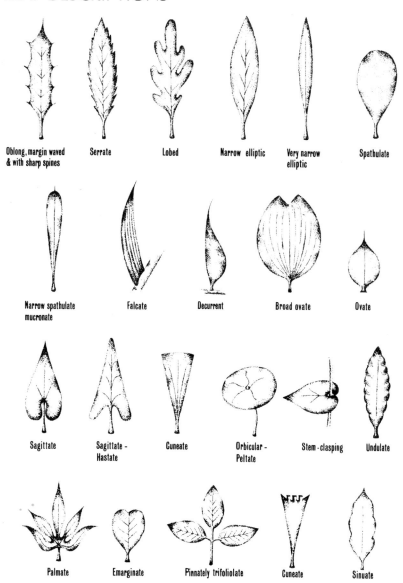

Oblong, margin waved & with sharp spines

Serrate

Lobed

Narrow elliptic

Very narrow elliptic

Spathulate

Narrow spathulate mucronate

Falcate

Decurrent

Broad ovate

Ovate

Sagittate

Sagittate - Hastate

Cuneate

Orbicular - Peltate

Stem - clasping

Undulate

Palmate

Emarginate

Pinnately trifoliolate

Cuneate

Sinuate

LEAF DESCRIPTIONS

Ovate in outline

Linear, apex subulate

Elliptic parallel venation

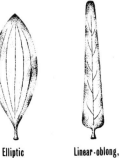

Linear-oblong, obtuse

Orbicular Stem-clasping

Narrow-spathulate obtuse, parellel venation

Narrow-elliptic, linear

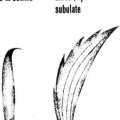

Falcate, serrate

Bipinnate

Deeply-serrate

Serrate

Dentate

Ovate

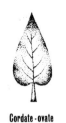

Cordate-ovate

Linear

Cuneate

Denticulate

Linear-oblong dentate

FRONT EDGE VIEW

Revolute

Recurved

Inrolled-involute

Incurved

Convolute

LEAF DESCRIPTIONS

BIPINNATE—Twice pinnately divided.

CAULINE—Attached to or pertaining to the stem (e.g. leaves on the stem).

CONVOLUTE—Rolled together so margins overlap.

CORDATE—Heart shaped, this is often applied to the leaf base only.

CUNEATE—Wedge shaped.

DECURRENT—Extending downwards from the place of insertion; this is applied to leaves when their blades continue down the stem, forming raised lines.

DENTATE—Toothed.

DENTICULATE—Finely toothed.

ELLIPTIC—Shaped like an ellipse.

EMARGINATE—Notched at the apex.

FALCATE—Sickle or scythe shaped.

HASTATE—Spear shaped or triangular with rounded basal lobes.

INCURVED—Curved inwards.

INROLLED—Rolled inwards.

INVOLUTE—Rolled inwards.

LANCEOLATE—Shaped like the head of a lance or spear.

LINEAR—Long and narrow, having parallel sides.

LOBED—A division in the leaf.

MUCRONATE—A sharp, abrupt terminal point.

OBTUSE—Rounded at the apex.

ORBICULAR—Circular or almost.

OVATE—Egg shaped.

PALMATE—Divided into five leaflets, coming from the same point.

PELTATE—The stalk is attached at the back and in the centre of the leaf.

PINNATE—A compound leaf whose leaflets are arranged on the opposite sides of a common petiole.

PINNULES—Leaflets of the smallest order, in a doubly-pinnate leaf as in many wattles.

RADICAL—Springing from the root.

RECURVED—Curved backwards.

REVOLUTE—The margins of leaves rolled back towards the mid-rib.

SAGITTATE—Arrow-head shaped.

SERRATE—Toothed like a saw.

SINUATE—Wavy margin.

SPATHULATE—Spoon shaped.

STEM-CLASPING—Leaf basal clasping around stem.

SUBULATE—Narrow and tapering to a fine point.

TERETE—Almost rounded, cylindrical, not angular.

TRIFOLIATE—Having three leaflets.

UNDULATE—Wavy sides.

VENATION—The way the veins of the leaves are arranged.

BOTANICAL TERMS

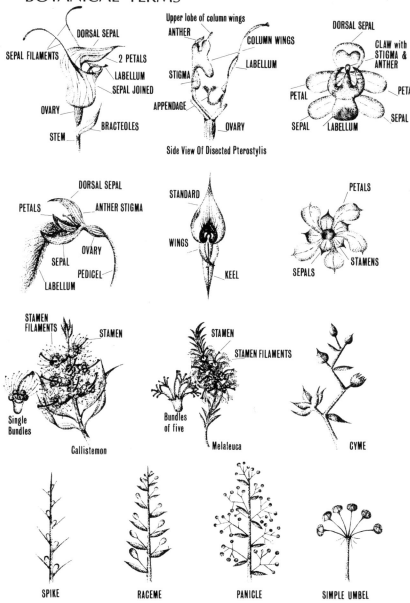

DORSAL SEPAL
SEPAL FILAMENTS
2 PETALS
LABELLUM
SEPAL JOINED
OVARY
BRACTEOLES
STEM

Upper lobe of column wings
ANTHER
COLUMN WINGS
LABELLUM
STIGMA
APPENDAGE
OVARY

Side View Of Disected Pterostylis

DORSAL SEPAL
CLAW with STIGMA & ANTHER
PETAL
PETAL
SEPAL
SEPAL
LABELLUM

DORSAL SEPAL
PETALS
ANTHER STIGMA
OVARY
SEPAL
PEDICEL
LABELLUM

STANDARD
WINGS
KEEL

PETALS
STAMENS
SEPALS

STAMEN FILAMENTS
STAMEN
Single Bundles
Callistemon

STAMEN
STAMEN FILAMENTS
Bundles of five
Melaleuca

CYME

SPIKE

RACEME

PANICLE

SIMPLE UMBEL

BOTANICAL TERMS

ABERRANT—Differing from the normal.
ABUNDANT—Ample, plentiful.
ACHENE—A small, dry, indehiscent, one-seeded fruit.
ACUMINATE—Tapering in long hollow curves to a point.
ACUTE—Pointed.
AGGREGATED—Placed singly, with change of sides at each node.
ALTERNATE—Scattered, not opposite.
ANNUAL—A plant completing its life in one year.
ANTHER—The top of the stamen, holding pollen.
APICULATE—Ending in a sharp point on an otherwise blunt end.
APPENDAGE—A subordinate or subsidiary part.
AQUATIC—Growing in water.
AROMATIC—Fragrant.
ARIL—Covering or appendage of seed.
ARTICULATE—Jointed.
ASCENDING—Climbing, moving upward.
AURICULATE—Having ear-like appendage.
AWN—A stiff bristle-like appendage. (The beard of barley.)
AXIL—The angle formed by a leaf with the branch.
AXILLARY —Arising from the axil.
AXIS—A line passing through the centre of a body, e.g. the stem.
BARB—One of the hairs of a plumose bristle.
BERRY—A succulent, the seeds scattered about in a fleshy pulp.
BESET—To surround, to press on all sides.
BI—Two.
BIENNIAL—A plant completing its life in two years.
BISEXUAL—A flower containing both stamens and pistil.
BRACT—Leaf bearing flower in its axil.
BRACTEATE—Having bracts.
BRACTEOLE—A small bract immediately below the calyx of a flower.
BULB—A short thickened, underground stem.
CAESPITOSE—Tufted, matted.
CALLOUS—Thickened.
CALYX—The outer whorl of a flower, consisting of sepals.
CAPSULE—A dry, dehiscent fruit of two or more united carpels.
CARPEL—A modified leaf forming the whole or part of an ovary, and extending
    to form the style and stigma.
CILIATE—Bordered by hairs.
CLAW—Lower part of petal or bract.
COHERING—Sticking together.
COLUMN—Combination of stamens and pistil into a solid body.
COMPOUND—Made of several parts, as a leaf of several leaflets.

17

CONE—A woody, globular collection of fruits consisting of scales surrounding a central axis.

CONNATE—Closely united to each other.

CONVOLUTE—Rolled together.

COROLLA—The whorl of the flower inside the calyx, consisting of petals.

CORYMB—Flattish raceme (*corymbus* = cluster).

CULMS—Stems of grass, usually hollow except at nodes.

CRENATE—Rounded teeth between sharp notches.

CYANOGENETIC—1. Cyano—blue; genetic—genetically; the genus is blue. 2. Producing hydrocyanic acid (prussic acid).

CYLINDRICAL—Cylinder-like in shape.

CYME—Main shoot ending in flower, with other flowers on successive branches.

CYPSELLAS—Small, dry, one-seeded fruit developed from inferior ovary, having hairy pappus attached as in dandelions.

DECIDUOUS—Falling off, not remaining.

DECLINATE—Inclined to one side.

DECUMBENT—Lying flat, except for the tip, which ascends.

DEFLEXED—Bent downwards.

DEHISCENT—Splitting open along definite lines.

DICHOTOMOUS—Having divisions always in pairs.

DIFFUSE—Spreading over the ground.

DIGITATE—A compound leaf whose leaflets spread from a common centre, like fingers of a hand.

DILATE—To expand; to extend.

DISC—An extension of the receptacle of a single flower.

DISTINCT—Separate.

DIVERGENT—Diverging; receding from each other.

DORSAL—Relating to the back.

DRUPACEOUS—Applied to fruit with a structure of a drupe, but derived from more than one carpel.

DRUPE—An indehiscent fruit of one carpel.

DRUPEL—A small drupe.

ENDEMIC—Prevalent in a particular region.

ENTIRE—Without any division.

EPICALYX—An involucre outside the true calyx and resembling the second calyx.

EPIPHYTE—A plant which grows upon trees but does not derive nourishment from them.

FAMILY—A group of genera botanically related.

FASCICULATE—Arranged in bundles or clusters.

FILAMENT—The stalk of a stamen.

FILIFORM—Thread-like.

FLEXUOSE—Bending.

FLORAL—Belonging to the flower.

FLORET—One of the small flowers in a compact head.

FLOWER—Part of the plant which produces seed.

FOLIATE—Leaf-like.

FOLLICLE—A dry fruit formed from single carpel containing more than one seed and splitting open along a definite lateral line (fruit of Telopea and Grevilleas).

FRUIT—The matured ovary with fertilized seeds.

FUNGUS—Plants of the lowest groups (*fungus* = mushroom).

GALEA—Petal shaped like a helmet.

GENUS—The smallest natural group of species having certain essential characters in common.

GLABROUS—Without hairs, smooth surface.

GLAND—An excrescence usually secreting a fluid.

GLAUCOUS—Dull green with whitish-blue lustre.

GLOBULAR—Globose, rounded.

HABITAT—The natural home of a plant.

HERBACEOUS—Without woody tissue.

HERB—A plant which does not have a woody stem. (Unlike trees or shrubs.)

HISPID—Rough, with strong hairs or bristles.

HIRSUTE—Covered with long, spreading hairs.

HOARY—Covered with very short hairs, white or grey in colour.

IMBRICATE—Overlapping.

INCISED—Deeply cut.

INDIGENOUS—Native.

INFERIOR—Applied to an organ below another.

INFLEXED—Turned abruptly inwards or downward or towards the axis.

INFLORESCENCE—The general arrangement of flowers.

INVOLUCAL—Belonging to any collection of bracts around a cluster of flowers. One or more whorls of bracts at base of single flower or flower cluster.

INVOLUCRE—A number of bracts surrounding the base of a head of flowers or leaves.

INVOLUTE—Applied to floral organs whose edges are rolled inwards.

KEEL—Applied to the two lowest petals of pea flowers.

LABELLUM—The lip-like petal of orchids.

LACINIATE—Cut into narrow slender teeth or lobes.

LATERAL—Fixed on or near sides of an organ, arising from a leaf-axil.

LAMINA—Leaf-blade or expanded portion of a leaf.

LEAFLET—A division of a compound leaf.

LEGUME—A dry fruit of one carpel splitting along two sides. A characteristic fruit of Leguminosae, Caesalpiniaceae and Mimosaceae.

LENTICEL—A breathing pore in bark.

LIGNO TUBER—A woody, often conspicuous, swelling at the base of the stem; as well as storing food, a ligno tuber has dormant buds from which new shoots develop.

LIMB—Spreading upper part of a calyx or corolla.

LOBE—A division in a leaf, petal or sepal.

MEDIAN—The thickened rib of a petal as in the Goodenaceae family.

MERICARP—A separating one-seeded part of a schizocarp, especially half of a cremocarp.

MUCRONATE—Terminating abruptly into a sharp point.

NECTARY—Glands at the base of a flower which secrete nectar.

NERVED—See vein.

NODE—Part of stem where leaf or leaves emerge.

NUT—A dry fruit of one carpel with a woody covering.

NUTLET—A small nut; example: *Isopogon*.

OBOVATE, OBOVOID—Egg shaped with the broad end towards the apex.

OPPOSITE—Applied to branches, leaves and flowers when two come from the same level.

ORBICULAR—Circular or almost.

OVARY—The lowest part of the pistil containing the ovules which, when fertilized, becomes the fruit.

OVULE—Unfertilized seed.

PANICLE—An inflorescence in which the axis is divided into branches.

PAPILLOSE—Having short protuberances.

PAPPUS—A ring of fine hairs or down, representing the calyx limb, which grows above the seed and helps in wind-dissemination in composites and some other plants.

PARASITE—A plant obtaining its nourishment from another plant.

PEDICEL—The stalk of an individual flower of an inflorescence.

PEDUNCLE—Stalk of a flower cluster or individual flower, when flower is sole member in an inflorescence.

PEDUNCULATE—On a peduncle.

PENDULOUS—Hanging.

PENICILLATE—Arranged like a tuft of hairs.

PENNIVEINED—Feather-veined.

PERENNIAL—A plant living for several years.

PERFECT—Finished, complete, faultless.

PERIANTH—Single term for calyx and corolla.

PERICARP—Matured wall of ovary which encloses a seed.

PETALOID—Resembling a petal, as a petal-like sepal.

PETIOLE—The leaf-stalk.

PHYLLODES—Flattened leaf-stalks resembling and functioning as leaves. Found in Acacias.

PINNULES—Leaflet of smallest order on a bipinnate leaf.

PLUMOSE—Feathery, or feather-like as sepals of Verticordia plumosa or style of Clematic achene.

POD—(Legume) dry fruit of one carpel.

POLLEN—Powdery substance on the anthers.

POLYGAMOUS—Bearing both unisexual flowers within the inflorescence.

PROCUMBENT—Trailing along the ground.

PROSTRATE—Lying flat on ground.

PSEUDO-BULBS—(Pseudobulbs) The swollen bulb-like part of the stems of many epiphytic orchids.

PUNGENT—Penetrating.

RACEME—An indefinite inflorescence with undivided axis and equally pedicellate flowers.

RADICAL—Springing from the root.

RADICLE—The embryonic root.

RAY—Outer part of a Compositae flower-head which has disc florets and outer florets.

RHIZOME—A prostrate or subterranean stem.

RHOMBOID—Nearly square, with petiole at one of the acute angles.

SAGITTATE—Having the form of a barbed arrow-head, with two basal lobes pointing backwards.

SCABROUS—Rough to touch, scabby.

SCARIOUS—Dry, thin, more or less transparent, and usually brownish as if scorched, especially at the tip and along the edges.

SCHIZO-CARP—A dry fruit which on dehiscence breaks into individual carpels, each of which is called a mericarp.

SCLEROPHYLL—A plant or tree with hard textured leaves.

SEGMENT—Each division of a divided leaf or an individual perianth division.

SENSITIVE—Applied to parts of plants such as leaves which show movement on being touched.

SEPAL—An individual calyx segment.

SESSILE—Without stalk.

SHRUBS—Woody plants not growing to the size of a tree and having several branches coming from the roots.

SPATHE—Bract or leaf enclosing in the bud stage a spike of fleshy flowers.

SPECIES—A division of a genus, each species having characters distinguishing it from other species of the genus.

SPIKE An indefinite inflorescence of sessile flowers.

SPUR—A hollow projection from the calyx or corolla.

STAMEN—Individual parts of the flower, consisting of a stalk or filament to which the anther is attached.

STAMENATE—Having stamens but no pistil.

STAMINODE—A sterile stamen.

STANDARD—The large posterior petal of the pea flowers.

STELLATE—Star-like, giving a flannel-like appearance.

STEM—The ascending axis of a plant.

STIGMA—The top of the pistil which is the receiving surface for the pollen.

STIPE—Small stalk.

STIPITATE—Stalked, applied to the ovary.

STIPULE—Appendage at the base of the petiole.

STRIATE—Marked with parallel lines.

STYLE—The stalk joining the ovary to the stigma of the pistil.

SUCCULENT—Juicy.

SUPERIOR—Applied to the flower in which sepals, petals and stamens are inserted below the ovary.

TAXONOMY—Classification—establishment of identification.

TENDRIL—The clasping organ of a climbing plant.

TERETE—Almost cylindrical.

TERMINAL—At the extremity.

TERRESTRIAL—Growing in the earth.

TESTA—Outer coat of seeds.

TETRA—A prefix meaning four.

THROAT—Opening in the upper part of the flower tube.

TOMENTOSE—Covered in woolly hairs.

TORUS—The swollen head of the flower stalk in which the parts of a single flower are arranged.

TRUNCATE—Appearing as though chopped off.

TUBER—Swollen piece of an underground stem or root which contains a food reserve.

TUFTED—Stems or leaves growing close together.

TURBINATE—Shaped like a top.

UMBEL—An indefinite inflorescence, branches all starting from the same point.

UNDERSHRUB—A small shrub whose flowering branches die off during the winter.

UNISEXUAL—A flower having stamens or pistil only.

VALVATE—Edges meeting but not overlapping—opening by valves.

VILLOUS—Covered with long soft hairs.

VISCID—Sticky.

WHORL—A set of organs coming from the same node and arranged in a circle round the axis.

WING—The membranous margin of a seed or fruit; also applied to the two lateral petals of pea flowers.

FRUITING BODIES

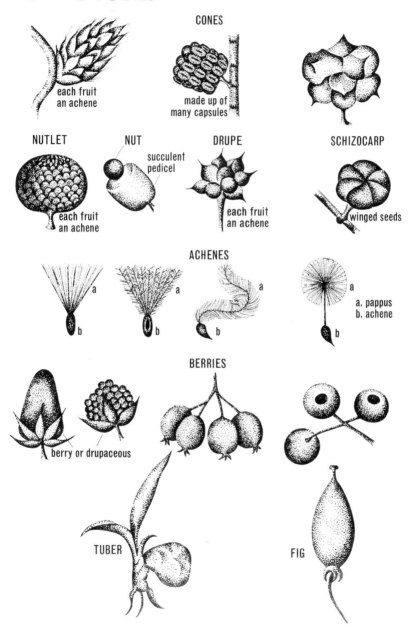

CONES

each fruit
an achene

made up of
many capsules

NUTLET

each fruit
an achene

NUT

succulent
pedicel

DRUPE

each fruit
an achene

SCHIZOCARP

winged seeds

ACHENES

a

b

a

b

a

b

a

b

a. pappus
b. achene

BERRIES

berry or drupaceous

TUBER

FIG

FRUITING BODIES

CAPSULES

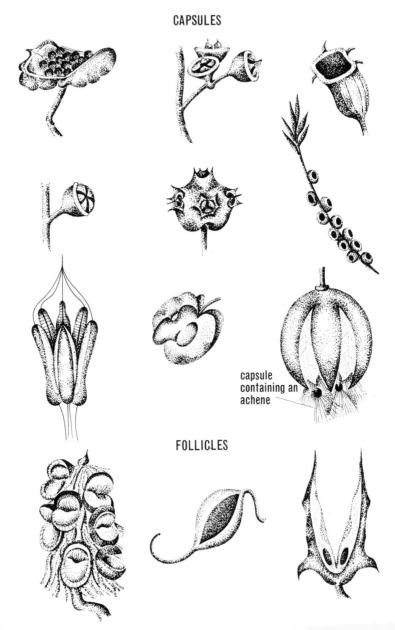

capsule
containing an
achene

FOLLICLES

FRUITING BODIES

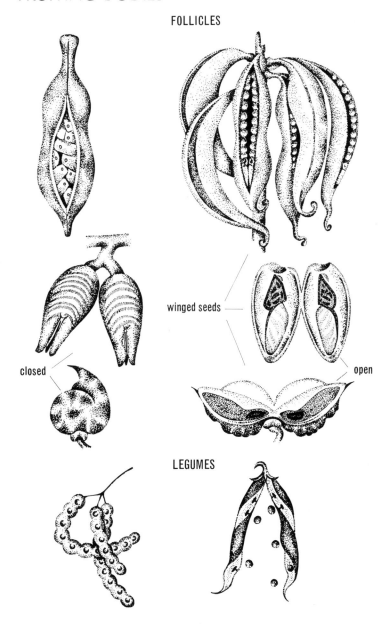

FOLLICLES

winged seeds

closed

open

LEGUMES

GLOSSARY OF NAMES AND TERMS

ABELIA—After Dr Abel, an English physician, 1780–1826.
ACACIA—A wattle; any plant of the genus *Acacia*.
ACANTHOCLADA—With thorny branches.
ACANTHUS—Plants of prickly-leafed genus *Acanthus* (*akantha*, prickle).
ACAULESCENT—Having a very short stem.
ACHILLEA—After Achilles, a mythical warrior slain by an arrow in the heel.
ACIANTHUS—*Acus*, a needle; *anthos*, a flower.
ACICULAR—Needle-shape.
ACINACEA—Dagger-like.
ACMENA—Nymph of Venus.
ACONITIFLORUS—*Aconitum*, poisonous plant; *floris*, a flower.
ACRID—Sharp; hot or biting to the taste; corroding; harsh.
ACROTRICHE—*Akros*, a point; *thrix*, a hair.
ACTINOSTRUBUS—Rayed cones.
ACTINOTUS—With rays.
ACULEATISSIMA—With prickles.
ACUMINATA—Narrow, foliage spikes.
ACUMINATE—Tapering to a narrow point.
ACUMINATUM—Pointed (*acumen*, a point).
ACUS—A needle.
ACUTE—Ending in a sharp point.
ADEN—A gland.
ADENOPHORA—*Aden*, a gland; *phora*, bearing.
ADNATE—Connected to another part throughout its whole length.
ADPRESSA—Pressed close.
AEMULA,—UM—Rivalling; emulating.
AEQUALIS—Equal.
AESTIVALIS—Of summer.
AFUGA—Not joined.
AGGREGATE—Closely packed but not confluent (of flowers or fruit).
AGONIS—Without angles.
AKANTHOS—A thorn.
AKAZO—To sharpen.
AKRIS—A mountain.
AKROS—A point.
ALBA,—US—White.
ALBIZIA—From the family name Albiza.
ALBUMEN—Nutritive substance stored in the seed; in many cases surrounding the embryo.
ALLIONII—After Carlo Allioni, an Italian botanist, 1705–1804.
ALPESTRIS—Of the mountains, the lower Alps.
ALPINA—Of the mountains, the highlands, the higher Alps.

ALTERNATE—Not opposite each other but arranged successively at regular intervals; of leaves on a stem, or petals in a flower in relation to sepal and stamen position.

ALSTROEMERCIA—After Baron Charles Alstroemer, Swedish agriculturalist, 1736–94.

ALYSSUM—A genus of cruciferous plants with white or yellow flowers, grown in rock-gardens.

AMARYLLIS—A country woman in the works of Virgil.

AMBIGUA—Doubtful (referring to whether it was a Melaleuca or Tea Tree).

AMOENUS—Pleasing.

AMPLEXICAUL—Stem-clasping.

AMYGDALIFOLIUS—*Amygdalus*, the almond; *folium*, a leaf.

AMYGDALUS—The almond.

ANACARDIUM—Of the Anacardiaceae family, the trees or shrubs of which have resinous, milky, acrid juice.

ANCEPTS—Two-edged.

ANCHOUSA, ANCHUSA—A paint used for skin.

ANCHUSA—A genus of hairy-stemmed plants.

ANDROMEDA—After daughter of Cephes rescued by Perseus.

ANDROS—A man (only the inner row of anthers are fertile).

ANEMONE—Wind flower.

ANEMONIFOLIUS—Anemone-leafed.

ANETHUM—A plant of the Flannel Flower family.

ANEURA—Without nerves (reference to the leaves, which appear to be without veins until viewed with lens).

ANGIOSPERM—Plant which has the seed enclosed in an ovary.

ANGOPHORA—Vessel-bearing (from the shape of the fruits).

ANGOPHORAS—Apples ("apple trees"), common name applied to several species of Eucalpyts.

ANGOS—A vessel.

ANGUILLARIA—After Anguillara, Professor of Botany in the sixteenth century.

ANGULOSA—Angular.

ANIGOS—Unequal.

ANIGOZANTHOS—Unequal flowers (*anigos*, unequal; *anthos*, flower).

ANNUAL—Plant that completes its life cycle in one year.

ANNULAR—Ring-shaped, arranged in a circle.

ANNUUS—Annual.

ANOPTERUS—Referring to the winged seeds.

ANTHEMON, ANTHOS—A flower.

APICULATE—Abruptly ending in a short sharp point.

APPENDAGE—An attachment developed on and projecting from the surface of an organ.

ARIL—Fleshy appendage found on some seeds arising from seed stalk or surface of the seed.

ARISTATE—Having a narrow, bristle-like, stiff, pointed appendage.
ARTICULATE—Jointed.
AURICLE—Ear-shaped lobe at the base of a leaf or another organ.
AUSTRALIS—Southern or Australian.
AUTUMNALIS—Of the autumn.
AVICULARE—Belonging to little birds.
AXIL—Angle between a stem, and leaf or other organ.
AXILLARE,—IS—With flowers in the leaf axis.
AXILLARY—Coming from an axil.
AXIS—Central part of a plant on and around which the organs are placed.
AZEDARACH—From the Persian name of a tree.

BAECKEA—After Baeck, who collected the first known species.
BAILEYANA—After botanist F. M. Bailey.
BALAUSTION—Pomegranate flower.
BALONENSIS—After the Balone River, Queensland.
BANKSIA, BANKSII—After Sir Joseph Banks.
BARBATUS—Bearded.
BARKLAYA—Syringafolia, a tree with conical growth and golden flowers with
    deep green lilac-like foliage. It is in the Papilionaceae family.
BASIFIXED—Attached by the base.
BAUERI—After Ferdinand and Frederick Bauer, botanical artists.
BAUERLENII—After Bauerlen, a botanical collector.
BAUHINIAS—After James and Casper Bauhin, twin brothers; sixteenth century
    herbalists.
BAXTERI—After William Baxter, an English botanical collector.
BEAKED—Having a pointed appendage.
BEARDED—Having a tuft or tufts of hair.
BEAUFORTIA—After the Duchess of Beaufort, a patron of botany.
BEAUFORTIODES—Like a beaufortia.
BECKLERI—After Dr Beckler.
BEGONIA—After Michel Begon, French patron of botany, 1638–1710.
BEHRII—After H. Behr, botanist.
BETONICIFOLIA—With leaves like a betonica plant.
BICOLOR—Of two colours.
BIENNIAL—Plant that completes its life cycle in two years, not flowering in first.
BIFURCATE—Twice forked.
BILLARDIERA—After Labillardière, a French botanist.
BILOBA—Two lobes of the corolla segments.
BINATA—Paired.
BIOS—Life.
BIPARTITE—Divided into two portions.
BIPINNATE—Leaves of primary and secondary divisions both pinnate.
BIPINNATIFIDA—Leaves almost divided to the central vein.

BISEXUAL—Having both male and female parts in the same flower, inflorescence or individual plant.

BLANDFORDIA—After the Marquis of Blandford.

BLECHNUM—From the Greek name of a fern.

BOREALIS—Of the north.

BORONIA—After Borone, Italian eighteenth-century botanist.

BORONIAEFOLIA—Boronia-like leaves.

BOTRYCEPHALA—Flowers in raceme.

BOWMANII—After Bowman, an English botanist.

BRACHANDRUS—Having short stamens.

BRACHYCHITON—*Brachys*, short; *chiton*, shirt or tunic; reference to the coating of hairs over the seeds.

BRACHYCOME—Short hair.

BRACHYS—Short.

BRACHYSEMA—Short sign referring to the standard (uppermost petal).

BRACT—Modified leaf subtending in its axil.

BRACTEATUM—Bearing bracts; conspicuous with bracts.

BRACTEAUS—Having bracts.

BRACTEOLE—Small bract-like appendage

BREDEMEYERA—Is now listed as comesperma.

BRISTLE—Stiff hair.

BROWNII, BRUNONIA—After Robert Brown, the botanist.

BUDDLEIA—After English botanist, Adam Buddle, 1660–1715.

BULB—Short underground stem with overlapping leaf bases or scales (onion-like) in which food is stored, and enclosing the bud of next year's growth.

BULBOSUS—Having bulbs or bulb shaped.

BULBINE—Ancient name for a species of bulb-bearing plants.

BURCHARDIA—After H. Burchard.

BURSA—A purse.

BUXIFOLIA—Broad flowers; *buxa*, broad or stiff; *folia*, flower.

BUXIFOLIUS—*Buxis*, the ancient box tree; *folius*, leafy.

BUXUS—Box, the ancient box tree.

CAERULEUS—Blue.

CAESIA—Silver-grey.

CAESPIS, CAESPITOSA—Turf, in reference to the habitat of plant.

CAIRICA—From Cairo, one of its habitats.

CALAMIFOLIA—Leaf-like.

CALADENIA—From *kalos*, beautiful; *aden*, a gland.

CALANDRINA—After J. Calandrini.

CALCEOLARIA—*Calceolus*, a slipper.

CALECTARIA—Beautiful development.

CALENDULACEA—Resembling calendula, a plant of the daisy family.

CALEYI—After George Caley, a botanical collector.

CALLICOMA—*Calli*, beautiful; *comb*, hair.

CALLISTEMON—*Kallistos*, most beautiful; *stemon*, stamen.

CALLISTEPHUS—*Kallistos*, most beautiful; *stephos*, crown; referring to the seed.

CALLITRIS—Beautiful threads, referring to the leaves.

CALLUNA—*Kallunein*, to beautify, to sweep.

CALLUS, CALLI—Tissue produced by cambial activity protecting damaged surfaces of plants or outgrowth found on the labella of some orchids.

CALLYTHRIX—*Calix*, a cup; *thrix*, a hair; referring to the awns on the sepals.

CALOCEPHALUS—Beautiful heads.

CALOSTEMMA—With a beautiful crown.

CALOTHAMNUS—Beautiful shrub.

CALOTIS—*Callos*, beautiful; *ous*, an ear.

CALYCINE—Belonging to the calyx.

CALYTHRIA—Has only one seed per flower.

CALYTRIX—*Calix*, cup; *trix*, hair; hair-like.

CALYX—Outer series of floral organs, each one a sepal.

CAMASSIA—North American Indian.

CAMBRICUS—From *Cambria* (Wales).

CAMELLIA—Camellus, after George Josef Kamel, Moravian Missionary, botanist, 1661–1706.

CAMPANULA—Bell-flower.

CAMPHOROSMAE—With camphor-like scent.

CAMPO—From Greek, meaning bent.

CAMPYLONYHA—Reference to the bent shape of the wing petals.

CANDIDUS—White.

CANTABRICUS—Cantabria, north-west Spain.

CANTABRIGIENSIS—Of Cambridge.

CAPENSIS—The Cape of Good Hope.

CAPITATA—Large-headed, in reference to the crowded flowers.

CAPITULUM—Close head of stalkless flowers as in *Compositae*.

CAPPARIS—Caper bush (Graeco-Latin).

CARDIOPHYLLA—Heart-shaped leaves.

CARMICHAELIA—After Dugald Carmichael, 1722–1827.

CARNEA, CARNEOUS—Flesh-coloured.

CARPEL—Organ containing the ovules of seed plants.

CARPUS—Fruit.

CASIA, CASSIA—From the Hebrew Qaseah—cinnamon laurel (in error, a name devised by a later botanist who thought it meant bark strips).

CASSIAS—From *kasia*, a plant of the senna family.

CASSINIANUM—A reference to the plant cassiniae.

CASSIOIDES—Like cassia.

CASSIOPE—Mother of Andromeda.

CASSYTHA—A semi-parasitic plant.

CASSYTHOIDES—*Cassytha*, a semi-parasitic plant; *oides*, like.

CASTANA—Chestnut.

CASTANOSPORUM—From castana, the Spanish chestnut used as castanets, and *sporum*, seed.

CASUARINA—Named from its resemblance to Cassowary plumage.

CATKIN—Pendulous spike or narrow raceme of numerous unisexual flowers with scale-like bracts, falling as a whole.

CAUDEX—Axis of a plant, i.e. stem and root.

CAULINE—Pertaining to or attached to the stem.

CELL—Unit of a plant structure; or cavity of ovary or fruit containing ovules or seed.

CELMISIA—Celmisius, son of the nymph Alciope.

CEPHALANTHA—Flowers in a head.

CERATAPETALUM—Horny petals: *ceratos*, horny; *petalon*, petals.

CHALCEDONICUS—Chalcedon, part of Asia Minor.

CHAMAE—Dwarf, on the ground.

CHAMELAUCIUM—Geraldton Wax.

CHILUS—A lip.

CHION—Snow.

CHIONODOXIA—Glory of the snow.

CHLAOA—Yellowish-green.

CHLOANTHES—*Chloa*, yellowish-green; *anthos*, a flower.

CHLOROPHYLL—Green pigment found in higher plants.

CHOLOROS—Green.

CHORDOPHYLLA—Cord-like leaves.

CHORIZEMA—Separated threads: *chorizo*, to separate; *nema*, a thread.

CHORIZO—To separate.

CHRIPSOPHAEA—Yellow-brown.

CHRYSOS—Gold.

CICHORIUM—The chicory and endive genus of Compositae.

CIENFUGOSIA—From the name of a Spanish botanist.

CILIATE—Fringed with hairs.

CINEREA, CINERIUM—Ashy.

CINERARIA—Ash coloured: from *cinereal*, ashy.

CINNABARINA—Of a cinnabar, or red-brown colour.

CIRCUMSCISSILE—Opening by a circular fissure for top to come off as a cap.

CITRATUM, CITRIODORA—Lemon-scented, lemon.

CLADODE—Stem functioning as a leaf and bearing scale leaves.

CLADOCALYX—Branched calyx.

CLAVATE—Club shape.

CLAW—Narrow base of sepals or petals.

CLIANTHUS—From *clio*, glory; *anthos*, a flower.

CLIO—Glory.

COCCINEA—Scarlet.

COCCINEUS—Crimson.

CODONACARPUS—Bell fruit.

COLCHICUM—Colchis—ancient Black Sea region.

COLLINA—Found on the hillsides.

COLUMELLARIS—With very small columns.

COMA—Silky tuft of hair attached to a seed.

COME—Hair, beard.

COMESPERMA—Hairy seeds: *come*, beard; *sperma*, seed.

COMPANA—A bell.

COMPOUND (LEAF)—Having two or more parts (leaflets).

COMPTONIA—Native wistaria or W.A. corral pea.

COMPTONIANA—After the family of the Marchioness of Northampton, who introduced this plant.

CONDON—A bell (from the Greek).

CONFERTA—Crowded (flowers close together).

CONFLUENT—Lit. passing gradually one into another; blending together.

CONNATE—Fused to each other.

CONOS—Cone.

CONOSPERMUM—*Conos*, a cone; *spermum*, seed.

CONOSTEPHIOIDES—Like a conostephium plant.

CONVALLARIA—Of the valleys.

COPROSMA—*Copros*, dung; *osme*, a smell.

COR, CORDIS, CORDATUM,—US—Heart, heart shaped.

CORDATE—With two equal rounded lobes at base.

CORDIFOLIA—With heart-shaped leaves; *cor*, *cordis*, the heart; *folium*, leaf.

CORIARIUS—Of curriers or tanners, certain plants they used.

CORIACEOUS—Leathery in texture.

CORM—Solid underground stem of one year's duration, with next year's arising from top.

COROLLA—Series of floral organs or petals—Collective term for the petals of a flower.

CORNICULATUM—Referring to the horn-shaped fruit.

CORONA—Ring of appendages or ring-like appendage inside the corolla or perianth.

CORONATUS—Crowned.

CORREA—From Portuguese botanist Jose Francesco Correa da Serra, 1750–1823.

CORYBAS—After the priest of Cebele, possibly in reference to the hooded perianth.

CORYMB—Usually flat-topped raceme of flowers with flower stalks becoming shorter nearer the top.

CORYMBOSA—Clustered, in reference to the flowers.

COSMOS—*Kosmos*: order, harmony, beautiful.

COSTA—A midrib or vein (of leaves).

COSTATE—Ribbed.
COTINIFOLIUS—Foliage like a cotinus plant (from the Greek *kono*, cone; *stephos*, crown, wreath).
COULTERI—After Thomas Coulter, Irish botanist, 1793–1843.
CRENATIFOLIA—With leaf margins, having rounded teeth.
CRINON, CRINUM—From the Greek; a lily.
CROCUS—A genus of plants of the iris family with long grass-like leaves.
CROTALARIA—*Crotalum* (Greek): A rattle or castanet, reference to the seeds rattling in the pods.
CROTALUM—A rattle.
CROWEA, CROWEI—After J. Crowe, an English botanist.
CRYPTOSTYLOS—*Cryptos*, hidden; *stylos*, a column.
CRYPTOS—Hidden.
CUCULLATA—Hooded, in reference to the upper sepal.
CULTRIFORMIS—With the shape of a knife.
CUMIFORM—Cucumber like.
CUNEATUS—Wedge shape.
CUNEIFOLIA—*Cuneus*, a wedge; *folium*, a leaf.
CUNEUS—A wedge.
CUNNINGHAMII—After the botanist Alan Cunningham, 1791 1839.
CUPANIOPSIS—Cupania, a kind of plant; *opsis*, appearance.
CUPRESSUS -Cypress pine.
CUTICLE—Outermost skin.
CYANEA—Blue.
CYANOCARPI—With blue fruit.
CYATHEA—Spore corers like small ladles.
CYCLAMEN—A genus of Primulaceae, with nodding flowers and bent-back petals.
CYMOSA—Clustered.
CYMOSUM—Bearing a cluster of flowers.

DALLACHIANA—After John Dallachy.
DAMASCENUS—Damascus.
DAMPIERA, DAMPIERI—After William Dampier.
DAPHENOIDES—*Oides*, like; *daphne*, cultivated plant, resembling a daphne.
DARIESIA—Triangular pod.
DARWINIA—After Charles Darwin, English scientist, 1809–82.
DEALBATA—Silver wattle.
DEBILE—Weak.
DECIDUOUS—Falling off (leaves of non-evergreen trees or petals after flowering).
DECOMPOSITA—Much divided.
DECORE—Showy.
DECUMBENT—Lying along the ground.

DECURRENT—Continued down the stem.

DECUSSATA—With each pair of opposite leaves at right angles to the next pair.

DEFOLIATUM—Without leaves.

DEHISCENT—Bursting along definite slit or pore to release spores or seeds as in anthers and fruits.

DELAVAYI—After Jean Marie Delavay, French botanist 1834–95.

DELTOID—Triangular.

DENDROBIUM—Lives on trees; *dendron*, a tree; *bios*, life.

DENDRON—A tree.

DENDROPHOE—From *dendron*, a tree; *phthoe*, infection.

DENSA—Thick or dense.

DENDATA, DENDATUM—Toothed.

DENTATE—Toothed.

DENS,—TIS,—TEX—Tooth, toothed.

DENTICULATE—Finely toothed.

DENTICULATUS,–UM—Small toothed or fine toothed.

DENUDATA—Without leaves.

DESERTII—Of the desert.

DI—Away; two.

DIANELLA—After Greek goddess Diana.

DICHOTOMA—Cut in two, referring to the disposition of the flowers.

DICHOTOMOUS—Divided into two more or less equal branches and again divided into two, and so on.

DICKSONIA—After botanist James Dickson.

DICTAMNUS—From Mount Dicte in Crete.

DIFFUSE—Widely spreading.

DIGITALIS,—US—Digitatus, a finger

DIOECIOUS—Plants having unisexual flowers, the female being on one plant and the male flowers on another.

DIOICA, DIOECIOUS—*Di*, away; *oicos*, a house; referring to male and female sex organs on separate individual plants.

DIPLOLAEMA—Double cloak (referring to the bracts).

DIPLOPELTIS—Double shield.

DIPODIUM—From *di*, two; *podium*, a balcony or projection.

DIPTERA—Two-winged.

DIPTERACANTHUS—*Diptera*, two-winged; *acanthus*, horned.

DIS—Two.

DISC FLOWERS—Cental flowers borne on the capitulum of some of the *Compositae* family.

DISCOLOR—Variegated.

DISCRASTYLIS—Forked, from Greek *dickroos*.

DISSECTED—Divided into segments.

DISTICHA—In two rows.

DIURIS—From *di*, two; *ouros*, a tail.

DIVARICATE—Spreading at a wide angle.

DIVERSIFOLIUS—*Diversus*, different; *folium*, a leaf.

DIVERSUS—Different.

DODOENAEA—After Dodoens, a French botanist. A hop bush.

DODOENAEFOLIA—With leaves like Dodoenaea.

DORATA—A spear.

DORATOXYLON—*Doru, dorata*, a spear; *xylon*, wood.

DORSAL—Related to the back.

DORU—Spear.

DOUGLASII—After David Douglas, a Scottish collector, 1798–1834.

DOXA—Glory.

DRACAENA—The dragon plant.

DRACO—From Dracaena.

DRACOPHYLLUM—From *draco, dracaena*, the dragon plant; *phylos*, a leaf.

DROSEROS—Dew, dewy (Greek).

DRUMMONDII—After James Drummond, Western Australian botanist.

DRY SCLEROPHYLL FOREST—A forest in which the undergrowth is composed of drought-resisting plants.

DRYANDERA—After Dryander, a Swedish botanist.

DRYOPTERIS—An oak fern.

EARLII—After G. W. Earl.

EDINENSIS—Of Edinburgh.

EDULIS—*Esculentis*; edible.

ELAEAGNUS—One of the wild olives.

ELAEOCARPUS—*Elaeagnus*, one of the wild olives; *carpos*, fruit; olive-fruited.

ELATIOR,—TOR,—TUM—Taller, tall.

ELEGANS—Elegant.

ELLIPTICA—Elliptical.

ELLIPTICAL—Oblong with regularly rounded ends.

ELONGATA—Very long leaves.

EMARGINATE—Having a shallow notch usually at the top.

ENDEMIC—Confined geographically to a given region or country.

ENTIRE—Of the margins when without teeth, lobes or divisions.

EPACRIS—From *epi*, upon; *acris*, a hilltop.

EPI—Upon.

EPICALYX—Involucre closely resembling an outer calyx and beneath the true calyx.

EPIPHYTE—Plant perched on another or rocks, attached but not deriving nourishment from the attachment as does a parasite.

ERANTHIS—Spring.

ERECTA—Straight.

EREMAEA—Desert.

EREMOPHILA,—OS—Desert-loving.

ERICA—The heath.
ERICIFOLIA—Heath-leaved; *erica*, heath; *folia*, leaf.
ERICINUM—Heath-like.
ERINACEA—Like a hedgehog.
ERIOS—Wool.
ERIOSTEMON—Woolly stamens: *erios*, wool, *stemon*, thread, stamen.
ERUBESCENS—Reddish.
ERYNGIUM—A kind of thistle.
ERYTHOS, ERYTHRINA—Red (Greek).
ERYTHROCORYS—With red caps.
ERYTHRONEMA—With red stamens.
ESCALLONIA—After Antonis Jose Escallon, Spanish botanist.
ESCULENTIS—Edible.
EU—Well (Greek).
EUCALYPTUS—Well covered.
EUGENIA—After Prince Eugene of Saxony.
EUSTREPHUS—Of twining habit.
EUTAXIA—In good order.
EXALATA—Without wings.
EXALTATA,—US—Tall or raised high; lofty.
EXIMIUS—Choice, rare.
EXONIENSIS—Of Exeter.
EXOTIC—Introduced from a foreign country.
EXSUCCOSA|—Without sap.

FALCATE—US—Scythe or sickle shape.
FALCIFOLIA—Sickle shaped leaves.
FALCOROSTUM—Falcon's beak, from the shape of the column.
FAMILY—Group of genera resembling each other by a combination of characters
    more closely than they resemble other groups: given a Latin name with the
    suffix—*aceae* or *ae*.
FARINOSIS—Floury, mealy.
FARNESE,—ESIANA—From the Farnese Palace, Rome.
FARRAGEI—After Dr Guilielmo Farrage.
FARRERI—After William Farrer, an English collector, 1880–1920.
FERRUGINEA,—US—Rust coloured, rusty.
FERTILE—Capable of sexual reproduction.
FICUS—The fig.
FILAMENT—Stalk of a stamen.
FILIFORMIS—Thread like.
FIMBRIATE—Fringed.
FLACCIDUM—Drooping, feeble.
FLAVUS,—UM; FLAVIDA, FLAVESCENS—Yellow.
FLEXILIS—Flexible.

FLEXUOSA—Flexible, bent from side to side.

FLORET—One flower of a cluster, e.g. in capitulum of *Compositae*.

FLORIBUNDA,—AS,—UM—Many flowers; free flowering.

FLORIDA, FLORIS—Flowering.

FLOS—A flower.

FLUVIATILIS—Belonging to a river, stream.

FOLIUM,—US; FOLIA—A leaf; leaves.

FOREST—A large tract of land populated by a community of plants in which trees with long trunks and spreading tops are predominant.

FORMOSA,—US,—UM—Beautiful, charming.

FORRESTIANA—After Sir John Forrest.

FORSYTH—William Forsyth (1737–1804), Scottish royal gardener, one-time curator of Centennial Park.

FORSYTHIA—From Forsyth.

FORTUNEI—After Robert Fortune, collector, 1812–80.

FREE—Not united with any other organ or part.

FREELINGII—After Captain Freeling.

FRITILLARIA—A dice box.

FRUIT—Nature ovary and whatever accessory structures of the flower may be attached to it at the time the seed ripens.

FRUTICOSUS—Shrubby.

FUCHSIA—After Leonhardt Fuchs, botanist, 1501–66.

FULGENS—Bright.

FULVUS—Tawny.

FUNICLE—Stalk of the ovule or seed.

FUSIFORUS—Spindle shape.

GALA—Milk.

GALANTHUS—*Gala*, milk; *anthos*, a flower.

GALEGA—A genus of small leguminous plants (goat's rue).

GALEGIFOLIA—From galega, and folium; leaves like a goat's rue (*galega*).

GALLICUS—From Gaul (France).

GAULTHERIA—After Gaulther, a botanist.

GEITON—A neighbour, in reference to its similarity to the genus *Similax*.

GEITONOGAMY—Pollination from another flower on the same plant.

GENTIANA—After Gentius, King of Illyria, 180–167 B.C.

GENUS—Group of species resembling each other by a combination of characters more closely than they resemble other groups; generic name is the first of the two denoting a particular species.

GEODORUM—Referring to the flowers being near to the earth.

GEORGINAE—After the Georgina River, Queensland.

GERANIUM—A crane.

GERMINATION—When seeds begin to grow.

GIBBOUS—With short pouch-like spur at base of an organ.

GIBBERULA—A swelling, in reference to the flower.

GIGANTEA—Very large.

GLABROUS—Without hairs.

GLABERRA, GLABRATA—Smooth.

GLADIOLUS—A little sword.

GLAND—A single or group of secretory cells.

GLANDULAR—Having glands.

GLAUCA—Blue-grey; with a bluish tint.

GLAUCESCENT—Bluish.

GLAUCIFOLIA—From *glaucous*, bluish.

GLAUCOUS—Bluish.

GLOBOSE—Nearly spherical.

GLOSSA—A tongue.

GLOSSODIA—From *gloss*, tongue; *odos*, tooth (tooth shaped).

GLUME—Bracts subtending the flower in a spikelet of *Cyperaceae*, or *Gramineae*.

GLUTINOSA—Sticky.

GOMPHOLOBIUM—From *gomphos*, a nail; *lobos*, a pod; referring to the way the seed pods are attached.

GOMPHOS—A nail, referring to the attachments.

GOODIA—After Good, a botanist.

GOSSYPIUM—Softness (Arabic).

GRACILA,—IS—Slender.

GRACILICAULE—Slender canes.

GRAMINEUM—Grass-like.

GRANDIFLORA,—US,—UM—With large flowers.

GRANDIS—Large.

GRAPHTOPHYLLUM—With leaves that are "written on", or marked.

GREGORII—After A. C. Gregory, explorer.

GREVILLEA—After C. E. Greville, an English horticulturist, 1749–1809.

GROSSA—Thick.

GUNNIANA—After R. Gunn, a Tasmanian botanist.

GUMMI—Gum.

GUMMIFERUM—From *gummi*, gum; *ferum*, bearing (gum-bearing).

GYMNOSPERM—Plants whose ovules are not enclosed in a seed vessel or ovary, and are consequently naked.

GYPSOPHILA—A lover of chalk.

HAIR—Outgrowth from an epidermis.

HAKEA—After Christian Ludwig Hake, botanist.

HAKEIFOLIA—With leaves like a hakea plant.

HALGENIA—After Halgen, a French admiral.

HARDENBERGIA—After Countess von Hardenburk, sister of Baron von Hugal, a German who collected plants in Western Australia in 1933.

HASTATE—Spear shaped.

HEAD—Cluster of sessile flowers, essentially a spike with a much reduced floral axis.

HEATH—An open area often peaty or sandy, mostly flat with a plant community which consists mainly of small shrubs with small leaves.

HEBE—After the daughter of Zeus.

HEDERACEA—Ivy-like, resembling ivy.

HELIANTHI,—US—Resembling the sunflower (from *helios*, sun; *anthos*, flower).

HELICHRYSUM—From *helios*, the sun; *chryos*, gold; referring to the colour of the flower.

HELIPTERUM—From *helios*, the sun; *pteron*, a feather; referring to the feathery seed pappus.

HEMEROCALLIS—From *hermera*, day; *kalas*, beauty (day-lily).

HENRYI—After Augustine Henry, Irish botanist, 1857–1930.

HERB—Non-woody plant.

HERBACEOUS—Without woody tissue.

HERBERTIANA—After Lady Carnarvon (Herbert).

HERMAPHRODITE—A flower containing functional female and male parts; bisexual.

HERMERA—Day.

HETEROPHYLLA—*Heretos*, different; *phylos*, a leaf (variable leaves).

HETEROS—Different.

HIBBERTIA—After George Hibbit, botanist.

HIBISCUS—An ancient name for the mallow, Greek-Latin plant name.

HILEMALIS—Of winter.

HILLII—After W. Hill, an English botanist.

HIRSUTE—Hairy.

HISPANIA,—ICUS—From Hispania (Spain).

HISPID—Having rough hairs.

HOARY—Densely covered with almost microscopic hairs, giving a white-grey appearance.

HOMALANTHUS—With all flowers alike.

HOOKERIANA—After Sir Joseph Hooker, an early botanist.

HORTENSIS—Of gardens.

HOREA—After Hore, a Polish botanist.

HOWITTII—After Howitt, a collector.

HOYA—After Thomas Hoy, a gardener.

HUEGELII—After Baron von Hugel.

HUMEA—After Sir Abraham Hume, an English patron of the arts and science.

HUMIFUSUM—Spread over the ground.

HUMILIS—Lowly.

HUMUS—Organic portion of the soil, formed from decaying vegetable and animal matter.

HYACINTHUS—After the youth accidentally slain by Apollo.

HYBANTHUS—Spurred or pouched; from *hybos*, a bump.

HYBOS—A bump.

HYBRID—Progeny resulting from fertilization of a member of one subspecies, species or genus by another member.

HYBRIDUS—Hybrid.

HYD—From the Greek, *hydor*, water.

HYMEN—A membrane

HYMENOSPORUM—From *hymen*, a membrane; *sporos*, a seed.

HYPERICUM—Old name of the St John's wort genus of plants. The family name was Hypericaceae.

HYPOCALYMMA—Under the veil of the falling calyx.

HYPORYTHIS—Seeds above the petals and stamens.

HYSSOPUS—Hebrew.

IBERICUS, IBERIS—Iberia (Spain and Portugal).

IBISCUM—Old name for the marsh-mallow.

ILICIFOLIA,—UM— With holly-like leaves.

IMBRICATE—With edges overlapping.

IMPLEXA—Entwined.

IMPRESSA—Indentations near the base of the flower.

INCANA,—US—Grey, hoary.

INCARNATA—Flesh-coloured.

INCISED—Margin cut sharply and deeply into teeth or lobes.

INCURVED—With the edges curved inwards.

INDEHISCENT—Not opening to release spores or seeds.

INDIGOPHERA—Dark blue (indigo) dye obtained from some species.

INDUSIUM—Cup-like fringe surrounding the stigma of species in the *Goodeniaceae* family; of some ferns an epidermal membrane covering the spore case.

INDUTA—Covered.

INFERIOR OVARY—With perianth and stamens inserted above the ovary.

INFLEXED—Incurved; bent inwards.

INSIGNIS—Noticeable, conspicuous.

INSULARE—Of the islands.

INTEGER—Complete.

INTEGRIFOLIUS—With entire leaves (*integer*, complete; *folium*, leaf).

INTERNODE—The portion of stem between two nodes.

INUNDATUS—Overflowing.

INVOLUCRE—One or more whorls of bracts at base of flower cluster or capitulum.

INVOLUTE—Rolled inwards at the edges.

IPO, IPOMOEA—From *ipo*, bindweed (erroneous); *homotos*, like.

IRIS—The goddess of the rainbow.

IRREGULAR—With members of the same series within a flower different in form or size from one another, having only one vertical plane of symmetry.

ISOPOGON—Equal beard: *isos*, equal; *pogon*, a beard.
ISOS—Equal.
ISOTOMA—Equal cut of the petals: *isos*, equal; *toma*, petal.
ITEAPHYLLA—Willow-leaves.
IXIOIDES—Ixia-like.

JACEA, JACEOIDES—Resembling the jacea (plant), a genus of the Compositae family.
JASMINUM—Persian.
JONESII—After Dr Sydney Jones.
JOVELLANA—After C. M. de Jovellanos, a student of flora (Peru).
JUNCEA—Rush-like.
JUNCIFOLIA—Rush-like leaves.
JUNIPERNA—Foliage like a juniper.

KAEMPFERI—After Engelbert Kaempfer, a German botanist, 1651–1716.
KALLANEIN—To sweep.
KALLISTOS—Most beautiful.
KALLOS; KALOS—Beauty; beautiful.
KALMIA—After Petr Kalm, a Finnish botanist, 1715–79.
KASIA—Bark strips.
KALYPTOS—Covered.
KEEL—Ridge like the keel of a boat; or the two united lower petals of a pea flower.
KEMPEANA—After Rev. H. Kemp of Hermannsburg.
KENNEDIA,—YA—After Lewis Kennedy, an English nurseryman, 1775–1818.
KEPHALE—A head.
KERAUDRENIA—After Keraudren, a French nobleman.
KEWENSIS—Of Kew (the famous London botanic garden).
KHRYSOS—Gold.
KISSOS—Ivy.
KNIGHTIA—After T. A. Knight, 1758–1838, President of the Royal Horticultural Society (London).
KNIPHOFIA—After Johann Hieronymus Kniphof, a German botanist, 1704–63.
KORIS—Long.
KOSMOS—Order, harmony.
KUNZEA—After Gustav Kunze, a German botanist.

LABELLUM—The third upper petal (but often apparently lower by twisting of the ovary) of the flower of species of *Orchidaceae* family; usually different and larger than the other two petals; or the fifth and different petal of flowers in the *Stylidiaceae* family.
LABIATAE—Lipped ones.
LABIATE—Lipped.
LABICHIOIDES—Like labichea, compound lip.

LABURNIFOLIA—Leaves resembling laburnum.
LABURNUM—A leguminous plant.
LACINIATUS—Slashed, jagged.
LAEVIGATUM, LAEVIS—Smooth.
LAGERSTROEMIA—After Magnus Lagerstroem (Swedish).
LAGUSTRIS—Of a lake.
LAMBERTIA—After A. B. Lambert, an English botanical writer, 1761–1842.
LAMINA—The expanded blade of a petal or leaf.
LANATUS—Woolly.
LANCEA—Lance shaped.
LANCELATUS,—OLATA,—OLATUM—Lance shaped, or with lance shaped
    leaves.
LANIGERUM—Woolly.
LANUGINOSUS—Wool-bearing.
LAPPACEUS—Burr-like.
LARICIFOLIUM—With leaves like those of a larch.
LASIANTHOS—With hairy flowers.
LASIOPETALUM—With hairy petals.
LASIOS—Hairy.
LATERITA—Orange-scarlet or brick-red in colour.
LATIFOLIA, –IUM—Broad leaves; *latus*, broad; *folium*, leaf; or with leaves like
    a lotus plant.
LATROBEI— After Governor La Trobe of Victoria.
LATUS—Broad.
LAURENTIA—Neck.
LAURINA—Laurel-like.
LAUTUS—Elegant.
LAVARE—To wash.
LAVANDULA—From *lavare*.
LAVANDULACEA—Lavender-like.
LAWRENDULACEA—From the surname Lawrence.
LEAFLET—Division of a compound leaf.
LEDIFOLIA—Simple leaves.
LEDUM—A kind of plant.
LEHMANNII—After Lehmann, a German botanist.
LEPIS—A scale.
LEPROSA—Scaly.
LEPTOPHYLLA—Slender leaves.
LEPTORHYNCHUS—*Leptos*, slender; *rhynchos*, a beak.
LEPTOS—Small, slender, tiny.
LEPTOSPERMUM—Tiny seeds: *leptos*, tiny; *spermum*, seeds.
LESCHENAULTIA—After Leschenault de la Tour, a French botanist,
    1773–1826.
LEUCOCEPHALUS—White-headed.

LEUCOS—White.

LEUCOXYLON—With white wood: *leucos*, white; *oxylon*, wood.

LIBERTIA—Spreading.

LIGNOTUBER—Conspicuous woody swelling at the base of a stem, as in *Eucalyptus* and *Telopea*; as well as storing food, a lignotuber has dormant buds from which new shoots develop. An adaptive feature for survival, the growth of the dormant buds is stimulated when the aerial stem is destroyed, e.g., by fire.

LIGULATE—Furnished with a ligule as in corolla of ray florets of members of *Compositae* family.

LIGULE—Strap-shaped limb of the corolla of ray florets in many of the *Compositae* family, or chaffy projection of leaf sheath of grasses.

LIMB—Upper free and spreading portions of a connate corolla as distinct from tube formed by the united parts.

LIMNANTHES—*Limne*, a marsh; *anthes*, on another.

LIMNE—A marsh.

LEIMON—A meadow.

LIMONIUM—From lemon.

LINEA, LINARIA,—EARIS—Narrow.

LINAR—,LINEAR—, IFOLIA (—UM)—With narrow leaves or foliage.

LINGUIFORME—Tongue shaped.

LINIFOLIA—Flax leaved; narrow leaved.

LINUM—Latin name for flax.

LITTORALIS—Of the coast or shore.

LOBE—Any rounded segment of a structure.

LOBELIA—After Lobel, Flemish botanist, 1538–1616

LOBOS—A pod.

LOCHAE—After Lady Loch, wife of a Governor of Victoria.

LOCULE = LOCULUS—A cavity within an ovary or another.

LOMATIA—Referring to the wings or borders of the seeds.

LONGICOMA—With long hairs.

LONGIFLORA—With long flowers.

LONGIFOLIA—Long leaves or foliage.

LONGIPEDATA—Long peduncles.

LONGISSIMA—Very long.

LONGUS—Long.

LONICERA—After Adam Lonicer, a German botanist, 1528–87.

LUSITANICUS—Portugal.

LUTEUM,—US—Yellow.

LYPERANTHUS—*Lyperos*, sad; *anthos*, a flower.

LYPEROS—Sad.

LYNCHNE (S)—From *lynchos*, lamp. Its leaves were used for wicks.

MACDONNELLII—After Sir Richard Graves MacDonnell, Governor of South Australia.

MACROCARPA,—UM—With large fruit.

MACROCEPHALUS—With large or long head.

MACROSTYLIS—With large or long styles.

MACROZAMIA—With large or long zamia.

MACULATA—Blotched, spotted.

MAGNIFICUS—Showy.

MAGNOLIA—After Pierre Magnol, French botanist, 1638–1715.

MAJALIS—Of May.

MAJOR—Greater.

MALLEE—A shrubby Eucalypt with slender stems arising from a woody base.

MANGLESII—After Robert Mangles, a collector.

MANNI—After Sir Frederick Mann, in whose garden the species first appeared as a seedling.

MARGINALE—Bordered.

MARGINATA,—US—Having a margin.

MARIESII—After Charles Maries, an English collector, 1850–1902.

MARITIMUS —Of the sea.

MATTHIOLA—After Pierandrea Matthioles, an Italian botanist and physician, 1500–77.

MECONOPSIS—The Welsh poppy genus. *Mekon*, a poppy; *opsis*, appearance.

MEGA—Large.

MEGACEPHALA—With large heads.

MEGASTIGMA—Large stigma.

MEKON—A poppy.

MELALEUCA—*Melas*, black; *leukos*, white (black and white).

MELANOXYLON—Black wood (*melas*, black; *oxylon*, wood).

MELAS—Black.

MELIA—The nim tree genus, giving name to the family Meliaceae (mahogany, Cedrela). From the Greek *melia*, ash-tree.

MELOSTOMA—*Melo*, black; *stoma*, mouth or opening (Greek).

MELUM—Fruit.

MEMBRANOUS—Thin, semi-transparent.

MERICARP—One of the single-seeded carpels of a schizocarp.

METROSIDEROS—*Metra*, middle; *sideros*, iron; alluding to the heart-wood.

MICRO—Small.

MICROMYRTUS—Small myrtle.

MICROPHYLLA—Small leaves.

MICROSPORE—Small male spore or pollen grain.

MIDRIB—The central vein of a leaf.

MIMOSA—The sensitive plant genus, popularly extending to *Acacia* and other genera of the Mimosaceae, a regular-flower family of Leguminosae. From the Greek, *mimos*, a mimic.

MIMOSEAE—From mimosa.

MIMULUS—A little actor (flowers are mask-like).

MINURIA—*Minyros*; small, thin.

MINYROS—Small.

MIQUELLI—After F. A. W. Miquel.

MITCHELLI—After Sir Thomas Mitchell, surveyor and explorer.

MITRA—A cap.

MITRATA—Conical and dilated at the base.

MOLLIS—Soft.

MOLLISIMA—From Mollis.

MONADELPHA—With filaments joined into one bundle.

MONOPETALUS—Single petal.

MONIMIACEAE—From moschatus.

MONTANUM—Of the mountains.

MONTICOLA—Mountain dwelling.

MONOECIOUS—Of a plant that has separate female and male flowers on the one plant.

MONOPHYLLA—Single leaves.

MOSCHATUM,—US—Musk-scented, the musk.

MOSCHOS—Musk.

MUCRONATE—Terminating suddenly in a sharp, stiff point called a mucro.

MUCRONULATAS—With little points.

MUELLERI—After F. von Mueller, 19th century Victorian Government botanist.

MULTIFLORA,—US—Many flowers.

MULTILINEATA—With many lines.

MULTUS—Many.

MURALIS—Of the walls.

MURRAYANA—After Murray, a member of Howett's exploring party.

MUSCARI—From *moschus*, musk; referring to the scent.

MUSSINII—After Count Appollos Appollosvich Mussin Puschkin, a Russian chemist and collector.

MUTABILIS—Changeable.

MYO—To shut.

MYOPOROIDES—Like a myoporum plant.

MYOPORUM—Closed pores.

MYRIOS—Many, numberless.

MYRSINOIDES—Like a primulate plant.

MYRTLEFOLIA—Leaves like the myrtle.

MYRTIFOLIA—Myrtle-leaved.

MYRTUS—(Greek) myrtle.

MYRIOCEPHALUS—From the Greek—very many.

NARCISSUS—From *narkau*, to grow stiff.

NEMOPHILA—A lover of the grove.

NERINE—A South African amaryllid genus, with scarlet or rose-coloured flowers, including the Guernsey lily. From the Latin *nerine*, a sea-nymph of Greek mythology.

NERIIFOLIA—From *nerium*, the oleander; and *folia*, a leaf.

NERVE—Fibrous tissue of a leaf, also see VEIN.

NERVOSA—A rib.

NESOPHILA—Island-loving.

NEWCASTLIA—After the Duke of Newcastle.

NICOTIANA—After Jean Nicot, a French traveller, 1530–1600.

NIGELLA— *Niger* (black).

NIGER—Black.

NIGRICANS—Blackish.

NITENS—Brilliant.

NITIDA,—UM—Shining.

NIVALIS—Of the snows.

NIVEA—Snowy.

NOBILIS—Well known.

NODE—Part of stem, often swollen, from which the leaf arises.

NU—Without, naked.

NUDICAULIS—Naked stemmed.

NUDUM—Without any hairs or scales.

NUMMUL—A coin.

NUMMULARIUM—Coin shaped.

NUTANS—Nodding.

NYMPHAEA, NYMPHE—Water sprite.

OBCORDATE—Inversely heart shaped with broadest part at tip.

OBCUNEATA—Reverse, wedge-shaped leaves.

OBLANCEOLATE—Lance shaped but broadest toward the tip.

OBLONG—Longer than broad, having almost parallel sides, and rounded at both ends.

OBORATA—Reverse, heart shaped.

OBORALIS—Reverse oval of the leaves. broader part outwards.

OBOVATE—Inversely egg shaped, broadest toward the tip.

OBTUSIFOLIA—Blunt-leaved: *obtusus*, blunt; *folia*, a leaf.

OBTUSE—Blunt.

OCCIDENTALIS—Of the west.

ODORATUS—Scented.

OFFICINALIS—From apothecaries.

OICOS—A house.

OIDES—Like.

OLEA—Olive.

OLEOIDES—Olive-like: from *olea*; olive; *oides*, like.

47

OLIGANDRA—With few stamens.

OLIVACEUS—Olive green.

OPIS—Resemblance, similarity, likeness.

OPPOSITE—Organs arising at the same level but with the axis between them.

ORBICULAR—Flat and circular in outline, or nearly so.

ORDER—Groups of families resembling each other by a combination of characters more closely than they resemble other groups; given a Latin name with suffix—*ales*.

ORIENTALIS—Of the east.

OSME—A smell.

OUROS—A tail.

OVALES—Oval.

OVALIFOLIA—Oval-leaved: *ovalis*, oval; *folia*, leaf.

OVARY—Part of the pistil that contains the ovules or immature seeds.

OVATE—Flat and egg shaped, with broad end towards the base, e.g., leaf.

OVOID—Solid and egg shaped, e.g. fruit.

OVULE—Structure containing the egg which develops into a seed on fertilisation.

OXY—Sharp.

OXYCEDRUS—Sharp-edged leaves.

OXYLOBIUM—Sharp-edged or pointed pods: *oxy*, sharp, *lobos*, a pod.

PACHYPHYLLUS—Leathery or thick leaves.

PAEANIA—After Paean, Homeric physician of the gods.

PALLASII—After Simon Peter Pallas, a German explorer and naturalist, 1741–1811.

PALLIDUS—Pallid or pale in colour.

PALMATE—Arranged like palm of a hand, leaflets spreading fanwise from a petiole.

PALMATIFID—Leaf cut into lobes in a palmate manner.

PALUDOSA—Boggy.

PALUSTRIS—Of the marshes.

PANDOREA—(Greek mythology) Pandora was the first woman.

PANDORANA—Gifted, from the same origin as pandorea.

PANICLE—Much branched loose inflorescence.

PANICULATUM—Paniculate (branching).

PANICULATUS—Flowers in panicles, branching.

PAPILIO—Butterfly.

PAPILIONACEAE—From *papilio*, referring to the winged shape of the flowers.

PAPPUS—Late maturing calyx generally found at the top of the fruit in the *Compositae* family.

PARASITE—Organism growing upon or inside another so as to derive its nourishment.

PARIPINNATE—Of a pinnate leaf that has two terminal leaflets.

PARTHENOS—A virgin.

PARVIFLORUS—Small flowers: *parvus*, small; *floris*, flower.
PARVIFOLIA—With small leaves: *parvus*, small; *folia*, a leaf.
PARVUS—Small.
PASSIFLORA—Flowers spread out: *passus*, spread out; *flora*, a flower.
PASUS—*Passus*: spread out.
PATERSONIA—After Col. W. M. Paterson.
PARVINIA—After Pavon, a Spanish botanist.
PEDATE—Of a palmate leaf that has its lateral leaflets cleft into two or more segments.
PEDICEL—Stalk of an individual flower.
PEDICELLATE—Borne on a pedicel.
PEDUNCULARIS—With long flower stems.
PEDUNCULATA,—UM—Stalked, with long flower stalks.
PELARGONIUM—From *pelegos*, a stork.
PELTATE—Generally orbicular leaf with the petiole attached beneath the middle and not at the edge.
PHEBABIUM—A name for the myrtle.
PENNIGERA—Winged.
PENNIVEINED—Pinnately veined.
PERENNIAL—Plant that lives for two or more years, generally flowering each year.
PERENNIS—Perennial.
PERFOLIATA—A leaf having the base joined around the stem, so as to appear pierced by the stem.
PERSICA—Peach.
PERSICIFLORUM—Peach-flowered.
PERSISTENT—Parts of the flower that remain after flowering.
PERSOONIA—After Christian Hendrik Persoon (1761–1836), South African mycologist.
PETAL—Unit of a corolla between sepals and stamens, usually conspicuous.
PETALOID -Resembling a petal.
PETALOCALYX—Referring to the petal-like calyx.
PETALON—Petal, hence leaf.
PETALOSTYLIS—From the Greek *petalon*, petal; *stylis*, styles.
PETERSONII—Also known as citratum.
PETIOLE—leaf-stalk.
PETIOLARIS—With prominent leaf stalks.
PETRA—Rock.
PETROPHILE—Rock-loving: *petra*, rock; *philos*, loving.
PHILLYRAEOIDES—Resembling phillyrea, the jasmine box.
PHILYDIUM—Water loving.
PHOENICEUS—From Phoenicia, where a crimson dye was produced.
PHOENICIUS—Bright red.
PHORA—Bearing.

PHTHOE—To destroy.

PHYLLODE—Flattened petiole which functions as a leaf (common to *Acacia*).

PHYLLON—A leaf.

PHYSA—A bladder.

PHYSALLIS—From *physa*, a bladder.

PHYSODES—Inflated.

PICTUM—Painted.

PILEANTHUS—Cap-flower, referring to the buds.

PILIFERA—Bearing hairs.

PILOSA,—UM—Hairy, woolly.

PIMELE—Fat, fatty. referring to the oil seeds.

PINIFOLIA—US—Pine-like leaves or needles.

PINNA,—ATA,—ATE—A feather; feather-like.

PINNATIFID—Pinnately cleft on both sides and extending not more than halfway to the midrib.

PINNATISECT—Pinnately cleft on both sides with lobes extending almost to the midrib.

PINNULE—Secondary pinna or leaflet in a bipinnate leaf, e.g. as in many *Acacia* species.

PINUS—Pine.

PISTIL—Female part of the flower, generally consisting of a stigma, style and the ovary.

PITTA—Resin, pitch.

PITTOSPORUM—Sticky seeds: *pitta*, pitch; *sporum*, seeds.

PLAGIOPHYLLA—Transverse-leafed.

PLATYCARPUS—With broad, flat pods or fruit; *platys*, broad, flat or plate-like; *carpus*, lobes, pod, or fruit.

PLATYLOBIUM—With broad fruit.

PLECTRANTHUS—From *plectron*, a cock's spur; *anthus*, a flower.

PLECTRON—Cock's spur.

PLEURA—A side rib.

PLEUROCARPA—*Pleura*, a side rib; *carpos*, fruit.

PLICATE—Plaited, in the manner of a closed fan.

PLICATUS—Folded.

PLUMULE—Primary shoot of a seed.

PLUMOSE—Feather-like; feathery.

PLURINERVIA—Many nerves or veins.

POD—Dry and dehiscent many seeded fruit: includes legume, sihigua etc.

PODALYRIA—A silver-leafed shrub.

PODALYRIAEFOLIA—Leaves like a podalyria.

PODOCARPUS—From *podis*, a foot; *carpus*, fruit.

PODIS—Foot.

PODOLEPIS—From *podis*, a foot; *lepis*, a scale.

POGON—A beard.

POINCIANA—After Monsieur de Pointei, 17th century French governor of Antilles.

POLLEN—Male spores of a flowering plant produced by anthers (microspores).

POLLINATION—Transfer of pollen from the stamen to stigma.

POLLINIUM—Mass of cohering waxy pollen grains facilitating wholesale pollen transfer found in *Asclepiadaceae* and *Orchidaceae* families.

POPULIFOLIUS—Poplar-leafed.

POPULNEUM—Poplar-like.

POLY—Many.

POLYANTHUM—Many flowers.

POLYBOTRYA—Many branches.

POLYSTACHYUS—Many spikes.

POLYSTICHUS—Arranged in several to many rows.

POMIFERA—Apple-bearing.

POROS—A pore.

PRATENSIS—Of the meadows.

PRAVIFOLIA—With small leaves.

PRAVISSIMA—Twisted.

PREISSICANA—After Preiss, a botanical collector.

PRIMULA—Of the Primula family, or from *primus*, the first.

PROCUMBENT—Trailing, or spreading along the ground.

PROLIFERUM—Bearing offsprings.

PROMINENS—Prominent.

PROSTANTHERA—From *protos*, a vessel; *anthera*, an anther.

PROSTHEKE—(Greek) a process.

PROSTRATE—Lying flat on the ground.

PROSTRATA—Prostrate.

PROTEA,—EACEA—From Proteus, the sea god, who assumed many shapes.

PSEUDOBULB—Swollen internode(s) of many Orchids.

PTERIS—A fern.

PTEROSTYLIS—Hooded, style.

PTILOTUS—Winged or feathered.

PUBESCENS—Downy.

PUBESCENT—Covered with a short soft, downy hairs.

PUGIONIFORMIS—Dagger form.

PULCHELLA,—CHERRIMUM—Beautiful.

PULTENAEAE—After R. Pulteney, an English botanist, 1730–1801.

PULVERULENTA—Dusted with a fine powder.

PUNCHELL—A Western Australian Boronia.

PUNCTATA,—UM—Dotted, spotted.

PUNGENS—Sharp, pointed.

PUNGENT—Ending in a stiff, sharp point.

PUNICEUS—Scarlet.

PURPUREA,—UM, -US—Purple.

PYANATHER—With dense heads.
PYRACANTHER—*Pyr*, fire; *akanthos*, a thorn.
PYRAMIDALIS—Pyramid-like.
PYRIFORM—Pear shaped.
PYRO—Fire.

QUADRIFIDUS—Refers to the four bundles of stamens; from *quadri-*, four in composition.
QUADRILOCULATUM—Four-celled.
QUINQUENERVIA—Five-nerved: *quinque*, five; *nervia*, sinews.

RACEME—Rasem, flowers having a common stem.
RACEMONS—Flowers in racemes.
RADIATE—Spreading from or arranged around a common centre.
RADICAL—Arising from the root or its crown as basal leaves forming a rosette at the soil surface.
RADICLE—Primary root of the seed.
RADULA—Rasp-like.
RAIN FOREST—Closed plant community dominated by soft-leaved trees with lianas and herbaceous and woody epiphytes. Classed according to latitude as tropical, sub-tropical and temperate rain-forest.
RAMOSSIMA—Much branched.
RAY—Marginal series of showy florets of capitulum of certain members of the *Compositae* family.
RECEPTACLE—That part of the floral axis from which the floral parts arise.
RECURVED—Curved downwards or backwards.
REFLEXA—Bent back.
REGELIA—After Dr von Regel, director of St Petersburg Botanical Gardens.
REGULAR—Flower with the perianth segments alike and symmetrical in more than one plane.
RENIFORM—Kidney shaped.
REPENS—Creeping.
RESEDA—To calm or soothe.
RESIN,—OUS—Similar to resin in taste or smell.
RETICULATE—A net-work.
RETORTA—Bent back.
RETUSE—Having a shallow notch at the rounded apex.
REVOLUTE—Edges of the leaves rolled back from the margin.
REVOLUTUM—Rolled back.
RHACIS or RACHIS—Primary axis of an inflorescence or compound leaf.
RHAGODIA—Berry-bearing.
RHETINODES—Resinous.
RHIN—Snout.
RHIZOME—Underground stem lasting for more than one season.

RHODON—Rose.

RHOMBOID—Approaching quadrangular, with the lateral angles obtuse.

RICINOCARPOS—With fruit (*carpos*) like the castor oil plant (*ricinus*).

RIGIDA,—US—Stiff.

RISINOSUM—Gum-bearing.

RIVULARIS—Of the rivers.

ROBINIA—After Jean Robin, French royal gàrdener, 1550–1629.

ROBUSTA,—UM—Sturdy.

RODNEYANUM—After Lord Rodney.

ROEI—From the surname Roe.

ROSA,—EA,—ERI,—EUM—Rosy.

ROSEUS—Rosy-pink.

ROSIFOLIUS—From *rosa*, a rose; *folius*, a leaf.

ROSMARINIFOLIA—Foliage like a rosemary.

ROSMARINUS—Rosemary.

ROSTELLUM—Small protruding beaklike appendage at the upper edge of the stigma of orchids.

ROSTRATUM—From *rostrate*, beaked.

ROTUNDIFOLIUM—With round leaves: *rotundus*, round; *folia*, leaf.

ROTUNDUS—Spherical, round.

RUBEUS,—ER—Red.

RUBIA—The madder plant.

RUBICUNDA—Reddish.

RUBIDA—Red stem.

RUBIGINOSA—Rusty-brown.

RUBIOIDES—Like the rubia or madder plant.

RUBERA—Red.

RUBRIFLORUS—Red flowers: *rubri*, red; *florus*, flowers.

RUBUS—The raspberry and bramble genus of the rose family.

RUE—An aromatic shrubby plant.

RUELLIA—A genus of the Acanthus family, named after the French botanist Jean Ruel (1479–1537).

RUFUS—Reddish.

RUGOSE—Covered with wrinkles.

RUPESTRIAN—Of rock.

RUSCIFOLIA—Ruscus-leafed.

RUTACEAE—From rue (see above).

RUTHENICUS—From Ruthenia in the Carpathians.

SAGITTATE—Shaped like the barbed head of an arrow.

SAINTPAULIA—After Baron Walter von Saint Paul Illaire, a German traveller (1869–1910).

SALICIFOLIA—Willow-leafed.

SALIGNA,—US—Like a willow.

SALSOLA--A plant; the saltwort genus of the goosefoot family.

SALSOLIFOLIA—With leaves like a salsola.

SALVEO,—IO—To heal; to save.

SAMBUCIFOLIUS—With leaves like a sambucus (elder tree).

SAPO,—ONARIA—Soap; soapy. The saltwort genus.

SAPROPHYTE—Plant using dead organic matter for food.

SARCOCHILUS—*Sarx*, flesh; *cheilos*, a lip.

SAXICOLA—The wheatear genus. Living or growing on rocks.

SAXIFRAGA—Of the rocks.

SCABROUS—Rough to touch.

SCABIOSA—Plants of the genus *Scabiosa*; once thought to cure skin eruptions (*scabies*, the itch).

SCALE—Thin membranous process of hair or rudimentary leaf.

SCAPE—Leafless or bracteate flower stem of plant with basal leaves.

SCANDENS—Climbing.

SCAREVOLA—Left-handed.

SCARIOUS—Thin, dry and membranous.

SCHELHAMMER—After G. C. Schelhammer, a German botanist.

SCHIZO—To cut or split.

SCHOLTZIA—After H. Scholty, a German botanical writer.

SCLEROPHYLL —Hard, stiff foliage.

SCOPARIA,—US,—UM—Brush or broom-like.

SECUNDUM—Following.

SEDUM—The stone-crop genus of Crassulaceae. From the Latin *sedum*, house-leek.

SEED—Reproductive body that contains the embryo, often with associated food reserve, with a protective covering, the seed coat.

SEGETUS—Of the cornfields.

SEMIPAPPOSUM—From *semi*, half; *pappus*, a cluster of hairs.

SENECIO—(Latin) *senex*, an old man, referring to the white pappus.

SEPIARIUS—Showy.

SEPULERAL,—ALIS—Weeping habit; *poss*, from *sepultus*, to bury.

SERICA,—EA—Silk; silky hairy.

SERRATIFOLIA—From *serratus*, saw-edged; *folia*, leaves.

SERRATUS,—ULATE—Saw-edged; serrated.

SESSIFLORA—Without flower stalks.

SESSILE,—IS—Having no stalks.

SETACEOUS—Bristle-like.

SHIRLEYAE—After Mrs J. Shirley.

SHRUB—Woody perennial that generally has several stems arising at or near the ground and smaller than a tree.

SIDEROS—Iron.

SIEBERA—After F. W. Sieber, a botanist.

SILAIFOLIA—Leaves like the silays plant.

SILOUS—Pepper sassifrage (Flannel Flower family).

SILVESTRIS—Of the woods.

SIMPLE—Undivided.

SINUATUS—Wavy.

SMITHII—After Smith, a 19th century botanist.

SOLITARY—Single, one only from the same place.

SPADIX—Fleshy or succulent axis in which flowers are frequently partly embedded.

SOLANUM—The potato and nightshade genus (*solanum*, nightshade).

SOLLYA—After R. H. Solly, an English botanist.

SOMNIFERUS—Sleep-inducing.

SOWERBAEA—After J. Sowerby, a naturalist.

SPARSA—Scattered.

SPATHE—Bract(s) enclosing a spadix or inflorescence.

SPATHULATE—Spoon shaped.

SPECIES—Group of individual plants resembling each other by a combination of constant characters: usually infertile, but often not so with individuals of another species; the basic unit in biological classification.

SPECIOSA,—US,—UM—Beautiful, handsome, showy.

SPECIOSISSIMA—Most beautiful.

SPECTABILIS—Showy, graceful, fern-like.

SPEIRA—A coil.

SPERMA,—UM—Seed.

SPICATE—In form of a spike.

SPIKE—Arrangement of sessile flowers along an unbranched axis.

SPINE—Stiff, sharp-pointed process.

SPINOSA,—US—Thorn, thorny.

SPINULOSA—Spiny.

SPIRANTHES—*Speira*, a coil; *anthos*, a flower.

SPLENDENS—Brilliant, resplendent (*splendere*, to shine).

SPOROS—Seed.

SPRENGELIA—After Sprengel, a German botanist.

SPRENGELOIDES—Sprengelia-like (*oides*, like).

SQUAMATUS—Scaly.

SQUAMULOSUM—With scales.

SQUARROSA,—UM—Ragged, scaly.

STACHYS—A spike.

STAMEN—The male reproductive organ of the flower, which produces the pollen; generally comprising an anther and filament.

STAMINODE—Sterile modified stamen.

STANDARD—Name given to the large upper (posterior) petal of the pea flower (*Papilionaceae* family).

STEEDMANII—After H. Steedman, a botanical collector.

STELLATE—Star shaped, hairs.

STELLIGERA--Starry.

STEMON—Stamen or thread.

STENOCARPUS—Narrow or small fruit.

STENOPHYLLUM—With narrow leaves.

STENOS—Narrow.

STEPHELIA,—OS—From *stephelos*, rough; of stiff habit.

STEPHOS—Crown.

STERILE—Incapable of sexual reproduction, infertile.

STIGMA—Top of the pistil (*stigme*, a point).

STIPULARIS—Having stipules.

STIPULES—A small leaf-like appendage to a leaf.

STOECHADIS—From the stoechas plant.

STOLON—A creeping, leafy, aerial stem capable of forming a new plant at its tip.

STOLONATE—Reproducing by stolons.

STOLONIFEROUS—Reproducing by stolons.

STOMA—A mouth.

STRELITZIA—After Charlotte of Mecklenburg Strelitz, wife of George III of England, 1744–1818.

STRIATIFLORA—Flowers having striata (see below).

STRIATA—Marked with fine parallel streaks or lines.

STRICTA—Upright, erect, straight.

STROPHIOLE—An appendage to the hilum of some seeds.

STUARTII—After J. McDouall Stuart, explorer.

STURTADUM—After explorer Charles Sturt.

STYPANDRA—*Stype*, two; *andros*, a man.

STYPE—Two.

STYLIDIUM, STYLOSUS—From *stylos*, a column.

SUAVEOLENS—Sweet-scented.

SUB—Below.

SUBALPINA—Of the lower mountains.

SUFFRUTICOSE—Of an herbaceous perennial with that part of the stem immediately above soil level more or less woody and perennial.

SULCATA—Furrowed.

SULLIVANII—After David Sullivan, a botanist.

SWAINSONIA—After Isaac Swainson, an English botanist and gardener, about 1790.

SYRINGA—Popular name for mock-orange; generic name for the lilac (from *syrinz*, Pan-pipes).

SYZYGIUM—Joining together.

TASMANICA—Tasmanian.

TELOPEA—Seen from afar (*tele*, far; *ophthalmos*, eye).

TEMPLETONIA—After John Templeton, an Irish botanist.

TENELLA—Delicate.

TENTELLA—Small-flowered, narrow-leafed.

TENUIFOLIA—*Tenuis*, slender; *folia*, leaves (with slender leaves).

TENUIFOLIUM—*Tenuis*, slender; *folium*, a leaf.

TENUIOR,—US—Slender.

TENUISSIMA—Very narrow leaves.

TERETIFOLIUS—Bearded bottle brush.

TESTACEUS—Terracotta, tile-coloured.

TETRAGONOUS—Four-angled.

TETRATHECA—With four parts to the seed case.

THELEMANNIANA—From the surname Thelemann.

THELYMITRA—*Thelys*, a woman; *mitra*, a cap; referring to hooded column.

THOMASIAE—After Thomas, a plant collector.

THRIX—A hair.

THRYPTOMENE—Made small (has only one seed per flower).

THUNBERGII—After Karl Per Thunberg, a Swedish botanist, 1743–1822.

THYME,THYMUS—Low half-shrubby plants with two-lipped corolla and calyx
and four diverging stamens.

THYMIFOLIA—Thyme-leafed.

THYSANOTUS—From *thysanos*, a fringe.

TIEGHEMOPANA—After von Tieghem, a French botanist, and the panax plant.

TILIACEOUS—Belonging to the *Tiliaceae* family (*Tilia*, the lime or linden
genus).

TINCTORIUS—For dyeing.

TINGITANUS—From Tingi (now Tangiers).

TOMENTOSUS—Felt-like.

TORQUATA—Twisted cóllar.

TORULOSA—Swollen (of the cones).

TRACHYMENE—From *trachys* (rough) referring to the shape of fruit.

TRADESCANTIA—After John Tradescant, English royal gardener, 1638.

TRACHYS—Rough, shaggy.

TREMULA—Trembling.

TRICOPHYLLA—With hairy leaves.

TRIDENTIFERA—Bearing a "trident"; three prongs or points.

TRIFOLIATE—Three leaves.

TRIFLORA—Three flowers.

TRILOBA,—LOBATUM—Three lobes upon a leaf; three segments.

TRILOCULARIS—Having three cells.

TRIMESTRIS—Every three months.

TRINERVIS—With three sinews (three veins).

TRIPLINERRIUM—Three-nerved.

TRISPERMA—With three seeds.

TRISTANIA—After M. Tristan, a French botanist.

TROPAEON,—ION—A trailing plant.

TROPAROLUM—From tropacon.

TUBER—Thickened underground root or stem of one year's duration that acts as a food reservoir.

TUBEROSUS—With tubers.

TUBIFLORA—*Tubus*, a pipe or trumpet; *floris*, a flower; hence trumpet flower.

TULIPA—With showy or solitary flowers, from *tulbend*, turban.

TURNBULLI—After J. Turnbull of Adelaide, South Australia.

TWINER—Plant, the stem of which twists around an adjoining object in order to climb.

ULICIFOLIA—Leaves like gorse.

UMBEL,—LATE,—ATA—A flower head; flower heads starting from the same point; flowers in umbels.

UNCINATA,—UM—Hooked.

UNDERSHRUB—Low shrub.

UNDULATE—Wave-like.

UNILATERAL—One-sided.

UNISEXUAL—Of one sex, flower having only male or female parts present.

UTILES—Useful.

UTRICULARIA –The bladderwort genus of *Lentibulariaceae*; having a bladder-like envelope on fruits (*utris*, bag or bottle).

VAGUS—Rambling.

VALVATE—Dehiscing by doors or valves; or parts without over-lapping margins.

VALVE—Segment remaining after dehiscence of a capsule.

VARIABLE,— BILIS—Variable, changing.

VARIETY—Group of individuals departing from the true species by a constant single or small combination of characters but lacking a coherent geographic distribution.

VARIEGATA—Variegated.

VEIN—Strand of conducting tissue forming the framework of fibrous tissue of a leaf.

VEITCHII—After members of the nursery firm of Veitch, 1891–1914.

VELLOREIA—In honour of Major Vellor (British).

VELUTINA—Covered with soft hairs.

VENINATUS—Poisonous.

VENOSA—Veined.

VERNICIFLUA—Of varnished appearance.

VERRUCOSA—Warty.

VERSATILE—Swinging freely on its support.

VERTICILLATE—Arranged in whorls.

VESPERTILES—,—IO—Pertaining to the evening; shaped like the wings of bats which fly in the evening.

VESTILA—Clothed.

VEXILLATA—Standard, prominent.

VICTORIAE—After Queen Victoria.

VIGNA—After Domine Vigna.

VILLOUS, VILLOSA—With long, soft hairs.

VILMORINII—After members of the French nursery firm of de Vilmorin, flourishing since mid-19th century.

VIMINALIS—Bearing osiers (drooping leaves).

VIMINARIA—Twiggy.

VIOLA,—ACEA,—ACEUS—Violet in colour or resembling the violet.

VIRGATE—Twiggy.

VIRGALUS—Twiggy, wand-like.

VIRIDIS—Green

VIRISCOLOR—Of changing colour.

VISCOSA—Sticky.

VITTADINIA—After Vittadinia, an Indian botanist.

VOLUBLE,—LIS—Changing, twisting.

WAHLENBERGIA—After the Swedish botanist, Wahlenberg, early 19th century.

WEDELIA—After G. W. Wedel, a 17th century botanist.

WESTRINGIA—After Johann Peter Westring, a Swedish physician, 1753–1833.

WHORL—Radial arrangement of organs around an axis.

WILLSII—After W. J. Wills.

WILLMOTTIAE—After Ellen Anne Willmott, an English gardener, 1869–1934.

WILSONII—After I. B. Wilson, a 19th century English botanist.

WING—Membranous expansion of an organ.

WISTERIA—After Casper Wistar, an American scientist, 1761–1818.

WOOLLSIA—After Dr Woolls.

XANTHOS—Yellow.

XANTHOCARPUM—Yellow fruit; *xanthos*, yellow; *carpos*, fruit.

XEROPHYTE—Plant subsisting on small amounts of water.

XYLOMELUM—*Xylo*, wood; *melum*, fruit.

XYLON—Wood.

XYRIS—A genus of sedge-like plants, usually with yellow flowers, of the family *Xyridaceae*. An old name for Iris.

YOMERIFORMIS—Low-growing.

YUCCA—A genus of plants of the family *Liliaceae*, natives of Mexico, New Mexico, the Caribbean area, etc.

ZIERA—Has four petals like boronia, but four stamens.

ZIER, ZIERA—After Polish botanist Zier.

VEGETATION AREAS

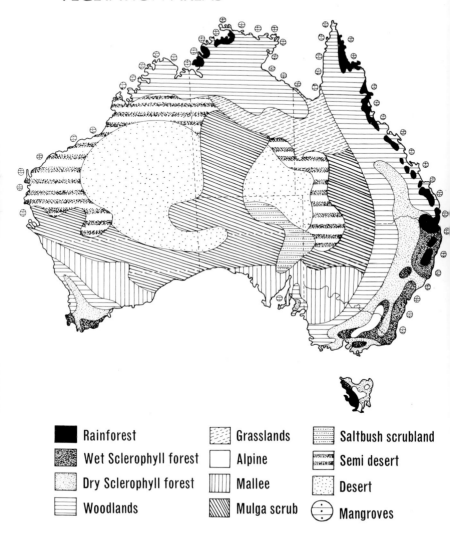

■ Rainforest	▨ Grasslands	☰ Saltbush scrubland
▦ Wet Sclerophyll forest	▢ Alpine	▤ Semi desert
▨ Dry Sclerophyll forest	▥ Mallee	⦂ Desert
≣ Woodlands	▧ Mulga scrub	⊕ Mangroves

COLOUR PLATES

and

WILDFLOWER DESCRIPTIONS

ROSTELLULARIA PEPLOIDES

FAMILY: Acanthaceae. COMMON NAME: None. COLOUR: Mauve. SIZE: Up to 9 cm high.

DESCRIPTION: A rare perennial herb. Leaves are petiolate, ovate-lanceolate 3 to 7 cm long. Calyx is tubular and deeply five lobed. Flower is 2 to 3 cm long, irregular, bisexual. Corolla: tubular, two lipped (upper lip not greatly developed), five lobed, four stamens, epipetalous, ovary superior, two locular. Fruit a capsule, opening loculicidally into two valves, seed flat and attached to hooked process.

AREA: North N.S.W. and Qld. TIME: September to January.

ROSTELLULARIA PROCUMBENS

FAMILY: Acanthaceae. COMMON NAME: None. COLOUR: Mauve. SIZE: 30 cm high.

DESCRIPTION: Erect perennial herb. Leaves simple, opposite, entire, up to 3 cm long. Flowers are in terminal, narrow raceme. Calyx lobes are linear, 3 to 5 mm long. Corolla tube is short, two lipped, upper linear 2 cm long, two undeveloped lobes, lower 2 cm long not lobed deeply, white throat with striate markings. Fruit a capsule, seeds flat.

AREA: North N.S.W. and Qld. TIME: August to December.

CORDYLINE SP. (undescribed)

FAMILY: Agavaceae. COMMON NAME: Pink Cordyline. COLOUR: Pink. SIZE: Up to 3 metres high.

DESCRIPTION: Botanically undescribed; very similar to *C. stricta*. An erect spreading shrub with a long ringed stem and long sheathing leaves more lanceolate than linear, tapering both ends. As the leaf matures the apex splits and frays; this is typical of this species. The leaves tend to bunch on a short branch from which hangs a long panicle of small flowers. The inflorescence is about 25 to 30 cm long. Flowers are bell-shaped, perianth about 15 mm long, six lobed, three smaller than the other three; the lobes are spreading or recurved, the six stamens are as long as the lower lobes. The fruit is a succulent, globular and three celled with few seeds.

AREA: South Qld., rainforest. TIME: October to December, seeds in December to January.

CORDYLINE STRICTA

FAMILY: Agavaceae. COMMON NAME: Narrow Leaf Cordyline. COLOUR: Lilac to purple. SIZE: Up to 2 metres high.

DESCRIPTION: An erect shrub with slender ringed stem. Leaves are about 60 cm long, linear, sheathing, crowded at upper ends of stems. Flowers are small, bell-shaped up to 8 mm long, six lobed spreading. The inflorescence forms long terminal panicles up to 30 cm long. Six stamens, usually white at base. Fruit is globular, more or less succulent, three celled with several seeds.

AREA: North N.S.W., south Qld., rainforest. TIME: October to December.

canthaceae
ostellularia peploides

Acanthaceae
Rostellularia procumbens

gavaceae
ordyline sp. (undescribed)

Agavaceae
Cordyline stricta

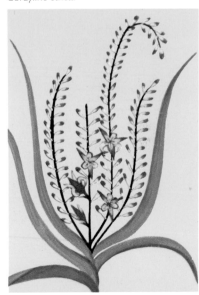

CORDYLINE TERMINALIS

FAMILY: Agavaceae. COMMON NAME: Broad Leaf Cordyline. COLOUR: Rose pink and mauve. SIZE: Up to 2 metres high.

DESCRIPTION: Erect shrub. Leaves are linear-lanceolate up to 45 cm long, 8 cm wide tapering at base to channelled petiole, stem-sheathing at base. Terminal panicle, racemes up to 20 cm long, peduncles 18 cm long. Perianth tubular, 6 to 10 mm long, crimson outside, five lobes, recurved, mauve, up to 12 mm across, five stamens, white, anthers yellow. Fruit, a berry.

AREA: North N.S.W. and Qld., marginal and rainforest. TIME: Spring to early Summer.

DORYANTHES PALMERI

FAMILY: Agavaceae. COMMON NAME: Spear Lily. COLOUR: Light red. SIZE: Flower stem up to 3 metres long.

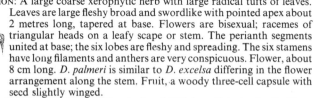

DESCRIPTION: A large coarse xerophytic herb with large radical tufts of leaves. Leaves are large fleshy broad and swordlike with pointed apex about 2 metres long, tapered at base. Flowers are bisexual; racemes or triangular heads on a leafy scape or stem. The perianth segments united at base; the six lobes are fleshy and spreading. The six stamens have long filaments and anthers are very conspicuous. Flower, about 8 cm long. *D. palmeri* is similar to *D. excelsa* differing in the flower arrangement along the stem. Fruit, a woody three-cell capsule with seed slightly winged.

AREA: North coast N.S.W. (Mt Warning) and Qld. in well drained soils. TIME: October to December.

CARPOBROTUS GLAUCESCENS

FAMILY: Aizoaceae. COMMON NAME: Angular Pigface. COLOUR: Purple-red. SIZE: Prostrate creeper.

DESCRIPTION: Glabrous succulent perennial with prostrate stems, rooting at the nodes. Leaf and stem are pale green-blue in colour. Leaves are thick, fleshy, triquetrous, opposite. Flowers are pedunculate or subsessile within a pair of terminal leaves, with numerous, narrow shiny cerise-coloured petals. Calyx tube is top-shaped, having five three-sided unequal lobes. Petaloid staminodes are numerous. (Glaucescens: blue-green with a bloom.) Fruit obovid, berrylike capsule and edible.

AREA: Native to Australia: N.S.W., Fraser Island, occurring from central Qld. coast southwards, favouring sand dunes and in abundance along beach front. TIME: All year round.

PTILOTUS SPATHULATUS

FAMILY: Amaranthaceae. COMMON NAME: None. COLOUR: White tipped with pink. SIZE: Up to 7.5 to 15 cm high.

DESCRIPTION: A prostrate perennial, growing from a thick woody rhizome. Leaves: rosette, stalked, round contrast to narrow stem leaves. Flowers are small and numerous, clothed in dense hairs, terminal, with fluffy spikes or heads and five perianths over lapping segments with five stamens. Fruit is a small circumscissile hairy nut often infertile or slow to germinate; will propagate from cuttings.

AREA: W.A., S.A. and Tas., usually in dry scrub. TIME: September to March, most of the year.

Agavaceae
Cordyline terminalis

Agavaceae
Doryanthes palmeri

Aizoaceae
Carpobrotus glaucesens

Amaranthaceae
Ptilotus spathulatus

ANIGOZANTHOS HUMILIS

FAMILY: Amaryllidaceae (Haemodoraceae). COMMON NAME: Cat's Paw. COLOUR: Yellow and red. SIZE: 20 to 45 cm high.

DESCRIPTION: A small growing, vigorous herb with short rhizomes. The straplike green leaves arise from above, while the roots extend from below the rhizome. The flowers, in racemes on a simple rhachis, are short. The perianth which is not contracted above the middle is under 5 cm long. The anther is inappendiculate (without appendages); the fruit is a three-cell capsule with several seeds in each cell.

AREA: South-western W.A. in sand. TIME: June to November.

ANIGOZANTHOS MANGLESII

FAMILY: Amaryllidaceae (Haemodoraceae). COMMON NAME: Common Green Kangaroo Paw, Red-stemmed Green Paw, Mangles or Kings Park Kangaroo Paw. COLOUR: Green and red. SIZE: Up to 90 cm high.

DESCRIPTION: A perennial herb having short rhizomes with rosettes of ribbonlike shiny green leaves. The raceme is at the end of a long red woolly stem. The flowers are green and red, rarely yellow at the base. Perianth tube is approx. 8 cm long and not contracted above the middle. Anthers are much longer than the filaments. In *A. viridis* the perianth tube is approx. 8 cm long not contracted above the middle, but the anthers are more or less as long as the filaments. Fruit is a three-cell capsule; when ripe it opens to release a number of small grey-brown seeds.

A. MENGLESII

FILAMENT   ANTHER

A. VIRIDIS

AREA: South-western W.A. in sandy-gravel soils. TIME: June to December.

BLANCOA CANESCENS

FAMILY: Amaryllidaceae (Haemodoraceae). COMMON NAME: Red Bugle. COLOUR: Red. SIZE: Up to 25 cm high.

DESCRIPTION: A small caespitose (tufted) herb with a small rhizome. Narrow, iris-like, stem-clasping green leaves, 17 to 25 cm long. Flowers are bell-shaped and pendulous in a terminal cluster which hangs low to the ground. The calyx and petals unite in a perianth with six petal lobes. Fruit is a three-cell capsule.

AREA: South-western W.A., in the Avon and Darling districts, in white sand. TIME: May to October.

CRINUM FLACCIDUM

FAMILY: Amaryllidaceae. COMMON NAME: Darling Lily or Sandover Lily. COLOUR: White. SIZE: To 50 cm high.

DESCRIPTION: Small erect herb with underground bulb. Leaves are radical, linear, channelled up to 75 cm long. Cymose flower; six to eight umbels on pedicels. Perianth tube is about 6 cm long; lobes broadest of all Australian species, 6 cm long. Three ovaries, locular inferior; seeds have corky covering. *Crinum asiaticum* is stalkless. Crinums are a variable group and require further study.

AREA: N.S.W., Vic. and S.A., in wet and damp places, along banks of inland rivers; seed is distributed on water. TIME: October to February.

Amaryllidaceae
Anigozanthos humilis

Amaryllidaceae
Anigozanthos manglesii

Amaryllidaceae
Blancoa canescens

Amaryllidaceae
Crinum flaccidum

ALYXIA RUSCIFOLIA

FAMILY: Apocynaceae. COMMON NAME: Chain fruit. COLOUR: White. SIZE: 120 cm high.

DESCRIPTION: Low shrub. Leaves are narrow, lanceolate, 2.5 cm long, armed with pungent points, and in three to five whorls. Flowers are in cymes or solitary, bisexual. The five sepals are imbricate in bud. Corolla is tubular, five lobed; the lobes are imbricate and contorted, shaped like sails of a windmill. The five stamens are epipetalous, alternating with the corolla segments; the anthers are erect. Fruit are orange berries growing to form a chain, hence the common name. Alyxia— a chain.

AREA: Northern Australia, Qld. and N.S.W., in the sandy forest land of the coast, mostly tropical. TIME: Spring and Summer, August to December.

ALOCASIA MACRORRHIZOS

FAMILY: Araceae. COMMON NAME: Spoon Lily or Conjevoi. COLOUR: Green. SIZE: Up to 100 cm high.

DESCRIPTION: Large, erect, perennial herb with a stout tuberous rhizome. Leaves are radical, hastate-cordate with thick spongy petiole. Large, green, spoon-shape spathes on thick spongy peduncle. Female flowers are at the base of the spadix with the male at the top and rudimentary flowers between. All of the plant contains an intensely acrid and poisonous substance. Suitable cooking, it is said, will destroy the poisons in the rhizome. Fruit are globular red berries—this in itself is a beautiful display.

AREA: N.S.W., Qld., Vic., in moist forest. TIME: December to February.

ASTROTRICHA LONGIFOLIA

FAMILY: Araliaceae. COMMON NAME: None. COLOUR: White. SIZE: Up to 2 metres high.

DESCRIPTION: A tall shrub more or less clothed in stellate tomentum. Leaves are variable, usually not exceeding 1 cm wide, narrow-lanceolate, thin and flat with rather dull upper surface. Specimens from the north coast of N.S.W. are distinctively small-leaved, slender form of this variable species. The Qld. specimens are all of the larger coarser form. Illustrated is a specimen from Fraser Island. Flowers are about 5 mm across, articulate on pedicels in umbels in terminal panicle. Calyx teeth are minute; five petals, pubescent outside. Fruit compressed schizocarp.

AREA: N.S.W., Qld. and Fraser Island, widespread in gullies and dry sclerophyll forest. TIME: September to February.

HOYA AUSTRALIS

FAMILY: Asclepiadaceae. COMMON NAME: Australia Wax Plant. COLOUR: White—at times pink. SIZE: Climber.

DESCRIPTION: A twining perennial with leaves opposite; it is smooth, fleshy, broad-elliptic, almost egg-shape, 5 to 6 cm long. Flowers are highly perfumed with five calyx lobes and five waxy petals on a simple umbel, approximately 15 mm across. The stamens have a fleshy appendage known as a corona. The fruit is a follicle; seeds, silky.

AREA: North N.S.W. coast and nearby ranges, Qld. coast. TIME: October to early April, seeds in May to June.

Apocynaceae
Alyxia ruscifolia

Araceae
Alocasia macrorrhizos

Araliaceae
Astrotricha longifolia

Asclepiadaceae
Hoya australis

MARSDENIA ROSTRATA

FAMILY: Asclepiadaceae. COMMON NAME: None. COLOUR: White. SIZE: Vine.

DESCRIPTION: A robust twiner, glabrous, young growth may be tomentose. Leaves are up to 10 cm long, ovate to orbicular, acuminate, dark green above and paler underneath, on long petioles. Flowers are numerous in simple umbels up to 30 cm across. Corolla is 6 mm across, urn-shaped, bearded inside, with lobes longer than tube. Fruit is a follicle, broad, acuminate and 5 cm long.

AREA: N.S.W. along coast and nearby mountain ranges in or near rainforest in sheltered areas. TIME: October to February.

PANDOREA PANDORANA

FAMILY: Bignoniaceae. COMMON NAME: Wonga Wonga Vine. COLOUR: Cream with maroon markings. SIZE: Climber.

DESCRIPTION: A variable, twining woody climber. Leaves are opposite, smooth, light green, and pinnate. Flowers are in a loose inflorescence from the leaf axil. Calyx is bell-shaped with five short lobes. Corolla is tubular or trumpet-shaped with five irregular lobes, large up to 30 mm long and four stamens. The fruit is a large capsule 40 to 50 mm long, which releases a number of winged seeds.

AREA: N.S.W., Qld., N.T., Vic., S.A. and Tas. TIME: September to November, seeds in November to December.

ECHIUM LYCOPSIS

FAMILY: Boraginaceae. COMMON NAME: Paterson's Curse, Salvation Jane. COLOUR: Red changing to purple-blue. SIZE: 1 metre high.

DESCRIPTION: Erect biennial variable herb, scabrous to hairy. Leaves are sparingly scabrous to softly hairy; radical leaves are ovate, up to 10 cm long with prominent lateral veins; cauline leaves are oblong to lanceolate, cordate at base, 3 to 9 cm long. Flower cymes are arranged in a panicle, calyx is five cleft. Corolla tube has five unequal lobes, five stamens.

AREA: N.S.W., Qld. and Vic., widespread, introduced from the Mediterranean, considered a noxious weed; cultivated land, vacant land and roadsides. TIME: Winter to early Summer.

BRUNONIA AUSTRALIS

FAMILY: Brunoniaceae. COMMON NAME: Blue Pincushion. COLOUR: Blue. SIZE: 30 cm high.

DESCRIPTION: A small perennial herb with a basal rosette of leaves up to 10 cm long, grey green, ovate to spathulate. Flowers are a very dense terminal pincushionlike cluster on an erect slender stem, 2 to 4 cm across. Five sepals support the floral cluster. As the fruit ripens the five calyx lobes, which form a tube, harden and enclose the small nut. First discovered in 1804 on Mornington Peninsular, Victoria.

AREA: South N.S.W., S.A. and Vic. in sandy and clay soils. TIME: August to December.

Asclepiadaceae
Marsdenia rostrata

Bigoniaceae
Pandorea pandorana

Boraginaceae
Echuim lycopsis

Brunoniaceae
Brunonia australis

BURMANNIA DISTICHA

FAMILY: Burmanniaceae. COMMON NAME: None. COLOUR: Purple. SIZE: 60 cm high.

DESCRIPTION: A slender plant. Leaves are radical, lanceolate, green, up to 6 cm long. Inflorescence is terminal; flower has three petallike winged and angular sepals, and three petals of unusual shape, 3 cm long. Stamens are longer than the perianth. Fruit is a capsule containing numerous seeds.

AREA: North N.S.W. and Qld., swamps and open heath. TIME: August to December.

BYBLIS GIGANTEA

FAMILY: Byblidaceae. COMMON NAME: Rainbow Plant. COLOUR: Deep pink. SIZE: Up to 60 cm high.

DESCRIPTION: Small tufted, insectivorous herb. Leaves are very thin, sometimes channelled, clothed with two kinds of glands. Stalk glands secrete sticky mucilage which traps small insects. The tiny sessile glands appear to have digestive function. Striking similarity to Sundews. Flowers are solitary on axillary peduncles. Plant is named after Byblis, daughter of Miletus who, being in love with her twin brother when he ran away, collapsed into tears and was changed into a fountain. The glistening glands are likened to tears. *Byblis liniflora* is a low herb up to 75 cm high; flowers are blue, growing in bogs.

AREA: W.A., *B. gigantea* in Avon and Darling districts and *B. liniflora* in Kimberley area and N.T. TIME: *B. gigantea*—June to January; *B. liniflora*—April to July.

BAUHINIA VARIEGATA

FAMILY: Caesalpiniaceae. COMMON NAME: Variegated Bauhinia. COLOUR: White with red and purple markings. SIZE: Up to 14 metres high.

DESCRIPTION: Spreading tree. Leaves are broad ovate, folding, emarginate, predominantly five to seven nerved, penniveined; 7 to 15 cm long. Flower is up to 10 cm across. Flag deep red and purple markings; four petals, two marked, two clear; terminal cluster. An escaped exotic, originally cultivated as shade and ornamental trees.

AREA: Tropical Qld. and north and south N.S.W. TIME: Mainly June to November, often flowering from Spring into late Summer.

Burmanniaceae
Burmannia disticha

Byblidaceae
Byblis gigantea

Caesalpiniaceae
Bauhinia variegata

fruiting body of Bauhinia variegata

CASSIA SP.

FAMILY: Caesalpiniaceae. COMMON NAME: None. COLOUR: Yellow. SIZE: Up to 3 metres high.

DESCRIPTION: Small shrub. Leaves are pinnate, five to seven pairs of leaflets 2 to 5 cm long, linear; glands absent. Inflorescence panicle, axillary. Flower is 2 to 3 cm across; five sepals up to 6 mm; five petals; ovate; six stamens.

AREA: Central and western Qld., north-west N.S.W., central Australia in dry areas and close to desert. TIME: March to April.

CASSIA ARTEMISIOIDES

FAMILY: Caesalpiniaceae. COMMON NAME: Silver Cassia or Blue Bush Cassia. COLOUR: Yellow. SIZE: Up to 2 metres high.

DESCRIPTION: Erect shrub. Leaves are pinnate with three to six pairs of leaflets, linear-terete and hoary white; glands between leaflets are absent. Inflorescence axillary; five sepals, small. Flower is 18 mm across with five petals, ovate light-brown markings, style and ovary-curved and horn-shaped. The ten stamens are all perfect but not always all equal. Dried leaves and fruit of *Cassia senna* are used as laxative.

AREA: *C. artemisioides*: W.A., S.A., Vic., N.S.W. and Qld. *C. senna*: tropical and sub-tropical. TIME: July to January.

CASSIA COLUTEOIDES

FAMILY: Caesalpiniaceae. COMMON NAME: None. COLOUR: Yellow. SIZE: Up to 3 metres high.

DESCRIPTION: An erect divaricate shrub, glabrous or nearly so. Leaves are pinnate 5 to 10 cm long, with four to six pairs of leaflets, ovate, obovate to elliptic, slightly mucronate, 2 to 4 cm long, up to 15 mm wide, with a stout gland between the lowest pair of leaflets only. Flowers are terminal panicle.

AREA: N.S.W. and Qld., widespread, popular in gardens, coastal, garden escape, introduced from tropical America. TIME: March to May.

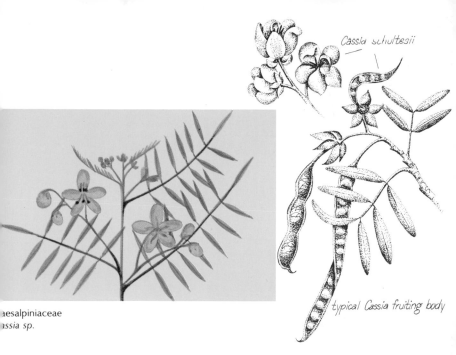

Cassia schultesii

typical *Cassia* fruiting body

Caesalpiniaceae
Cassia sp.

Caesalpiniaceae
Cassia artemisioides

Caesalpiniaceae
Cassia coluteoides

WAHLENBERGIA GLORIOSA

FAMILY: Campanulaceae. COMMON NAME: Royal Blue Bell. COLOUR: Azure purple. SIZE: Creeper.

DESCRIPTION: A creeping herb with woody root-stock or rhizome. Leaves are oblong, 2 to 3 cm long, with wavy margins. Flowers are on long peduncles, small calyx lobes, narrow-lanceolate. Corolla is five lobed and opens widely to 3 cm across. Taxonomic position of the genus is in process of revision.

AREA: N.S.W., Vic. and A.C.T., a wildflower of snow gum woodlands. TIME: January to March.

CASUARINA LITTORALIS

FAMILY: Casuarinaceae. COMMON NAME: Black She Oak. COLOUR: Female flower red, male rusty red. SIZE: Up to 6 metres high.

DESCRIPTION: A tall upright shrub or small tree. Bark is rough and furrowed. Branchlets are dark green; true leaves are minute teeth at the twig joints with six to eight leaf-teeth whorls. Trees, male and female. Male spike is slender and weak; male flower has one stamen tipped with rusty red pollen. Female flower is a cluster of red stigmas protruding from small swellings which mature to a chestnut brown; cone-nut is up to 3 cm long and 2 cm across; truncate cone valves are prominent and angular.

AREA: N.S.W., coast and foot of nearby mountains, in sandy or stony forest soils. TIME: March to October.

CEPHALOTUS FOLLICULARIS

FAMILY: Cephalotaceae. COMMON NAME: Albany Pitcher-Plant or Fly Catcher Plant. COLOUR: White; pitchers, green but red when growing in sunlight. SIZE: Up to 13 cm high.

DESCRIPTION: A small plant, the only species of *Cephalotaceae* family. The young plant has a deep tap root with a rosette of leaves around the top; in older plants the tap root may fork having a smaller rosette of leaves. The foliage leaves begin to grow in July and August and fully develop by September and October. The leaves which modify into pitchers begin their development during June and July and are not fully mature until December and January, by that stage they are 5 cm long and 19 mm across. Ants and insects are trapped in the pitchers which contain a fluid with digestive properties. The flowers have six petals, are in short terminal inflorescence on a long triquetrous stalk.

AREA: Albany swamps and King River swamps, W.A. TIME: Flower, September to October.

TRADESCANTIA ALBIFLORA

FAMILY: Commelinaceae. COMMON NAME: Wandering Jew. COLOUR: White. SIZE: Up to 30 cm high.

DESCRIPTION: An introduced, weak, procumbent or ascending perennial, glabrous herb with stems rooting at the nodes. Leaves are alternate, ovate, up to 5 cm long, ciliate at the base, indistinct petiole. Flowers are in a terminal cluster from leaf axils. The two bracts are unequal and leaflike in appearance. The three sepals are green. The three petals are free; the six stamens have hairy filaments. Three fruit, locular capsule. Considered a common weed as is *Commelina cyanea*.

AREA: Qld., N.S.W., Vic., S.A., along roadsides, forests, in shaded places. TIME: August to November.

Campanulaceae
Vahlenbergia gloriosa

Casuarinaceae
Casuarina littoralis

Cephalotaceae
Cephalotus follicilaris

Commelinaceae
Tradescantia albiflora

AMMOBIUM ALATUM

FAMILY: Compositae. COMMON NAME: None. COLOUR: White with yellow centre.
SIZE: Up to 1½ metres high.

DESCRIPTION: A perennial herb; leaves are basal, lanceolate, spathulate, undulate

to sinuate up to 20 cm long, light green and paler on underside. The
four stems are sided, coarse and enlarged by addition of membranous wings which more or less sinuate on the margins, and pale
green in colour. The small flower heads are surrounded by numerous
rows of papery involucal bracts. Bracts are sessile and flowers on
very short peduncle, making the inflorescence everlasting like the
Helichrysum genus. Only two species and both endemic to Australia.

AREA: N.S.W., sandy habitats, along roadsides, open grasslands. TIME:
November to February.

BRACHYCOME ACULEATA

FAMILY: Compositae. COMMON NAME: None. COLOUR: Pink, white, lilac or blue.
SIZE: Up to 60 cm high.

DESCRIPTION: A slender perennial. Leaves are radical and cauline, oblanceolate
to spathulate or linear up to 10 cm long. Flower head is on a long leafy peduncle,
the involucre up to 2 mm across. Bracts are herbaceous with rays up to 8 mm long.
The fruit is a smooth cypsella about 4 mm long, green-brown, with wings about 5
mm wide.

AREA: N.S.W., in dry well-drained places, coast and nearby ranges. TIME:
Mainly, October to February.

BRACHYCOME ANGUSTIFOLIA VAR. HETEROPHYLLA

FAMILY: Compositae. COMMON NAME: None. COLOUR: Mauve, pink or blue.
SIZE: Up to 35 cm high.

DESCRIPTION: A small stoloniferous perennial, glabrous or may be glandular-
hairy. Leaves are narrow to broad-elliptical, and pinnatisect (variable leaf) up to 5
cm long. Flower head is on a filiform, leafless peduncle. The involucre is 5 cm
across; the ray 6 to 10 mm long. The one-seed fruit is about 2 mm long, brown, and
flattened with narrow ciliate wings. For positive identification the herbarium
should be supplied fruit.

AREA: N.S.W., Qld., Vic., coastal and nearby mountains. TIME: Most of the year.

BRACHYCOME IBERIDIFOLIA

FAMILY: Compositae. COMMON NAME: Swan River Daisy. COLOUR: Purple, violet
or white. SIZE: Up to 40 cm high.

DESCRIPTION: A wiry perennial, branching and glandular-pubescent. Leaves are
pinnatisect with five to thirteen rather long linear segments; minute pappus.
Involucral bracts are ovate-oblong 2 to 5 mm; eight to twenty ligules, 10 to 20 mm
long. Fruit achenes are narrow-obconical, 2 mm long.

AREA: W.A., S.A., Central Australia, Musgrave Ranges. TIME: July to
December.

Compositae
Ammobium alatum

Compositae
Brachycome angustifolia var. *heterophylla*

Compositae
Brachycome aculeata

Compositae
Brachycome iberidifolia

CELMISIA LONGIFOLIA

FAMILY: Compositae. COMMON NAME: Snow Daisy or Silver Daisy. COLOUR: White. SIZE: Up to 25 cm high.

DESCRIPTION: Perennial herb. Leaves are radical, linear to linear-lanceolate, 20 cm long, sheathing at the base, margins revolute, densely white tomentose under surface, silvery tomentose (older leaves glabrous) on upper surface. Flower head is solitary; peduncle bracts linear; and lanceolate up to 3 cm long. Involucral bracts are imbricate; ray flowers are numerous with female 1 to 2 cm long. Disc flowers are bisexual and yellow.

AREA: N.S.W., Vic. and Tas., wet ground, high elevations. TIME: October to February.

CICHORIUM INTYBUS

FAMILY: Compositae. COMMON NAME: Chicory. COLOUR: Blue-mauve. SIZE: Up to 1 metre high.

DESCRIPTION: A short, erect, perennial herb. Leaves are radical, pinnatifid 10 to 25 cm long, lanceolate, cauline and stem-clasping. Flower head is solitary or two or three together, may be terminal or sessile and axillary. Involucre is small about 5 mm across, and oblong. The flower is ligulate or straplike; the rays blue up to 1 cm long. Fruit is a striate cypsella and only 2 mm long.

AREA: N.S.W., Qld., Vic., along road sides. Introduced from Europe, it is commercial chicory. The roots are dried and ground before being incorporated into coffee. TIME: December to November.

HELIPTERUM ALBICANS VAR. ALBICANS

FAMILY: Compositae. COMMON NAME: Hoary Sunray. COLOUR: Pure white, or tinged with pink, yellow or brown. SIZE: Up to 40 cm high.

DESCRIPTION: Tufted perennial herb. Leaves are softly grey-woolly on both upper and lower surface, radical or chiefly near base of stems or branches, linear to linear-oblong, and 4 to 10 cm long. Flower heads are on leafless scape 3 to 4 cm diameter. Involucral bracts are in many rows, petaloid, spreading, 8 to 18 cm long.

AREA: N.S.W., Qld., Vic. and S.A., in grassland and tall open forests. TIME: Summer.

HELIPTERUM FLORIBUNDUM

FAMILY: Compositae. COMMON NAME: None. COLOUR: White with yellow centre. SIZE: Up to 40 cm high.

DESCRIPTION: Rigid annual, sometimes perennial. Stems are prostrate and ascending. Leaves are linear, 1 to 3 cm long and 1 to 3 cm wide. Flower head is solitary at end of branches or often corymbosely arranged; involucral bracts are snow white, broad but acute; receptacle is conical. Fruit achenes are silky-villous, with six to ten pappus bristles, plumose, dilated, rigid.

AREA: West of S.A., N.T. and Central Australia, Nullarbor Plain, east to Lake Frome, north to Warburton river, N.S.W. and Vic. TIME: October to February.

Compositae
Celmisia longifolia

Compositae
Cichorium intybus

Compositae
Helipterum albicans var. albicans

Compositae
Helipterum floribundum

HELIPTERUM ROSEUM

FAMILY: Compositae. COMMON NAME: None. COLOUR: Pink and white with brown centre. SIZE: Up to 35 cm high.

DESCRIPTION: Slender tufted herb. Leaves are alternate; linear-lanceolate and 2.5 mm to 8 cm long. Head is solitary terminal up to 5 cm across. Disc flowers are bisexual tubular, brown, 5 mm across. Bracts are in many rows, all petaloid, pink, radiating clockwise 6 to 10 mm long.

AREA: W.A., Irwin District, Austin and Coolgardie District. TIME: August to September.

OLEARIA SP. NOV. (AFF. O. CHRYSOPHYLLA)

FAMILY: Compositae. COMMON NAME: None. COLOUR: White. SIZE: To 2 metres high.

DESCRIPTION: Erect shrub. Leaves are opposite, pedunculate, glabrous, pale-green above and finely stellate, silver-green underneath, lanceolate to oblong, margins sinuate-dentate, revolute 6 to 12 cm long. Heads are 2.5 cm across, numerous, with six to eight ray flowers up to 12 mm long. Disc flowers are bisexual, tubular, few. *O.* sp. is very close to *O. chrysophylla*. *O. chrysophylla* has leaves that are silver-white underneath, with two to four ray flowers.

AREA: N.S.W., coast and nearby mountains (Nandewar Ranges) and north Tablelands. TIME: November to February.

OLEARIA ELLIPTICA

FAMILY: Compositae. COMMON NAME: Sticky Daisy Bush. COLOUR: White. SIZE: About 2 metres high.

DESCRIPTION: Erect shrub. Leaves are dark green, glabrous with glandular dots, alternate, lanceolate to oblong, and 3 to 9 cm long. Heads are numerous, with clusters forming a terminal corymb; panicle is leafless, involucre is broad 8 mm across. Disc flowers are bisexual and tubular, the ray florets being six to eight in number, white, 6 to 12 mm long and 5 mm wide. Pappus-hairs are 6 mm long. Fruit is a silky-hairy cypsela.

PAPPUS HAIRS

RAY PETAL 10-12 mm.

AREA: Coast and nearby mountains, wet area and gullies. TIME: September to December.

OLEARIA GRAVIS

FAMILY: Compositae. COMMON NAME: Rough Olearia. COLOUR: White. SIZE: Up to 1 metre high.

DESCRIPTION: Erect herb with scabrous-pubescent stem. Leaves are alternate, petiolate, lanceolate, 2.5 to 8 cm long, upper surface shiny, dark green, deeply-veined, lightly pubescent; undersurface pubescent turning brown, edges undulate, dentate and recurved. Flowers are terminal panicle; six to eight ray flowers up to 14 mm long; disc flowers are bisexual, tubular, numerous and yellow, 6 to 8 mm in diameter.

AREA: North N.S.W. and New England tablelands, coast and nearby ranges. TIME: Spring and Summer.

Compositae
elipterum roseum

Compositae
Olearia sp. nova. aff. O. chrysophylla

Compositae
Olearia elliptica

Compositae
Olearia gravis

OLEARIA VISCIDULA

FAMILY: Compositae. COMMON NAME: Sticky Olearia. COLOUR: White. SIZE: Up to 2 metres high.

DESCRIPTION: Erect viscid shrub. Leaves are linear, 4 to 8 mm wide, opposite, viscid, 4 to 10 cm long, with white-green undersides. Flower heads are 1.5 cm in diameter, solitary or loose corymb. Involucre is 6 mm across; ray flowers number eight to ten; disc flowers are up to 4 mm in diameter.

AREA: N.S.W., Qld., coast and mountains, rainforest and wet sclerophyll forest. TIME: September to December.

PODOLEPIS LONGIPEDATA

FAMILY: Compositae. COMMON NAME: Native Dandelion. COLOUR: Yellow. SIZE: Up to 70 cm high.

DESCRIPTION: Small erect perennial plant, with stems often branched and lightly covered with woolly hairs. Leaves are linear or cauline, with radical leaves much broader. Flower heads are often solitary or a few together. Involucre is ovoid to hemispherical; unequal bracts; outer flowers are female, with two to four lobes or teeth; disc flowers are tubular and five-toothed.

AREA: N.S.W. and Qld., coastal and nearby mountains, preferring rich soils. TIME: Spring and Summer.

PODOLEPIS JACEOIDES

FAMILY: Compositae. COMMON NAME: Showy Podolepis. COLOUR: Yellow. SIZE: Up to 60 cm high.

DESCRIPTION: A perennial herb. Leaves are alternate, radical and cauline, lower, longest up to 20 cm long. Stem is lanceolate. Involucre to 3 cm diameter. There are thirty to forty ray flowers with three ray ligules lobed up to 25 mm long. Disc flowers are tubular, five-toothed. Pappus is up to 1 cm long.

AREA: N.S.W., Vic., Qld., widespread, coast and mountains (west in Nandewar Ranges) sub-alps, open country and roadsides. TIME: September to December.

SENECIO LAUTUS (form of)

FAMILY: Compositae. COMMON NAME: Variable Groundsel or Fireweed. COLOUR: Yellow. SIZE: Up to 1 metre high.

DESCRIPTION: Erect, glabrous, perennial, variable herb (at times spreading). Leaves are linear, lanceolate, toothed or pinnatisect, blade or lobes 5 mm wide, stem-clasping. Form illustrated has soft and fernlike leaves. Flower heads are several in a loose terminal corymb. Involucre is campanulate (bell-shaped). Ray flowers have ten to fifteen rays 1 cm long; disc flowers are numerous, tubular, pappus 6 to 8 mm long.

AREA: N.S.W., Vic., Qld., sandy soils in dunes, along roadsides and forests. TIME: September to March.

Compositae
Olearia viscidula

Compositae
Podolepis jaceoides

Compositae
Podolepis longipedata

Compositae
Senecio lautus ssp. (form)

SENECIO LAUTUS SSP. BIPINNATISECTUS

FAMILY: Compositae. COMMON NAME: None. COLOUR: Yellow. SIZE: Up to 2 metres high.

DESCRIPTION: An erect, glabrous herb with deeply-lobed, twice-pinnatisect leaves up to 10 cm long. Flower heads are solitary or several in a loose terminal corymb. Involucre is bell-shaped up to 1 cm diameter. Ten to fifteen ray flowers; ray ligule lobed, up to 15 mm long. Disc flowers are tubular; disc 10 mm across. *Senecio lautus*, a variable species, is at present being reclassified, with *S. lautus* ssp. *bipinnatisectus* being one of the variants.

AREA: N.S.W., marginal, sandy soils to gullies. TIME: September to February.

CUCUMIS AFRICANUS

FAMILY: Cucurbitaceae. COMMON NAME: Prickly Cucumber. COLOUR: Yellow. SIZE: Prostrate.

DESCRIPTION: Monoecious prostrate. Stems are slender scabrous. Leaves are ovate-cordate in outline 3 to 8 cm long, palmately divided into five- to seven-toothed lobes. Flowers are unisexual, with the male in clusters on short peduncles and the female solitary. Fruit is globular, 6 to 8 cm long and 4 to 5 cm diameter, nonpoisonous, beset with long soft bristles, yellow when ripe, pulp very bitter. Introduced from South Africa.

AREA: N.S.W. and Qld., coastal, along roadsides, fields, close to cultivated land and edges of watercourses. TIME: November to March.

DIPLOCYCLOS PALMATUS

FAMILY: Cucurbitaceae. COMMON NAME: Cucumber. COLOUR: Cream. SIZE: Creeper

DESCRIPTION: Creeping and herb-climbing plant by means of its simple tendrils. Leaves are alternate, five-lobed, palmately veined. Flowers are unisexual, with two to five males in leaf axil, and the female solitary. Calyx is five-lobed; corolla is five-lobed. Fruit is green with white longitudinal stripes, 4 cm in diameter. Thought to be introduced.

AREA: N.S.W., found along roadsides, open fields, widespread. TIME: Flower, in Spring; fruit in Summer.

ACKAMA PANICULATA

FAMILY: Cunoniaceae. COMMON NAME: Corkwood. COLOUR: Cream. SIZE: Small to medium tree.

DESCRIPTION: Small to medium tree, with thick and corky bark. Leaves are compound with five to seven leaflets. These leaflets are ovate to elliptic and 4 to 6 cm long. Flowers are bisexual, regular, with five sepals and five petals about 1 mm long and slightly longer than sepals. Styles are deciduous. Fruit is a capsule, subglobular, 2 to 3 mm long.

AREA: N.S.W. and Qld., coastal and nearby mountains in rainforest. TIME: Spring.

Compositae
Senecio lautus ssp. bipinnatisectus

Cucurbitaceae
Cucumis africanus

Cucurbitaceae
Diplocyclos palmatus

Cunoniaceae
Ackama paniculata

CALLICOMA SERRATIFOLIA

FAMILY: Cunoniaceae. COMMON NAME: Hazelwood or Black Wattle. COLOUR: White to Cream. SIZE: Up to 9 metres high.

DESCRIPTION: Small tree. Leaves are opposite, elliptic-oblong to broad lanceolate, serrated, 5 to 10 cm long, glabrous, shiny above and white-green to rusty tomentose underneath. Flowers are numerous in globular heads 10 to 20 mm diameter; they are solitary or have several peduncles 3 cm long. Petals are absent but stamens are longer than sepals.

AREA: N.S.W., Qld., Vic., marginal edges of rainforest and near creeks, rocky gullies and sandy soils. TIME: October to November.

CERATOPETALUM APETALUM

FAMILY: Cunoniaceae. COMMON NAME: Coachwood. COLOUR: Red sepals. SIZE: Up to 20 metres high.

DESCRIPTION: Small to tall tree. Bark is smooth, grey, and fragrant when broken. Leaves are three folioate (simple) articulate on the petiole, elliptic-narrow ovate, serrate, acuminate, and 9 to 16 cm long. Flowers: dense corymbose cyme. Petals are absent, with sepals enlarged 5 to 7 mm long. As in *C. gummiferum*, the sepals become the display of the tree.

AREA: N.S.W. and Qld., in rainforest and gullies. TIME: Flower, Spring; fruit, Summer.

CERATOPETALUM GUMMIFERUM

FAMILY: Cunoniaceae. COMMON NAME: Christmas Bush. COLOUR: White. SIZE: Up to 8 metres high.

DESCRIPTION: Tall shrub with rough brown bark. Leaves are opposite, three foliate; leaflets are 4 to 8 cm long, glabrous, ovate to lanceolate, obtusely serrated. Flowers are white in terminal cymes or panicles. Five sepals united at the base; lobes spreading; five small inconspicuous tiny-horned petals. Sepals enlarge from 2 mm to 15 mm, becoming red after flowering. It is the red sepals which attract attention. Member of the Coachwood family. Fruit is a nut.

AREA: N.S.W., well drained soils, coast and nearby ranges. TIME: November to December; fruit: December to January.

GAHNIA SIEBERANA

FAMILY: Cyperaceae. COMMON NAME: Red-fruit Saw-edge. COLOUR: Cream; fruit, red. SIZE: Up to 3 metres high.

DESCRIPTION: A coarse rushlike, perennial and tufted herb. Stems are hollow with six to ten nodes. Leaves are long, linear, stem-clasping, glumes (attending bracts) that are smooth or glabrous, upper and lower shorter or glabrous, upper and lower shorter than the middle ones. Inflorescence, paniculate. Spikelets are numerous, subtended by leafy bracts. Each pedicellate spikelet is with two flowers, the terminal one being apparently bisexual and fertile with a male or sterile one below it. Flowers are small and featherlike. Fruit is a globular nut.

AREA: N.S.W., Qld., Vic., S.A., coastal and nearby mountains, marginal edge of rainforest. TIME: January to March; fruit: February to April.

Cunoniaceae
Callicoma serratifolia

Cunoniaceae
Ceratopetalum gammiferum

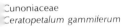

Cunoniaceae
Ceratopetalum apelalum

Cyperaceae
Gahnia sieberana

HIBBERTIA SP.

FAMILY: Dilleniaceae. COMMON NAME: None. COLOUR: Yellow. SIZE: Up to 60 cm high.

DESCRIPTION: Erect pubescent plant, covered with downy hairs. Leaves are spathulate to ovate, woolly tomentose, apex-pointed, and 1 to 3 cm long. Calyx is pubescent and densely covered with downy hairs. Flower is 4 cm in diameter, with five petals and emarginate.

AREA: Common in north-east N.S.W. and the New England tablelands; though rare in herbaria, as yet to be described. Another new species in the granite areas. TIME: Spring to Summer.

HIBBERTIA ASPERA

FAMILY: Dilleniaceae. COMMON NAME: None. COLOUR: Yellow. SIZE: Up to 1 metre high.

DESCRIPTION: An erect but, at times, ascending shrub. Leaves are opposite, obtuse to narrow-oblong, 5 to 25 mm long, light green and lightly-stellate hairs above, pale green and more or less tomentose underneath. Flowers are solitary on slender and often recurved peduncles, five sepals, five petals notched at the tips, usually ten to twelve stamens, ovary very pubescent.

AREA: N.S.W., Qld., Vic., widespread, coast and nearby mountains, sandstone. TIME: August to February.

HIBBERTIA LINEARIS

FAMILY: Dilleniaceae. COMMON NAME: Showy Guinea Flower. COLOUR: Yellow. SIZE: Up to 160 cm high.

DESCRIPTION: A diffuse glabrous shrub (very small in habit). Leaves are alternate, linear-oblong, 10 to 12 mm long. Flower: five sepals 5 to 6 mm long, petals 8 to 10 mm long notched at tip. Five to ten stamens. Buds and young shoots are at times woolly. *H. obtusifolia*: covered with short stellate grey tomentum. Leaves are broad-oblong, spathulate very obtuse, and flowers are large.

AREA: N.S.W., Qld., Vic., coastal and nearby mountains in dry and stony areas. TIME: August to November.

HIBBERTIA SERPYLLIFOLIA

FAMILY: Dilleniaceae. COMMON NAME: Thyme Leaf Guinea. COLOUR: Yellow. SIZE: Up to 60 cm high.

DESCRIPTION: Prostrate or decumbent shrub. Leaves are linear, oblong-ovate or spathulate, 3 to 6 mm long and 1 to 3 mm wide, margins revolute. Flowers are on short peduncles almost sessile; five sepals and five petals. Stamens are placed around carpels, at times unevenly. Carpels are tomentose.

AREA: Widespread, N.S.W., coast and nearby mountains, sandstone areas. TIME: October to January.

Dilleniaceae
Hibbertia sp. (undescribed)

Dilleniaceae
Hibbertia linearis

Dilleniaceae
Hibbertia aspera

.

Dilleniaceae
Hibbertia serphyllifolia

(A) DROSERA ARCTURI

FAMILY: Droseraceae. COMMON NAME: Alpine Sundew. COLOUR: White. SIZE: Up to 10 cm high.
DESCRIPTION: Leaves: blunt, linear, radical, rosette; peduncle 10 cm long. Flower: solitary, green sepals, petals 1.5 to 2 cm wide.
AREA: Plant restricted to high moors of N.S.W., Vic., Tas. and N.Z. in moss beds. TIME: Spring.

(B) DROSERA WHITTAKERI

FAMILY: Droseraceae. COMMON NAME: Scented Sundew. COLOUR: White. SIZE: Up to 4 cm high.
DESCRIPTION: Bulbous root stock. Leaves: spathulate, 4 cm long, large, radical rosette. Flower: solitary, peduncle 2 to 4 cm long, petals 12 to 15 mm wide, three styles.
AREA: Vic. and S.A., damp soils. TIME: July to September.

ELAEOCARPUS RETICULATUS SYN. E. CYANEUS

FAMILY: Elaeocarpaceae. COMMON NAME: Blue Berry Ash. COLOUR: White or pink; fruit, dark blue. SIZE: Up to 7 metres high.
DESCRIPTION: A small tree. Leaves are simple, alternate, lanceolate to elliptic-oblong, acuminate, slightly serrate or toothed, glossy, 5 to 12 cm long, petioles up to 2 cm long. Flowers are bisexual numerous, bell-shaped, with racemes up to 9 cm long. Four to five sepals, with as many petals, fringed on the edge. The fruiting body equals the flower display hence the common name. Fruit: drupe (succulent, indehiscent) blue berry, 12 to 18 mm across.
AREA: N.S.W., coast and nearby mountains, rainforest, and marginal. TIME: November to December; fruit, February to April.

BRACHYLOMA DAPHNOIDES VAR. LATIUSCULUM

FAMILY: Epacridaceae. COMMON NAME: Daphne Heath. COLOUR: White. SIZE: Up to 1 metre high.
DESCRIPTION: A variable shrub, with very twiggy branches. (*B. daphnoides* illustrated in *A Field Guide to Wildflowers*, Vol. 1, is a form which appears to be peculiar to east New England tablelands.) Leaves: sessile or nearly so, alternate, smooth, grey-green, oblong-ovate, 8 to 15 mm long. Young leaf tips are red-pink and soft. Flowers are in axillary clusters, corolla-tube is glabrous inside below middle, less than 6 mm long. Corolla throat is closed by reflexed hairs; petal tips are brown; anthers are enclosed within corolla tube. Fruit is drupaceous and seeds solitary. This genus is at present being revised.
AREA: N.S.W., Qld., Vic., coastal and nearby mountains, and tablelands in drier rocky soils and woodlands. TIME: September to December.

DRACOPHYLLUM SECUNDUM

FAMILY: Epacridaceae. COMMON NAME: None. COLOUR: White or pink. SIZE: Up to 1 metre high.
DESCRIPTION: A small erect or procumbent shrub. Leaves: lanceolate, linear, spreading, dark green to red, rigid, sheathing at the base and leaving annular scars at leaf fall, 5 to 10 cm long. Flowers: terminal raceme, one-sided inflorescence or narrow panicle, sepals 4 to 6 mm long. Corolla tube is 6 to 10 mm long; lobes are small, recurved. Bracts: sheathing and dropping away.
AREA: N.S.W., heathlands, moist rocky areas. TIME: July to October along coast; August to December in tablelands and mountains.

Droseraceae
(A) *Drosera arcturi* (B) *Drosera whittakeri*

Eleaocarpaceae
Elaeocarpus reticulatus syn. E. cyaneus

Epacridaceae
Brachyloma daphnoides var. latiusculum

Epacridaceae
Dracophyllum secundum

PLATE 17

EPACRIS IMPRESSA

FAMILY: Epacridaceae. COMMON NAME: Common Heath. COLOUR: Pink, red or white. SIZE: Up to 1 metre high.

DESCRIPTION: Slender erect shrub. Branches: minutely pubescent. Leaves: sessile, linear-lanceolate, pungent pointed, 7 to 10 mm long. Flowers: spreading, bracts and sepals white to pink; corolla tube 8 to 18 mm long, lobes short. Common but very variable in colour forms. *E. obtusifolia*: leaves and sepals oblong-obtuse. *E. lanuginosa*: leaves lanceolate, pungent; flowers in leafy spike.

AREA: N.S.W., Vic., Tas. and S.A., illustrated is the pink form of Victoria's State flower. TIME: May to November.

LEUCOPOGON ERICOIDES

FAMILY: Epacridaceae. COMMON NAME: White Beard. COLOUR: White. SIZE: Up to 1 metre high.

DESCRIPTION: Diffuse heath-like shrub with wiry branches. Leaves are small alternate, narrow-oblong, acuminate pungent pointed, 4 to 8 mm long, spreading. Sepals are glabrous outside, with anthers obtuse, and callous tip absent. Flowers are erect in small clusters in leaf axil.

AREA: N.S.W., south Qld., Vic., heathlands. TIME: August to October.

LEUCOPOGON LANCEOLATUS VAR. LANCEOLATUS

FAMILY: Epacridaceae. COMMON NAME: None. COLOUR: White. SIZE: Up to 150 cm high.

DESCRIPTION: A bushy shrub. Leaves: narrow-lanceolate, elliptic-lanceolate or oblong, flat obtuse with callous tip 4 to 10 mm wide and 1 to 4 cm long. Young stem is glabrous or minutely pubescent. Flowers are in loose inflorescence, spike 1 to 4 cm long. Sepals obtuse, flower 3 mm long, anthers with callous tip.

AREA: N.S.W., Qld., Vic., Tas., heathlands, coast and mountains. TIME: August to October.

LEUCOPOGON MELALEUCOIDES

FAMILY: Epacridaceae. COMMON NAME: None. COLOUR: White. SIZE: Up to 60 cm high.

DESCRIPTION: A low shrub. Leaves: alternate, linear, lanceolate, acuminate with hyaline tip 15 to 25 mm long. Flowers: numerous, showy in dense cluster on spike twice to three times as long as the leaves, corolla tube 8 mm long, five lobes, recurved, villous, 6 to 8 mm long.

AREA: N.S.W., Qld., Vic., heathland, coast and mountains. TIME: September to November.

Epacridaceae
Epacris impressa

Epacridaceae
Leucopogon ericoides

Epacridaceae
Leucopogon lanceolatus var. lanceolatus

Epacridaceae
Leucopogon melaleucoides

LEUCOPOGON MICROPHYLLUS

FAMILY: Epacridaceae. COMMON NAME: None. COLOUR: White. SIZE: Up to 1 metre high.

DESCRIPTION: Erect, at times straggling, shrub with wiry branches. Leaves: ovate-oblong to linear, 2 to 6 mm long obtuse. Flowers are in loose dense clusters in leaf axil. Sepals are very acute. Corolla tube is twice as long as sepals; lobes glabrous, recurved, and about 3 mm long.

AREA: N.S.W., Qld., Vic., Tas., widespread, heathland, dry forest, sandstone. TIME: Mainly Spring but most of the year.

LEUCOPOGON MUTICUS

FAMILY: Epacridaceae. COMMON NAME: None. COLOUR: White. SIZE: Up to 2 metres high.

DESCRIPTION: Slender, erect shrub. Leaves are alternate, erect or nearly so, light to grey-green underneath, prominently veined, elliptic or obovate to oblanceolate, 1 to 2 cm long and 3 to 4 mm wide. Flowers are erect, at times spreading. Corolla glabrous; lobes recurved.

AREA: N.S.W., Vic., coast and nearby mountains, New England plateau, heathlands and dry sclerophyll forests. TIME: August to November.

PENTACHONDRA PUMILA

FAMILY: Epacridaceae. COMMON NAME: Carpet Heath or Cushion Heath. COLOUR: Flower white; fruit red. SIZE: Up to 12 cm high.

DESCRIPTION: A low, mountain-inhabiting herb, forming a dense mat of crowded leaves. Leaves: linear, 3 to 6 mm long. Flowers: sessile, 6 mm diameter. Fruit is berrylike in shape, crimson, 6 to 8 mm diameter.

AREA: N.S.W., Vic., Tas. and N.Z., widespread on mountains and summits. TIME: Spring to Summer.

RICHEA CONTINENTIS

FAMILY: Epacridaceae. COMMON NAME: Candle Heath or Prickly Leafed Swamp Heath. COLOUR: White. SIZE: Up to 1 metre high.

DESCRIPTION: A rigid shrub. Leaves: recurved, lanceolate, 3 to 12 cm long, sheathing at base, possibly among the longest of heath leaves. Flowers: 5 to 10 mm long, massed in erect, cylindrical panicles, flower spike up to 12 cm long.

AREA: N.S.W., Vic. and A.C.T., in sphagnum bogs, this is the only species of *Richea* not endemic to Tasmania. TIME: Spring to Summer.

Epacridaceae
Leucopogon microphyllus

Epacridaceae
Leucopogon muticus

Epacridaceae
Pentachondra pumila

Epacridaceae
Richea continentis

RICHEA DRACOPHYLLA

FAMILY: Epacridaceae. COMMON NAME: Richea. COLOUR: White. SIZE: Up to 5 metres high.

DESCRIPTION: A tall branched palmlike shrub. Leaves are sheathing, 20 cm long, crowded at the ends of naked brown branches. The shedding leaves leave ring scars when they fall. The inflorescence subtended by brown or pink-brown bracts which shed as flower develops. Fruit is a hard brown capsule containing numerous small seeds.

AREA: Tasmania only. TIME: September to October.

RICHEA SCOPARIA

FAMILY: Epacridaceae. COMMON NAME: Kerosene Bush. COLOUR: White tinted with orange or pink. SIZE: Up to 1.5 metres high.

DESCRIPTION: Erect rigid bush with thin red-brown flaky bark. Leaves recurved, lanceolate, 4.5 to 5 cm long, sheathing at the base which decay very gradually, persisting for a long time and leaving a ring on the stem after falling. Flower appears to lack petals; petals acting as a cap are shed in early stage of flowering. The spike is up to 9 cm long. The flower has a strong pungent kerosene smell.

AREA: Tasmania only. TIME: August to November.

STYPHELIA BEHRII SYN. ASTROLOMA CONOSTEPHIOIDES

FAMILY: Epacridaceae. COMMON NAME: Flame Heath. COLOUR: Red. SIZE: Up to 1 metre high.

DESCRIPTION: Small erect herb with pubescent branchlets. Leaves: linear to linear-lanceolate, 6 to 20 mm long, pungent pointed, pubescent or glabrous, margins recurved. Flowers are drooping; bracts and sepals 12 to 15 mm long, turning red. Corolla is 18 to 22 mm long. Plant is better known as *Astroloma conostephioides*. Fruit succulent.

AREA: N.S.W., Vic. and S.A., heathlands. TIME: Most of the year.

STYPHELIA TUBIFLORA

FAMILY: Epacridaceae. COMMON NAME: None. COLOUR: Red or pink. SIZE: Up to 1 metre high.

DESCRIPTION: Spreading shrub. Branches are glabrous or very minutely pubescent. Leaves: oblong-linear or slightly cuneate, margins recurved, abruptly mucronate, corolla tube slender 20 to 25 mm long, bearded inside.

AREA: N.S.W., widespread in dry sclerophyll forest, sandstone, granite and heathlands. TIME: April to August.

Epacridaceae
Richea dracophylla

Epacridaceae
Richea scoparia

Epacridaceae
Styphelia behrii syn. Astroloma conostephioides

Epacridaceae
Styphelia tubiflora

RICINOCARPUS PINIFOLIUS

FAMILY: Euphorbiaceae. COMMON NAME: Wedding Bush. COLOUR: White. SIZE: Up to 2 metres.

DESCRIPTION: An erect monoecious shrub. Leaves: arranged spirally, linear, mucronate revolute margins, dark green, 2 to 5 cm long. Flowers: pedicels 1 to 2.5 cm long, calyx four- to six-lobed, mostly five petals but six is not uncommon, 10 to 15 mm long in terminal cluster, mostly one female with three to six males, often only female or male. Once in bloom this plant cannot be mistaken; the whole shrub is a mass of flower. Fruit is red-brown with short spiny protruberances.

AREA: N.S.W., Qld., Vic., Fraser Island and Tas., coastal heath and sand dunes. TIME: August to September.

GERANIUM NEGLECTUM

FAMILY: Geraniaceae. COMMON NAME: Snow Geranium. COLOUR: Mauve. SIZE: Decumbent.

DESCRIPTION: A weak ascending, often diffuse, perennial herb. Leaves: alternate, palmately lobed, 1 to 4 cm wide, often purple underneath. Plant is sparsely covered with flatly-pressed hairs. Flowers: solitary, five sepals, hairy, five petals, 20 to 30 mm diameter.

AREA: N.S.W. and Vic., mountains at high altitudes, in swamps and along creek banks. TIME: Spring and Summer.

GOODENIA GENICULATA

FAMILY: Goodeniaceae. COMMON NAME: Bent Goodenia. COLOUR: Yellow. SIZE: Up to 30 cm high.

DESCRIPTION: Perennial procumbent or ascending herb, clothed with pubescent short or spreading straight hairs. Leaves: almost radical, oblanceolate, rarely obovate-oblong, acute or obtuse, tapering to a petiole, usually with minute, distinct glandular teeth, 2 to 10 cm long and 3 to 8 mm wide. Flowers: solitary, peduncle slender and longer than the stem leaf, axillary, sepals linear and obtuse, corolla pubescent outside. Fruit is a capsule, seed flat.

AREA: N.S.W., Vic., S.A. and Tas., open woodlands. TIME: July to January.

GOODENIA OVATA

FAMILY: Goodeniaceae. COMMON NAME: None. COLOUR: Yellow. SIZE: Up to 3 metres high.

DESCRIPTION: Already illustrated in Volume 1 is a South Australian form *G. ovata.* This plant is very variable from area to area. Illustrated here is a specimen found throughout north N.S.W.; in comparison *G. ovata* on the tablelands is a much larger, more robust plant than in the drier areas. The leaf is more succulent in drier areas.

AREA: N.S.W., Qld., S.A., Vic. and A.C.T., widespread on coasts, mountains and tablelands. TIME: Spring to Summer.

Euphorbiaceae
Ricinocarpus pinifolius

Geraniaceae
Geranium neglecta

Goodeniaceae
Goodenia geniculata

Goodeniaceae
Goodenia ovata

SCAEVOLA RAMOSISSIMA

FAMILY: Goodeniaceae. COMMON NAME: Purple Fan Flower. COLOUR: Purple to mauve. SIZE: Up to 100 cm high.

DESCRIPTION: Shrubby herb that is ascending, hispid and scabrous. Leaves: linear to lanceolate, sessile, 2.5 to 5 cm long. Flowers: pedunculate in leaf axils, peduncles with leafy bracts, at times branching in cymes. Five sepals; corolla oblique 18 to 25 mm long; lobes have broad marginal wings.

AREA: N.S.W., Qld., and Vic., widespread in heathlands and dry sclerophyll forest, sandstone and granite. TIME: Most of the year.

VELLEIA SPATHULATA

FAMILY: Goodeniaceae. COMMON NAME: Wild Pansies. COLOUR: Yellow. SIZE: Flower stems up to 22 cm high.

DESCRIPTION: A weedlike plant with basal rosette and flowering stems. Leaves are oblong to spathulate, up to 15 cm long, entire or with teeth. Stems are weak branching. Inflorescence: terminal dichotomous cyme. Three sepals, lanceolate to ovate to oblong-lanceolate. Corolla: to 12 mm long, five-lobed. Fruit is a capsule.

AREA: N.S.W., Qld., along roadsides, clearings in poor soils and moist grounds. TIME: September to March.

OTTELIA OVALIFOLIA

FAMILY: Hydrocharitaceae. COMMON NAME: Swamp Lily. COLOUR: White. SIZE: Flower 4 to 15 cm above water.

DESCRIPTION: A fresh water, aquatic herb, with perennial root stock. Leaves: basal rising from root stock on bottom of pond, lake or stream, petioles long, radical, elliptical, with parallel venation, 4 to 12 cm long floating on the surface. Three sepals. Flowers: bisexual, 3 to 4 cm diameter, solitary within a two-lobed, tubular six-rib spathe, 25 mm long; three petals, very delicate and semitransparent. Male flowers are pedicellate; female flowers are sessile. Three to twelve stamens, with stigma divided into six to eight lobes.

AREA: Throughout Australia except Tas. in fresh water ponds, lakes and streams. TIME: January to May.

Goodeniaceae
Scaevola ramosissima

Goodeniaceae
Velleia spathulata

Hydrocharitaceae
Ottelia ovalifolia

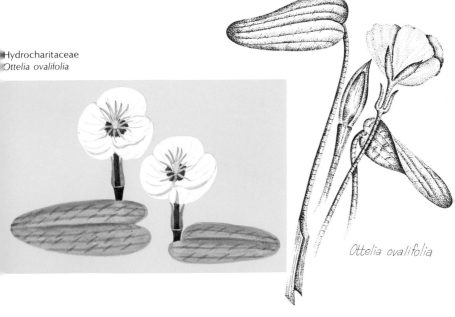

Ottelia ovalifolia

DIPLARRHENA MORAEA

FAMILY: Iridaceae. COMMON NAME: Butterfly Flag or Poorman's Orchid.
COLOUR: Pale blue-mauve. SIZE: Up to 60 cm high.

DESCRIPTION: Tall delicate herb. Leaves: linear, flat, radical, up to 60 cm long,
resembling *Patersonia*. Flowers are terminal in two long, green sheathing bracts.
Flowers appear one at a time over a long period, each lasting only one day. Calyx:
tube long and thin, three lobes, upper larger than the two lower ones, 25 mm
diameter. Three small petals are marked with yellow and occasionally lilac. Fruit is
an oblong, three-angled capsule.

AREA: Vic., Tas. and south-east N.S.W., moist areas. TIME: September to
December; seed, December to January.

PATERSONIA FRAGILIS

FAMILY: Iridaceae. COMMON NAME: Fragile Iris. COLOUR: Purple. SIZE: Up to 36
cm high.

DESCRIPTION: Erect herb with glabrous rhizome. Leaves are rigid and 15 to 40 cm
long. Scape is leafless, 20 to 35 cm long. Flowers are regular in terminal cluster
enclosed by two large, striate spathes. Outer perianth lobes are 10 mm long.

AREA: N.S.W., widespread in sandstone and granite, damp soils. TIME: Spring.

PATERSONIA SERICEA

FAMILY: Iridaceae. COMMON NAME: Bush Iris or Silky Purple Flag. COLOUR:
Blue-purple or deep purple. SIZE: Up to 30 cm high.

DESCRIPTION: Erect herb rising from underground rhizome, with stem leaves and
bracts covered with silky woolly hairs. Leaves: long, radical, linear (not much wider
than the stem), and stiff and flat, stem holding one or more blooms, wilting by
afternoon. Flowers: three sepals, three petals, three stamens.

AREA: N.S.W., Qld. and Vic., coastal and nearby mountains, in poor soils and
rock habitat. TIME: September to October.

AJUGA AUSTRALIS

FAMILY: Lamiaceae—syn. Labiatae. COMMON NAME: Australian Bugle. COLOUR:
Blue or purple. SIZE: Up to 30 cm high.

DESCRIPTION: An erect perennial herb. Leaves: obovate to oblong, radical,
bluntly toothed, 4 to 12 cm long. Scape carries small, sessile, almost entire, upper
floral leaves. Flowers form false whorls from leaf axil. Corolla upper lip is
inconspicuous, lower lip long and spreading, three-lobed, middle lobe large,
emarginate, variable in size up to 20 mm long, calyx five-toothed.

AREA: N.S.W., Qld., Vic., S.A. and Tas., widespread, roadsides, open forests and
fields. TIME: October to December.

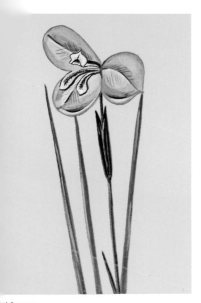

Iridaceae
Diplarrhena moraea

Iridaceae
Patersonia fragilis

Iridaceae
Patersonia sericea

Lamiaceae
Ajuga australis

HEMIGENIA DIELSII

FAMILY: Lamiaceae—syn. Labiatae. COMMON NAME: None. COLOUR: White, mauve, blue or violet. SIZE: Up to 120 cm high.

DESCRIPTION: Dense shrub. Leaves are very narrow, channelled and 25 mm long. Calyx: hairy, five-toothed, teeth as long as tube, young parts very hoary-pubescent. Flower: two-lipped, five-lobed, tube 20 mm long.

AREA: W.A., sandy heath. TIME: September to October.

PROSTANTHERA INCISA

FAMILY: Lamiaceae—syn. Labiatae. COMMON NAME: Cut-leaf Mint Bush. COLOUR: Blue-mauve. SIZE: Up to 2 metres high.

DESCRIPTION: Erect shrub, softly pubescent. Leaves: ovate, toothed, 1 to 3 cm long; floral leaves smaller or absent. Calyx lobes are unequal; flowers are bell-shaped, two-lipped with upper lip two-lobed and lower lip three-lobed; peduncle short in leaf axil.

AREA: N.S.W., Qld. and Vic., coastal and nearby mountains. TIME: August to October.

PROSTANTHERA LASIANTHOS

FAMILY: Lamiaceae—syn. Labiatae. COMMON NAME: Victoria Christmas Bush. COLOUR: White with mauve markings. SIZE: Up to 5 metres high.

DESCRIPTION: Erect shrub. Leaves: lanceolate to oblong-lanceolate, serrate, from 3 to 10 cm long, lighter on underside. Flowers are in large racemes or thyrses; the floral leaves are small often absent. Corolla is often spotted, up to 12 mm long, with wide or broad lobes.

AREA: N.S.W., Vic. and Tas., in forests. TIME: Summer.

PROSTANTHERA NIVEA

FAMILY: Lamiaceae—syn. Labiatae. COMMON NAME: White Mint Bush. COLOUR: White with orange marking. SIZE: Up to 125 cm high.

DESCRIPTION: An erect shrub. Leaves: linear to linear-lanceolate, 20 to 40 mm long, light green. Calyx is two-lipped, lobes unequal. Corolla perianth: 10 mm long, two-lipped, upper lip short not deeply lobed but lower lip deeply lobed, middle lobe up to 20 mm long, terminal raceme.

AREA: N.S.W., Qld. and Vic., coastal and inland, central areas. TIME: September to January.

Lamiaceae
Hemigenia dielsii

Lamiaceae
Prostanthera incisa

Lamiaceae
Prostanthera lasianthos

Lamiaceae
Prostanthera nivea

PROSTANTHERA OVALIFOLIA

FAMILY: Lamiaceae—syn. Labiatae. COMMON NAME: Oval Leaf Mint Bush. COLOUR: Mauve-purple. SIZE: Up to 2 metres high.

DESCRIPTION: Large shrub. Leaves: opposite, entire or crenate, thick, lanceolate to oblanceolate, 1 to 4 cm long, tapering to petiole 5 to 15 mm long. Raceme is short; floral bracts acuminate, broad, noticeable on young buds. Corolla is 6 to 10 mm long with lower lip deeply three-lobed.

AREA: N.S.W. and south Qld., in mountains and marginal rainforest. TIME: September to November.

SCUTELLARIA HUMILIS

FAMILY: Lamiaceae—syn. Labiatae. COMMON NAME: Skull Caps. COLOUR: Mauve and purple. SIZE: Up to 15 cm high.

DESCRIPTION: Perennial herb stoloniferous with creeping root stocks and ascending stems, and pubescent with minute white appressed hairs almost glabrous. Leaves: opposite, petiolate, ovate, crenate to lobed, 12 mm long. Flowers are in pairs from leaf axil. Calyx has divided upper lip with hollow scalelike protuberance. Corolla: 5 mm long, lower lip longer than upper, convex, spreading and three-lobed, upper lip concave, emarginate.

AREA: N.S.W., widespread. TIME: Spring.

TEUCRIUM CORYMBOSUM (common form)

FAMILY: Lamiaceae—syn. Labiatae. COMMON NAME: None. COLOUR: Up to 1 metre high.

DESCRIPTION: Erect perennial herb. Leaves: ovate to ovate-lanceolate, deeply or irregularly toothed or lobed 2 to 5 cm long. Floral leaves are smaller and narrow. Flowers in loose cymes from floral leaf axils form terminal panicle. Calyx: five-toothed, 3 to 5 mm long. Corolla: two-lipped, five-lobed, four upper lobes equal, middle or lower lobe twice as long. Four stamens in pairs. Fruit is a schizocarp.

AREA: Eastern states, widespread. TIME: Summer and early Autumn.

WESTRINGIA EREMICOLA VAR. EREMICOLA

FAMILY: Lamiaceae—syn. Labiatae. COMMON NAME: None. COLOUR: Pale mauve with white and orange markings. SIZE: Up to 2 metres high.

DESCRIPTION: Shrub. Leaves: in whorls of three narrow-linear to linear, revolute, 7 to 20 mm long, 1 to 2 mm wide. Flowers: axillary, sessile; calyx has few hairs; lobes deltoid less than 2 mm long. Corolla: 4 to 7 mm long, two-lipped, upper lip erect, lower lip long and spreading with markings.

AREA: N.S.W., sandstone and granite. TIME: Most of the year.

amiaceae
rostanthera ovalifolia

Lamiaceae
Scutellaria humilis

amiaceae
eucrium corymbosum (common form)

Lamiaceae
Westringia eremicola var. eremicola

WESTRINGIA GLABRA

FAMILY: Lamiaceae—syn. Labiatae. COMMON NAME: Violet westringia. COLOUR: Mauve with orange markings. SIZE: Up to 150 cm high.

DESCRIPTION: Erect shrub. Leaves: dark green, ovate to lanceolate, glabrous, in whorls of four, 10 to 25 mm long. Flowers: axillary, often solitary or small terminal cluster, sessile; calyx campanulate, five-toothed. Corolla: two-lipped and five-lobed, middle lobe of lower lip spotted with orange, 18 mm long.

AREA: N.S.W., Qld. and Vic., coastal and mountains. TIME: Most of the year.

ENDIANDRA SIEBERI

FAMILY: Lauraceae. COMMON NAME: Native Plum or Hard Corkwood. COLOUR: Cream-green. SIZE: Up to 9 metres high.

DESCRIPTION: A medium glabrous tree. Leaves: alternate, ovate-lanceolate, oblong or elliptic, shiny green, 2.5 to 5 cm long, yellow-green mid vein, paler green underside. Flowers are very small in a compound cyme or panicles 5 to 8 cm long. Perianth has six segments. Fruit: a berry, oval, 18 mm long, black in colour when ripe. Fragrance similar to nutmeg.

AREA: N.S.W. and Qld., coast and nearby mountains, rainforest. TIME: October to December; fruit, December to March.

PLANCHONIA CAREYA

FAMILY: Lecythidaceae. COMMON NAME: Cocky Apple. COLOUR: White centre tipped with pink. SIZE: Up to 6 metres high.

DESCRIPTION: Small tree. Leaves: spathulate to obovate, margins slightly crenate, shiny, 6 to 10 cm long. Sepals: four-lobed, holding four petals, stamens numerous, long, delicate filaments. Flower is 5 cm across and very showy. Fruit is fig-shaped.

AREA: N.T. and Qld., tropical, coastal extending to dry areas such as Arnhem Land and Katharine Gorge. TIME: June to October, flowering in dry seasons.

UTRICULARIA MENZIESII

FAMILY: Lentibulariaceae. COMMON NAME: Red Coats. COLOUR: Red. SIZE: Up to 6 cm high.

DESCRIPTION: A slender carnivorous herb known as Bladderworts. Its basal leaves may be submerged or exposed. The bladderlike trap is also submerged. The trap draws insects inside by a sudden, powerful suction. The flowers are solitary on short stems. Each flower has a long tubular appendage with large apronlike petal hanging in front. This flower is unmistakable once seen.

AREA: W.A., in partly flooded areas in Darling, Eyre and Warren districts. TIME: June to September.

amiaceae
Vestringia glabra

Lauraceae
Endiandra sieberi

ecythidaceae
lanchonia careya

Lentibulariaceae
Utricularis menziesii

BLANDFORDIA NOBILIS

FAMILY: Liliaceae. COMMON NAME: Sydney Christmas Bell. COLOUR: Red and yellow. SIZE: Up to 50 cm high.

DESCRIPTION: Erect perennial herb with fibrous roots. Leaves: crowded at base of stem, linear, margins crenulate, rough. Flowers: three to ten per raceme, perianth tube cylindrical, narrowing above base, 20 to 40 mm long, 5 to 12 mm across, usually constricted at the lobes.

AREA: N.S.W., widespread, coastal and damp places in nearby mountains. TIME: November to January.

BLANDFORDIA PUNICEA

FAMILY: Liliaceae. COMMON NAME: Christmas Bells. COLOUR: Red and yellow. SIZE: Up to 90 cm high.

DESCRIPTION: Tall herb with fibrous roots. Leaves are crowded at base of stem, linear, ribbonlike up to 46 cm long, coarse, margins crenulated, rough. Flowers: terminal clusters five to twelve per raceme. Perianth: bell-shaped, 44 mm long, scarlet outside, except for the margins of the three inner perianth lobes which are yellow, and yellow inside. Fruit is a capsule 38 mm long.

AREA: Tas., coastal and mountains, sandy soils and acidic moorlands. TIME: December to February.

BULBINOPSIS BULBOSA SYN. BULBINE BULBOSA

FAMILY: Liliaceae. COMMON NAME: Bulbine Lily. COLOUR: Yellow with green markings. SIZE: Up to 40 cm high.

DESCRIPTION: A small variable herb with onionlike, soft fleshy basal leaves. Flowers: terminal raceme on stalks up to 40 cm long, pedicels 3 to 4 cm long. Perianth: six in number, segments subequal and free, 2 to 3 cm across, six stamens, filaments bearded. Underside of perianth is marked with green lines. Fruit is a capsule 6 to 8 mm wide.

AREA: N.S.W., Qld., Vic. and Tas. in coastal, mountain and grasslands areas. TIME: Spring, September to November.

BURCHARDIA UMBELLATA

FAMILY: Liliaceae. COMMON NAME: Milkmaids. COLOUR: White with red markings. SIZE: Up to 60 cm high.

DESCRIPTION: An erect herb. Leaves: basal, narrow, linear, sheathing at base, 15 cm long. Flowers: star-shaped in terminal umbels, three sepals, three petals, free, 15 mm long, six stamens, with filaments flat at base. Fruit is a capsule.

AREA: All states and Tas., widespread—woods and open fields. TIME: Spring and Summer.

Liliaceae
Blandfordia nobilis

Liliaceae
Blandfordia punicea

Liliaceae
Bulbinopsis bulbosa syn. Bulbine bulbosa

Liliaceae
Burchardia umbellata

DIANELLA CAERULEA

FAMILY: Liliaceae. COMMON NAME: Tufted Lily. COLOUR: Blue. SIZE: Up to 50 cm high.

DESCRIPTION: A glabrous perennial herb. Leaves are linear and sheathing at the base. Groups of leaves bunch along the stem on short branches. Sheath of young leaves close at the base but split with age; lamina folded more or less tightly just above the sheath; margins scabrous; a keel, 10 to 60 cm long and 2 to 15 mm wide. Flowers are in terminal panicles, spreading 10 to 30 cm long and 12 mm across. Fruit is a blue berry.

AREA: N.S.W. and Vic., coastal, mountains, sandy sandstone and granite soils. TIME: Summer.

DIANELLA REVOLUTA

FAMILY: Liliaceae. COMMON NAME: Tinsel Lily. COLOUR: Blue. SIZE: Up to 60 cm high.

DESCRIPTION: A glabrous perennial herb. Leaves: revolute, well-keeled sheath, 20 to 40 cm long. Flowers are in a loose or spreading panicle 20 to 50 cm long. Perianth: six segments, subequal, yellow stamens. Anthers are yellow-brown or black, three or more times as long as thickest part of the filament. Fruit is a blue berry.

AREA: All states, temporal Australia, mountains, open forest and heathlands. TIME: October to December.

DIANELLA REVOLUTA (form) (Described only)

FAMILY: Liliaceae. COMMON NAME: Blue Tinsel Lily. COLOUR: Blue. SIZE: 60 cm.

DESCRIPTION: Perennial herb. Leaves: glaucous, almost flat, not tightly folded above the sheath, give a channel appearance. A distinct form, unmistakably different, but for the present placed with *D. revoluta*.

AREA: N.S.W., Qld. and Vic., widespread, sandstone and granite areas. TIME: October to December.

DICHOPOGON FIMBRIATUS

FAMILY: Liliaceae. COMMON NAME: Chocolate Lily. COLOUR: Purple, rarely white. SIZE: Up to 1 metre high.

DESCRIPTION: Erect herb. Leaves: radical, flat 4 to 5 mm wide, 3 to 8 cm long. Flowers: in terminal loose raceme of three or four together or solitary, axil, in floral bracts. Perianth: six segments, free, spreading, do not twist after flowering, chocolate-scented. Fruit is an erect capsule.

AREA: N.S.W., widespread, grasslands and forests. TIME: September to February.

DRYMOPHILA MOOREI

FAMILY: Liliaceae. COMMON NAME: None. COLOUR: White. SIZE: Climber or Vine.

DESCRIPTION: A small herbaceous plant with erect stem. Leaves: alternate, lanceolate to elliptical, shiny, stiff, 3 to 5 cm long. Flowers: terminal raceme, six petals, free, 2 to 3 cm across, numerous stamens, yellow. Fruit is a yellow berry.

AREA: N.S.W., north coast, south Qld., nearby mountains. TIME: August to October; seed, November to December.

Liliaceae
Dianella caerulea

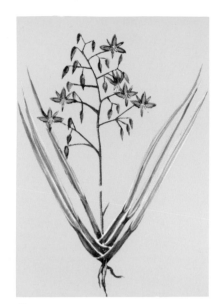

Liliaceae
Dianella revoluta

Liliaceae
Trichopogon fimbriatus

Liliaceae
Drymophila moorei

ISOTOMA AXILLARIS

FAMILY: Lobeliaceae. COMMON NAME: Rock Isotoma. COLOUR: Blue-mauve.
SIZE: Up to 30 cm high.

DESCRIPTION: Small, at times erect, bushy herb. Leaves: soft, fleshy, green,
fernlike, alternate, linear, deeply divided segments. Flowers: solitary in leaf axil,
pedunculate, five sepals, 10 to 15 mm long, perianth tube 25 mm long, five lobes, 18
to 30 mm long. Plant has foul smelling perfume which will cause headaches if
inhaled over long period. Stems have acrid, burning and poisonous milky sap
which is very harmful to eyes. Never allow children to come in contact with·
Isotomas.

AREA: N.S.W., Qld. and Vic., mountains, tablelands and open areas. TIME:
October to December.

ISOTOMA ANETHIFOLIA

FAMILY: Lobeliaceae. COMMON NAME: Mauve Isotoma. COLOUR: White tipped
with mauve. SIZE: Up to 60 cm high.

DESCRIPTION: Erect, glabrous herb. Leaves: alternate, linear 10 cm long with
narrow, linear segments. Flowers: solitary in leaf axil, pedunculate, five sepals
pointed 5 to 8 mm long, corolla tubular with five spreading lobes (two upper, three
lower, lower much longer at 2.5 cm), five stamens united to style and sickle-shaped.
Fruit is an urn-shaped capsule. Stems when broken produce an acrid milky sap
which is harmful to eyes.

AREA: N.S.W., tablelands. TIME: September to November; seed, November to
December.

LOBELIA GIBBOSA

FAMILY: Lobeliaceae. COMMON NAME: Tall Lobelia. COLOUR: Blue with white
markings. SIZE: Up to 45 cm high.

DESCRIPTION: An annual herb. Leaves are alternate, linear, toothed. Basal leaves
are generally broader and toothed. There is a terminal raceme of several blooms.
Flowers: five-lobed, upper two lobes are small and recurved, the lower three lobes
are longer and broader, 15 cm long. White markings on lower lobes quite
unmistakable.

AREA: All states, coastal heathlands, sub-alpine forest. TIME: November to
February.

LOBELIA GRACILIS

FAMILY: Lobeliaceae. COMMON NAME: None. COLOUR: Blue with white centre.
SIZE: Up to 45 cm high.

DESCRIPTION: An erect, glabrous herb. Leaves are alternate and linear with small
leaflets; leaf stems are radical forming basal tuft. Flowers are on slender pedicels in
terminal racemes. Corolla is 10 to 12 mm long, with the three anterior corolla lobes
broad-obovate 4 to 6 mm wide. Anthers are hairy and both flower and leaf stems
branched. Fruit is a capsule 4 mm across.

AREA: N.S.W., widespread open forests. TIME: Spring.

Lobeliaceae
Isotomo axillaris

Lobeliaceae
Isotomo anethifolia

Lobeliaceae
Lobelia gibbosa

Lobeliaceae
Lobelia gracilis

AMYEMA CAMBAGEI

FAMILY: Loranthaceae. COMMON NAME: Mistletoe. COLOUR: Red. SIZE: Up to 1 metre long.

DESCRIPTION: A parasitic shrub on trees. Leaves: terete, opposite, 3 to 10 cm long. Buds: scurfy, clavate, 15 to 20 mm long. Flowers are in umbels of two or three, with flower petals free. Host *Casuarina* spp. Fruit is a globular berry.

AREA: N.S.W. and Qld., along river banks. TIME: August to November.

AMYLOTHECA DICTYOPHLEBA

FAMILY: Loranthaceae. COMMON NAME: Red Mistletoe. COLOUR: Red with yellow tips. SIZE: Up to 1 metre long.

DESCRIPTION: A parasitic shrub on trees. Leaves: opposite, thick and leathery, oval to elliptic or broad-obovate, obtuse, narrowed to petiole, 5 to 12 cm long. Flowers are in raceme or umbel of three flowered cymes. Peduncles are axillary about 1 cm long. Corolla tube is six-lobed, straight, split on the upper side. Fruit is a globular berry.

AREA: N.S.W., coast and nearby mountains in rainforests. TIME: Spring to Summer.

DENDROPHTHOE VITELLINA

FAMILY: Loranthaceae. COMMON NAME: Mistletoe. COLOUR: Orange and red. SIZE: Up to 2 metres drop.

DESCRIPTION: A parasitic shrub on trees. Leaves: alternate, broad-ovate, narrow-ovate to narrow-lanceolate, obtuse, thick, glaucous, narrows into petiole, 4 to 8 cm long. Flowers are in short dense axillary raceme. Perianth tube is 2 to 3 cm long. There are five lobes, reflexed 1 to 2 cm long; many hosts.

AREA: N.S.W. and Qld. TIME: Spring or Summer according to season and situation.

HIBISCUS HETEROPHYLLUS

FAMILY: Malvaceae. COMMON NAME: Native Rosella. COLOUR: Pink or white with pink blush. SIZE: Up to 6 metres high.

DESCRIPTION: A tall shrub or small tree. Leaves are very variable, cordate to lanceolate and palmate being three-lobed, stiff, glabrous, finely toothed, 10 to 15 cm long. Flower: on short peduncles in upper axils, five petals 4 to 6 cm across, staminal tube and throat red-purple. Flower 10 to 12 cm across. Fruit is a five valve capsule, dehiscing loculicidally.

AREA: N.S.W. and Qld., coastal and nearby mountains and hills, marginal and scrub country. TIME: Spring and Summer.

Loranthaceae
Amyema cambagai

Loranthaceae
Amylotheca dictyopeleba

Loranthaceae
Dendrophthoe vitellina

Malvaceae
Hibiscus heterophyllus

HIBISCUS HUEGELII

FAMILY: Malvaceae. COMMON NAME: Huegelli Rose. COLOUR: Mauve. SIZE: Up to 2 metres high.

DESCRIPTION: Spreading shrub, scabrous with stellate hairs. Leaves: palmately lobed divisions crenate, 25 mm long, peduncles solitary and as long as the leaves. Calyx: 15 to 25 mm long, bracteoles united at base. Petal: 4 to 8 cm long, with one tooth at upper outer edge and with purple dot at base. Fruit is a capsule, ovoid and pubescent.

AREA: W.A., S.A. and parts of west N.S.W. TIME: September to October.

HIBISCUS SPLENDENS

FAMILY: Malvaceae. COMMON NAME: Native Rosella. COLOUR: Rose pink. SIZE: Up to 6 metres high.

DESCRIPTION: A straggly, spreading, stellate, tomentose, scabrous shrub, with prickles along branches and peduncles. Leaves: alternate, variable, elliptical, cordate-ovate to palmate, dentate 14 cm long. Flowers: delicate, solitary, with small and free involucre bracts. Calyx is five-lobed. Petals are large with deep red margins shading to white centres. Fruit is a capsule covered with silky hairs.

AREA: N.S.W. and Qld., mountains, marginal. TIME: September to December.

HIBISCUS TILIACEUS

FAMILY: Malvaceae. COMMON NAME: Cottonwood. COLOUR: Yellow turning red. SIZE: Up to 6 metres high.

DESCRIPTION: A small well-shaped tree. Leaves: cordate, upper surface light green, under surface hoary or lightly tomentose. Flower: five petals, imbricate, dark red centre, young roots edible, believed to have been used by the Aboriginals.

AREA: N.S.W. and Qld., coastal, tropical and subtropical, thrives along seaboard in salt breeze. TIME: September to March.

PAVONIA HASTATA

FAMILY: Malvaceae. COMMON NAME: None. COLOUR: White or pale pink with red centre. SIZE: Up to 60 cm high.

DESCRIPTION: Small, minutely stellate, tomentose shrub. Leaves are oblong-lanceolate 25 mm long, hastate with small lobes, crenate. Flowers are solitary, and peduncles axillary. Calyx is 6 mm long; five bracteoles, free, ovate. Petals are streaked with red or white from the five stamens. Fruit is a schizocarp.

AREA: N.S.W., Qld. and S.A., along roadsides. TIME: Spring and Summer.

Malvaceae
Hibiscus huegelii

Malvaceae
Hibiscus splendens

Malvaceae
Hibiscus tiliaceus

Malvaceae
Pavonia hastata

MELASTOMA POLYANTHUM

FAMILY: Melastomataceae. COMMON NAME: None. COLOUR: Pink, purple and white. SIZE: Up to 150 cm high.

DESCRIPTION: Small, softly tomentose shrub. Leaves are opposite, ellipticallanceolate to oval, curved with soft hairs, deeply veined, midribs raised and distinct, turning rich red before falling. Flowers are bisexual. Calyx is five-lobed. There are five petals, 12 to 18 mm across. Fruit is a capsule with seed embedded in a dark pulp. Resembles *Lasiandra* in appearance.

AREA: N.S.W., Qld., Fraser Island, warm tropical and subtropical climate. TIME: Late August and January.

ACACIA SP. NOVA

FAMILY: Mimosaceae. COMMON NAME: Granite Wattle. COLOUR: Yellow. SIZE: Up to 4 metres high.

DESCRIPTION: Erect thick shrub. Phyllodes are alternate, linear, 5 to 7 cm long, with gland one quarter to one third the length of phyllode from stem. Flowers are fluffy, ball-shaped, with up to ten balls on axil spike.

AREA: Granite area of north N.S.W., common along New England Tablelands fall over, only recently forwarded for identification. TIME: Spring.

ACACIA ALATA

FAMILY: Mimosaceae. COMMON NAME: Winged Wattle. COLOUR: Yellow. SIZE: Up to 1 metre high.

DESCRIPTION: Small shrub. Leafless, very prickly, stem wings of decurrent phyllodia, broad, tipped with sharp end. In var. *biglandulosa*, there are two glands present. Flowers are fluffy balls on 8 to 20 mm long, hairy peduncles.

AREA: W.A., Irwin, Dale and Warren districts, in forest undergrowth. TIME: April to October.

ACACIA BAILEYANA

FAMILY: Mimosaceae. COMMON NAME: Cootamundra Wattle. COLOUR: Yellow. SIZE: Up to 10 metres high.

DESCRIPTION: A large bushy shrub or tree. Branchlets are pilose or hispid, with hairs 1 to 2 mm long. Fine feathery 'leaves' bipinnate, pinnae blunt, glaucous, pinnules up to 1.5 mm wide, margins with fine cilia. There are several glands on base of petiole or between the lowest pair of pinnae. Inflorescence: twenty to thirty flowers in head, terminal panicle.

AREA: N.S.W., widespread at high altitudes. TIME: August to September.

Melastomaceae
Melastoma polyanthum

Mimosaceae
Acacia sp. nova

Mimosaceae
Acacia alata var. Biglandulosa

Mimosaceae
Acacia baileyana

ACACIA BRUNIOIDES SSP. BRUNIOIDES

FAMILY: Mimosaceae. COMMON NAME: None. COLOUR: Bright yellow. SIZE: Up to 1 metre high.

DESCRIPTION: Straggling shrub, branches terete. Phyllodes are light pubescent, pungent pointed, flat, short, linear, 8 to 10 mm long. Flower ball or head: up to twenty flowers, 12 to 18 mm diameter, peduncle much longer than phyllodes. Legume is blue-black, 3 to 6 cm long.

AREA: N.S.W., Qld., coast and nearby mountains. TIME: Summer.

ACACIA CRASPEDOCARPA

FAMILY: Mimosaceae. COMMON NAME: None. COLOUR: Yellow. SIZE: Up to 4 metres high.

DESCRIPTION: Spreading shrub. Phyllodes: ovate, elliptical to obovate, scattered, three to four obscure nerves, intricate reticulation, 15 to 25 mm long, 12 mm wide. Flower spike is pedunculate, oblong. Legume or.pod is flat, 10 to 15 mm long.

AREA: W.A., Kimberley and Eremean, in dry areas. TIME: August to October.

ACACIA CULTRIFORMIS

FAMILY: Mimosaceae. COMMON NAME: None. COLOUR: Yellow. SIZE: Up to 6 metres high.

DESCRIPTION: Tall shrubby bush or tree. Phyllode is curiously shaped to almost triangular, 20 mm long. Inflorescence: five to twenty fluffy globes or balls on stem in leaf axil, each globe with twenty to thirty flowers, and each flower with five sepals and five petals about 1.2 mm across.

AREA: N.S.W. and Qld., rocky dry ground, scrub forest. TIME: Spring.

ACACIA DECURRENS

FAMILY: Mimosaceae. COMMON NAME: Black Wattle or Green Wattle. COLOUR: Yellow. SIZE: 6 to 14 metres high.

DESCRIPTION: A small tree. Stem is broad with winglike ridges. Phyllodes are bipinnate, with beautiful feathery appearance. Four to twelve pairs of pinnae. Fifteen to thirty pairs of pinnules, 4 to 15 mm long, dark green. Several glands are often present between lowest pair of pinnae and along the common petiole. The twenty to thirty flowers are in axil panicles.

AREA: All eastern states; bark valuable for tanning. TIME: July to September.

imosaceae
cacia brunioides ssp. brunioides

Mimosaceae
Acacia craspedocarpa

imosaceae
cacia cultriformis

Mimosaceae
Acacia decurrens

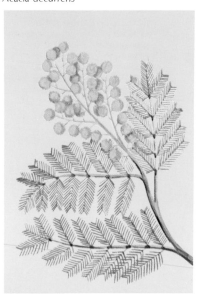

ACACIA ELONGATA

FAMILY: Mimosaceae. COMMON NAME: None. COLOUR: Bright yellow. SIZE: Up to 2 metres high.

DESCRIPTION: Erect shrub. Phyllodes are flat, rigid, glabrous with prominent veins, 7 to 13 cm long, 2 to 4 mm wide. Peduncles are pubescent. There are twenty to thirty flowers in each head. Legume is straight, 6 to 8 cm long and 5 mm wide.

AREA: N.S.W., usually in wet ground. TIME: Spring.

ACACIA FALCATA

FAMILY: Mimosaceae. COMMON NAME: None. COLOUR: Lemon or pale yellow. SIZE: Up to 3 metres high.

DESCRIPTION: A tall shrub or small tree. Phyllodes are lanceolate-falcate gradually narrowing towards base, glaucous, obtuse or acute, 8 to 18 cm long; marginal gland close to phyllode base. Flower head: fifteen to twenty flowers, 2 to 4 mm diameter. Fruit is a legume 6 to 10 cm long and 6 to 8 mm wide.

AREA: N.S.W. and Qld., along roadsides, cleared ground, open forests. TIME: May to June.

ACACIA FALCIFORMIS

FAMILY: Mimosaceae. COMMON NAME: Blue Leaf Hickory. COLOUR: Yellow. SIZE: Up to 9 metres high.

DESCRIPTION: A small tree. Phyllodes: elliptic-falcate, penniveined, 6 to 18 cm long, 17 to 35 mm wide. Marginal gland is very prominent and distant from base of phyllode, connected by a nerve to mid-vein. Peduncles and branches are silvery pubescent; there are up to twenty flowers in fluffy balls. Fruit is a legume 10 to 13 cm long and 18 to 25 mm wide.

AREA: N.S.W., south Qld. and into Vic., mountains and forests. TIME: Spring.

ACACIA FARNESIANA

FAMILY: Mimosaceae. COMMON NAME: None. COLOUR: Yellow. SIZE: Up to 7 metres high.

DESCRIPTION: Shrub or very small tree, almost glabrous. Phyllodes are bipinnate; with two thorny stipules 4 to 20 mm long, pinnae in one to four pairs with gland between each pair; pinnules are glabrous, linear, obtuse, four to ten pairs, 4 to 10 mm long. Up to fifty flowers in each head. Grown in Mediterranean for making perfumes. First cultivated in Rome in 1611.

AREA: N.S.W., S.A., N.T. and Qld., central and tropical Australia. TIME: Spring.

Mimosaceae
Acacia elongata

Mimosaceae
Acacia falcata

Mimosaceae
Acacia falciformis

Mimosaceae
Acacia farnesiana

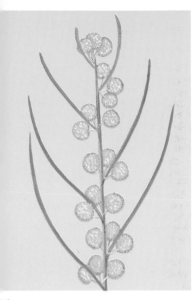

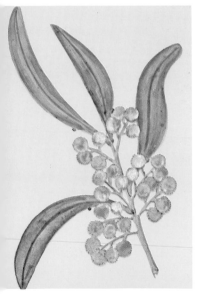

ACACIA FIMBRIATA

FAMILY: Mimosaceae. COMMON NAME: Fringed Wattle. COLOUR: Yellow. SIZE: Up to 10 metres high.

DESCRIPTION: Erect shrub or small tree. Phyllodes are linear to narrow-oblong-elliptic, 2 to 4 cm long. Mature phyllodes are ciliate at the margins, thin, with rounded gland at base or near base. Ten to thirty flowers in each head. Legume is straight, flat, 4 to 7 cm long.

AREA: N.S.W., coast and nearby mountains. TIME: July to September.

ACACIA IMPLEXA

FAMILY: Mimosaceae. COMMON NAME: Hickory. COLOUR: Pale yellow. SIZE: Up to 9 metres high.

DESCRIPTION: Tall shrub or small tree. Ribs on the young branches are not very conspicuous. Phyllodes: acute to acuminate, 8 to 16 cm long or longer up to 20 mm wide; four to twelve flower balls on thin peduncles about 0.5 mm diameter. Fruit is a legume, biconvex about 6 to 9 cm long, with the funicle folded under the seed. Very close to *A. melanoxylon*.

AREA: N.S.W., Qld., Vic. and Tas., very widespread. TIME: Most of the year.

Acacia melanoxylon. Common name: Blackwood. A tall shrub up to fifteen metres high. Phyllodes are shorter than *A. implexa*, ovate-obtuse to obovate lanceolate, with obtuse tips. Flower head has six to ten globes to flower spike. Area: North N.S.W. and south Qld. Time: August to October.

ACACIA LEIOCALYX

FAMILY: Mimosaceae. COMMON NAME: Cunningham's Wattle. COLOUR: Yellow. SIZE: Up to 3 metres high.

DESCRIPTION: Tall shrub. Phyllodes: green, falcate-lanceolate, 6 to 10 cm long, 12 to 20 mm wide. Flower spike is 3 to 8 cm long, terminal panicle, calyx soft and smooth. This species was once classified with *A. cunninghamii*; recent reclassification has placed it as a separate species.

AREA: South N.S.W. and south Qld.; *A. cunninghamii* occurs mainly in Qld. having been introduced into south N.S.W. and Sydney area. TIME: Spring.

ACACIA LONGIFOLIA VAR. SOPHORAE

FAMILY: Mimosaceae. COMMON NAME: Golden Wattle. COLOUR: Yellow. SIZE: Up to 2 metres high.

DESCRIPTION: A small shrub. Phyllodes: oblong-obovate, 4 to 10 cm long, 18 to 35 mm wide, mucronate apex with several prominent longitudinal veins. Flowers are densely packed to form a flower spike 25 mm long, giving cylindrical appearance, in phyllode axil. Fruit is a legume, convex often curved.

AREA: N.S.W., coastal, sand dunes. TIME: August to October.

Mimosaceae
Acacia fimbriata

Mimosaceae
Acacia implexa

Mimosaceae
Acacia leiocalyx

Mimosaceae
Acacia longifolia var. sophorae

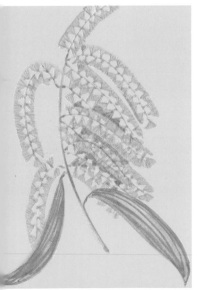

ACACIA MITCHELLII

FAMILY: Mimosaceae. COMMON NAME: Mitchell Wattle. COLOUR: Pale yellow. SIZE: Up to 1 metre high.

DESCRIPTION: The smallest wattle of the feather-leaf group. Phyllodes are very attractive, tiny, bipinnate. Pinnae: two to three pairs; pinnules: three to six pairs, 2 to 6 mm long. Flowers in a delicate globe on short peduncle in the phyllode axil. As the foliage ages the dainty shrub turns to a deep red-brown. Fruit is a flat pod.

AREA: N.S.W., Vic. and S.A., from New England tablelands to south-east S.A. TIME: August to December.

ACACIA PODALYRIIFOLIA

FAMILY: Mimosaceae. COMMON NAME: Queensland Silver Wattle. COLOUR: Lemon. SIZE: Up to 8 metres high.

DESCRIPTION: Large shrub or small tree. Phyllodes: pubescent, nearly glaucous, oblong, oblique, ovate, obovate or elliptic, 2 to 4 cm long, 12 to 25 mm wide. Margins are thick; racemes of flower heads terminal, twice as long as the phyllodes; twenty to thirty flowers. Fruit is a broad and glaucous legume.

AREA: N.S.W., introduced from Qld. TIME: Winter.

ACACIA SPECTABILIS

FAMILY: Mimosaceae. COMMON NAME: Mudgee Wattle or Pilliga Wattle. COLOUR: Yellow. SIZE: Up to 5 cm high.

DESCRIPTION: A bush shrub or small tree. It has powdery-white bark and silver-grey bipinnate leaves, with eight to sixteen pairs of pinnae and grey stems. Flowers are globular golden balls. Flower heads are often pendulous.

AREA: West N.S.W., west Qld. and tablelands. TIME: July to October.

Mimosaceae
Acacia Mitchellii

Mimosaceae
Acacia podalyriifolia

Mimosaceae
Acacia spectabilis

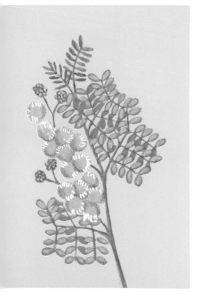

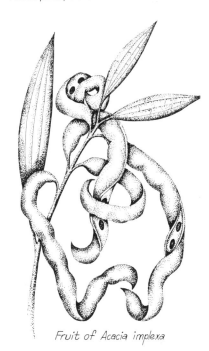

Fruit of Acacia implexa

MYOPORUM MONTANUM

FAMILY: Myoporaceae. COMMON NAME: Native Myrtle. COLOUR: White with mauve spots. SIZE: Up to 3 metres high.

DESCRIPTION: Handsome erect shrub. Leaves: alternate, lanceolate, very acute, 4 to 12 cm long, 5 to 12 mm wide. Narrow to short petiole. Flowers are in two to six axillary clusters, rarely solitary; peduncles 6 to 12 mm long. Calyx segments are lanceolate, 3 to 4 mm long. Corolla: 7 to 9 mm long, rounded lobes, bearded inside, four stamens. Fruit is a drupe, 6 to 8 mm diameter, purple when ripe.

AREA: N.S.W., Vic., S.A., central W.A. and Qld. TIME: September to November.

ANGOPHORA CORDIFOLIA

FAMILY: Myrtaceae. COMMON NAME: Dwarf Apple. COLOUR: Cream-white to lemon. SIZE: Up to 8 metres high.

DESCRIPTION: Shrub or small tree. Its bark is flaky, and its young branches and inflorescence are covered with red hairs. Leaves: opposite, ovate to oblong, obtuse up to 10 cm long. Flowers are in terminal corymbs. There are five sepals and five petals, spreading and free; stamens are numerous and free. Fruit is about 15 mm diameter, distinctly ribbed.

AREA: N.S.W., Qld. and Vic., widespread in dry sclerophyll forest. TIME: Summer.

BAECKEA UTILIS

FAMILY: Myrtaceae. COMMON NAME: None. COLOUR: White or red-white. SIZE: Up to 1 metre high.

DESCRIPTION: Small heathlike under-shrub. Leaves: small, opposite, linear to narrow, oblong-elliptic, keeled, 3 to 5 mm long. Flowers: 4 to 6 mm diameter, solitary or small, cymes in the leaf axil. Sepals are persistent. Fruit is a capsule.

AREA: N.S.W., damp places and mountains. TIME: Summer.

Myoporaceae
Myoporum montanum

fruit of Angophora species

Myrtaceae
Angophora cordifolia

Myrtaceae
Baecka utilis

CALLISTEMON ACUMINATUS

FAMILY: Myrtaceae. COMMON NAME: Red Bottlebrush. SIZE: Up to 3 metres high.

DESCRIPTION: Erect, rigid shrub. Leaves: almost opposite, linear to lanceolate, acuminate, distinct venation, 6 to 10 cm long, axillary bracts. Flowers are sessile, with terminal spike 5 to 8 cm long. Sepals are deciduous; petals green, orbicular; stamens numerous. Fruit is a woody capsule.

AREA: North N.S.W., in damp places (considered to be rare). TIME: Spring and Summer.

CALLISTEMON BRACHYANDRUS

FAMILY: Myrtaceae. COMMON NAME: None. COLOUR: Red. SIZE: Up to 3 metres high.

DESCRIPTION: Bushy shrub. Leaves: silky young, glabrous adult, terete, pungent pointed, 2 to 4 cm long, 1 to 2 mm diameter. Flower spike is 2.5 to 3.5 cm long. The rhachis and flowers are pubescent when young, becoming glabrous with age. Petals: green, 4 mm diameter; stamens, 5 to 8 mm long. Fruit is globular, 6 to 8 mm diameter.

AREA: Western N.S.W., north-west Vic., and S.A. TIME: October to February.

CALLISTEMON CITRINUS

FAMILY: Myrtaceae. COMMON NAME: Lemon Bottlebrush or Common Red Bottlebrush. COLOUR: Red. SIZE: Up to 3 metres high.

DESCRIPTION: Erect or spreading shrub. Leaves: dark-green, lanceolate 3 to 8 cm long, 6 to 12 mm wide with distinct mucro ridge. Flower spike is 6 to 12 cm long, with numerous filaments. Fruit is a woody capsule, 6 to 8 mm diameter.

AREA: N.S.W. and Qld., widespread, usually in damp places. TIME: Spring to early Summer, known to flower in Autumn.

CALLISTEMON PACHYPHYLLUS

FAMILY: Myrtaceae. COMMON NAME: Wallum Bottlebrush. COLOUR: Red or yellow-green. SIZE: To 2 metres high.

DESCRIPTION: Erect, bushy shrub. Leaves: stiff, narrow-spathulate, mucronate, 3 to 6 cm long. Flower spike is 5 to 8 cm long. Young buds are lightly pubescent. Filaments are red, and stamens are tipped with green anthers.

AREA: N.S.W. and south-east Qld., coastal, sandy and swampy soils. TIME: October to December.

Myrtaceae
Callistemon acuminatus

Myrtaceae
Callistemon brachyandrus

Myrtaceae
Callistemon citrinus

Myrtaceae
Callistemon pachyphyllus

Myrtaceae
Callistemon citrinus

CALLISTEMON PINIFOLIUS

FAMILY: Myrtaceae. COMMON NAME: Green Bottlebrush. COLOUR: Green (rarely red). SIZE: Up to 2.5 metres high.

DESCRIPTION: A small, rigid shrub. Leaves: alternate, narrow-linear, incurved margins almost terete, at times pungent pointed, 4 to 10 cm long. Filaments and stamens are a beautiful light-green, 10 to 15 mm long. Considered by many to be rather rare.

AREA: N.S.W., Royal National Park, Newcastle and Hunter Valley, in damp places. TIME: August to December.

CALLISTEMON RIGIDUS

FAMILY: Myrtaceae. COMMON NAME: Stiff Bottlebrush. COLOUR: Red. SIZE: Up to 4 metres high.

DESCRIPTION: Erect shrub. Leaves: linear, acute-acuminate 5 to 10 cm long, 3 to 5 mm wide. It has lateral veins from distinct ridges along the margins. Flower spike is 6 to 10 cm long; filaments 10 to 13 mm long, red. Fruit is 6 to 8 mm in diameter.

AREA: N.S.W., coastal and nearby mountains. TIME: November to February.

DARWINIA MEEBOLDII

FAMILY: Myrtaceae. COMMON NAME: Mondurup Bell. COLOUR: Red, white or purple. SIZE: Up to 2 metres high.

DESCRIPTION: Erect shrub. Leaves: not strictly opposite, linear, margins, entire, up to 15 mm long. Four to ten flowers in the flower head, involucre bracts entire, outer bracts green to white, red towards tips. Easily recognised by their prominent nodding flowers which in fact consist of a series of large, coloured bracts, completely obscuring the several tiny true flowers at base of the involucre. Flower has five petals and five sepals.

AREA: W.A., Stirling Range in stony ground. TIME: October to November.

KUNZEA AMBIGUA

FAMILY: Myrtaceae. COMMON NAME: Tick Bush. COLOUR: White with green centre. SIZE: Up to 3 metres high.

DESCRIPTION: Bushy shrub. Leaves: spreading, linear to linear-oblong, concave, 6 to 10 mm long. Flowers are crowded on leafy branches, in axils of upper leaves. Floral tube may be glabrous or pubescent; five petals; stamens are long and numerous; flower, 12 to 15 mm diameter. Fruit is a capsule but not woody.

AREA: N.S.W., Qld. and Vic., widespread, coastal and nearby mountains and plateau, open forest and heathlands. TIME: All Summer.

Myrtaceae
Callistemon pinifolius

Myrtaceae
Callistemon rigidus

Myrtaceae
Darwinia meeboldii

Myrtaceae
Kunzea ambigua

KUNZEA BRACTEOLATA

FAMILY: Myrtaceae. COMMON NAME: Granite Kunzea. COLOUR: White with green centre. SIZE: Up to 1.5 metres high.

DESCRIPTION: Dense shrub. Leaves: alternate, lanceolate, pungent tip, 3 to 8 mm long, 1.5 to 2 mm wide. Flowers: sessile in leafless terminal cluster, five sepals, five petals 4 mm long, floral tube short, stamens not many, anthers yellow, flower to 10 mm diameter.

AREA: N.S.W., common on granite heath in New England Tablelands and mountains, on well-drained soils. TIME: Summer.

KUNZEA CAPITATA

FAMILY: Myrtaceae. COMMON NAME: Pink Buttons. COLOUR: Mauve-pink. SIZE: To 1.5 metres high.

DESCRIPTION: Erect or ascending shrub. Leaves: alternate, oblanceolate to obovate, three-nerved, concave, 4 to 9 mm long, 2 to 3 mm wide. Flowers are crowded into a leafless terminal head. Sepals are deltoid to acuminate; floral tube is villous; petals are as long as sepals. Stamens are 5 to 6 mm long.

AREA: N.S.W., Qld. and Vic., widespread, coastal and nearby mountains. TIME: September to February.

LEPTOSPERMUM SP. NOVA

FAMILY: Myrtaceae. COMMON NAME: New England Tea Tree. COLOUR: White with green centre. SIZE: Up to 3.5 to 4 metres high.

DESCRIPTION: Slender, erect shrub. Leaves: in groups on short petiole 1 to 3 mm long, lanceolate, glabrous, 8 to 15 mm long. Flowers: five sepals, red-brown, deciduous, five petals, orbicular 15 to 18 mm diameter. Fruit is a woody capsule, 4 to 8 mm diameter. Common on tableland but only recently found to be undescribed. A beautiful showy bush.

AREA: N.S.W., New England Tablelands and Gibraltar Range, damp areas. TIME: Summer.

LEPTOSPERMUM ATTENUATUM

FAMILY: Myrtaceae. COMMON NAME: Weeping Tea Tree. COLOUR: White. SIZE: Up to 5 metres high.

DESCRIPTION: Tall shrub with papery bark. Branches: ascending, branching and becoming pendulous. Leaves: oblong, elliptic to linear, 6 to 13 mm long. Calyx tube and sepal lobes are silky. Stamens are numerous. Flower: 10 to 18 mm diameter, numerous on pendulous and delicate branches. Fruit is a capsule 4 to 8 mm diameter.

AREA: North N.S.W., granite areas. TIME: Summer.

Myrtaceae
Kunzea bracteolata

Myrtaceae
Kunzea capitata

Myrtaceae
Leptospermum sp. nova

Myrtaceae
Leptospermum attentuatum

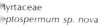

LEPTOSPERMUM FLAVESCENS (unusually narrow leaf form)

FAMILY: Myrtaceae. COMMON NAME: Yellow Tea Tree. COLOUR: White, cream white. SIZE: To 4 metres high.

DESCRIPTION: Tall shrub with hard bark. Leaves: unusually narrow, narrow-elliptic almost linear, acute to obtuse, lightly citron-scented, 6 to 25 mm long, 1 to 2 mm wide. Flower is glabrous, 5 to 15 mm in diameter. Fruit is a capsule 6 to 8 mm diameter.

AREA: Qld., very common in Maryborough District and Mary River Valley, in damp places. TIME: September to December.

LEPTOSPERMUM SEMIBRACCATUM

FAMILY: Myrtaceae. COMMON NAME: None. COLOUR: White. SIZE: To 3 metres high.

DESCRIPTION: Slender shrub. Leaves: oblanceolate to spathulate, glabrous, alternate 8 to 12 mm long, 2 to 4 mm wide. Flower: five sepals, white, deltoid; five petals, spathulate 8 to 10 mm long. Flower: 25 to 30 mm diameter; stamens are short and few.

AREA: Qld., coastal, sand soils, common on Fraser Island. TIME: Spring and Summer.

MELALEUCA BRACTEATA

FAMILY: Myrtaceae. COMMON NAME: White Paper Bark. COLOUR: White. SIZE: Up to 6 metres.

DESCRIPTION: Tall spreading shrub or small tree. It has papery bark on the tree trunk. Leaves: alternate, linear-lanceolate, bright green, glabrous, veins not prominent, 8 to 14 mm long. Flowers in spikes or terminal clusters 2.5 to 4 cm long. Staminal claw is very short, 0.5 to 1 mm long, 10 to 14 mm diameter.

AREA: N.S.W., Hunter Valley, coastal and nearby mountains; Qld., coastal, Lamington National Park. TIME: Spring, very showy and rich in nectar.

MELALEUCA NODOSA

FAMILY: Myrtaceae. COMMON NAME: Prickly Leaved Paper Bark. COLOUR: Cream to lemon. SIZE: Up to 3 metres high.

DESCRIPTION: A tall shrub. Leaves: alternate, veins linear, rigid, pungent pointed, 10 to 20 mm long. Flowers are in dense globular clusters, each flower being 15 to 20 mm in diameter. Five sepals, five petals, staminal claw 1 to 2 mm long. At first glance it is often mistaken for *Acacia* sp.

AREA: N.S.W. and Qld., coastal, open forest, sandy-poor soils and swampy areas. TIME: Spring and Summer.

Myrtaceae
Leptospermum flavescens var. sp.

Myrtaceae
Leptospermum semibraccatum

Myrtaceae
Melaleuca bracteata

Myrtaceae
Melaleuca nodosa

MICROMYRTUS CILIATA

FAMILY: Myrtaceae. COMMON NAME: None. COLOUR: White and red, with pink blush. SIZE: Up to 1.5 metres high.

DESCRIPTION: A spreading, glabrous shrub. Leaves: opposite, four-ranked, linear to oblanceolate, 3 to 4 mm long, minutely ciliate. Flowers: five petals, 3 to 4 mm diameter, floral tube short, ovate-turbinate, about 2 mm long, stamens opposite petals. Raceme is a small dense terminal cluster. Fruit is a nut.

AREA: N.S.W., Vic. and S.A., coast and nearby mountains and heathlands. TIME: September to December.

TRISTANIA LAURINA

FAMILY: Myrtaceae. COMMON NAME: Water Gum. COLOUR: Yellow. SIZE: Up to 10 metres high.

DESCRIPTION: Small tree. Leaves: alternate, lanceolate to narrow-elliptic, 10 to 14 cm long. Flower: cymes axillary, five sepals, five petals, staminal bundles distinct, claws about 1.5 to 2 mm long. Fruit is a distinctly domed capsule.

AREA: N.S.W., Qld. and Vic., creek banks, coastal and nearby mountains in rainforest, widespread. TIME: Summer: November to January.

NYMPHAEA CAPENSIS

FAMILY: Nymphaeaceae. COMMON NAME: Water Lily. COLOUR: Mauve. SIZE: Aquatic.

DESCRIPTION: An aquatic, perennial herb. Its rhizomes are prostrate, submerged. Leaves: floating, often submerged, orbicular, deeply cordate; veins radiate from the petiole. Flower is solitary and bisexual. Four sepals. Numerous petals, 3 to 6 cm long. Fruit is a spongy berry. Escaped and now naturalised in many areas.

AREA: South Qld., N.S.W., coastal. TIME: August to February, often later.

Myrtaceae
Micromyrtus ciliata

Myrtaceae
Tristania laurina

Nymphaeaceae
Nymphaea capensis

*fruiting body of
Tristania conferta*

JASMINUM CALCAREUM

FAMILY: Oleaceae. COMMON NAME: Poison Creeper. COLOUR: White to cream, fragrant and sweet scented. SIZE: Climber.

DESCRIPTION: Climber and twiner, minutely hoary-pubescent to almost glabrous. Leaves: simple, opposite, lanceolate to obovate-lanceolate, 4 to 12 cm long. Flowers: calyx teeth subulate, as long as or longer than the calyx tube. Corolla tube is funnel-shaped, lobes spreading, linear as long as or longer than tube, 12 to 18 mm across; style is two-lobed. Fruit is a black, globular berry 6 to 8 mm diameter.

AREA: N.S.W., Vic., S.A. and W.A., roadsides and watercourses. TIME: August to October.

NOTELAEA LINEARIS

FAMILY: Oleaceae. COMMON NAME: None. COLOUR: Pale yellow. SIZE: Up to 1 metre high.

DESCRIPTION: Small shrub. Leaves: coriaceous, linear, lanceolate to ovate, narrow-pointed, 4 to 8 cm long. Flowers are small, 6 to 8 mm diameter, in short simple, axillary raceme, often in sessile cluster; four petals often connected in pairs by the stamens. Fruit is 7 to 9 mm in diameter and drupaceous.

AREA: N.S.W., widespread north coast and nearby mountains, open forests. TIME: Spring to early Summer.

BULBOPHYLLUM SP. (possible cross between B. lageniforme and B. exiguum)

FAMILY: Orchidaceae. COMMON NAME: None. COLOUR: White with red and yellow markings. SIZE: Leaf 2 to 4 cm long.

DESCRIPTION: Small, epiphytic herb, with rhizome creeping extensively. Pseudobulbs: 5 to 8 mm diameter, 12 to 20 mm long, elongate, ovoid-globular. Leaf is solitary and 2 to 3 cm long. Flower somewhat bell-shaped with red and yellow or brown longitudinal nerves. Sepals: 5 to 8 mm long, three- to five-nerved, dorsal sepal lanceolate, cucullate, lateral sepal much broader at base. Petals: lanceolate, shorter than sepals, labellum leathery, channelled, margins recurved. Column is short and toothed.

AREA: Qld. and north N.S.W., widespread, rainforest above 750 metres. TIME: December to March.

BULBOPHYLLUM CRASSULIFOLIUM

FAMILY: Orchidaceae. COMMON NAME: Wheat Leaf Bulbophyllum. COLOUR: Off white to cream. SIZE: Leaf to 4 cm long.

DESCRIPTION: Small epiphytic herb, with stems creeping extensive, rather intricate. Pseudobulbs are minute. Leaf is thick, succulent, solitary, 2 to 4 cm long. Flowers are crowded, with pedicels 5 to 10 mm long. Perianth is white, and sheathing bracts are conspicuous.

AREA: N.S.W. and Qld., rainforest, humid areas. TIME: Spring.

Oleaceae
Notelaea linearis

Oleaceae
Jasminum calcareum

Orchidaceae
Bulbophyllum sp.

Orchidaceae
Bulbophyllum crassulifolium

CALADENIA DILATATA

FAMILY: Orchidaceae. COMMON NAME: Green Spider Orchid. COLOUR: Green and cream with red markings. SIZE: From 15 to 45 cm high.

DESCRIPTION: A robust, slender herb. Leaves are oblong to elliptical-lanceolate, hairy, 5 to 12 cm long. Flower is solitary, about 10 cm across. Sepals are up to 5 cm long, subequal, often clavate; petals are shorter and narrower, filiform, clubbed point, 5 to 5.5 cm long. Labellum lateral lobes are deeply fringed on a movable claw. Several variations to this species: *C. dilatata* var. *concinna*, and *C. dilatata* var. *patersonii*. The variations are in column, labellum and filaments.

AREA: N.S.W., Qld., Vic., Tas. and W.A., coastal and dry sclerophyll. TIME: August to January, later in Tas.

CALADENIA RETICULATA

FAMILY: Orchidaceae. COMMON NAME: Veined Spider Orchid. COLOUR: Deep red and green. SIZE: Up to 30 cm high.

DESCRIPTION: Slender herb. Leaf is solitary, radical, linear to lanceolate. Stem is more or less hirsute. Flowers are solitary but sometimes in a raceme of two to four flowers; dorsal sepal is erect; sepals are caudate, clavate, 2 to 5 cm long. Labellum is undivided, and calli are in four rows.

AREA: N.S.W., Qld. and Vic., widespread. TIME: August to October.

CALANTHE TRIPLICATIS

FAMILY: Orchidaceae. COMMON NAME: Scrub Lily or Christmas Orchid. COLOUR: White. SIZE: Up to 160 cm high.

DESCRIPTION: Tall perennial, terrestrial, herb with fleshy rhizomes. Leaves: large, broad, 90 cm long, rising from small pseudobulb. Scapes are up to 150 cm long, with few sheathing bracts. Flowers are in a terminal raceme of 3 cm diameter. Sepals and petals: equal, labellum spurred, lamina three-lobed, shaped like Lorraine Cross with several calli. Plant resembles *Phaius* in appearance.

AREA: Qld. and south N.S.W., coastal, deep shaded bush gullies in rich soil. TIME: November to February; seed in March to April.

CALEANA MINOR (recent reclassification—Paracaleana minor)

FAMILY: Orchidaceae. COMMON NAME: Duck Orchid. COLOUR: Green or dull red-brown. SIZE: Up to 18 cm high.

DESCRIPTION: Small glabrous herb with oblong tuber. Leaf: solitary, radical, red-brown underneath, linear 4 to 12 cm long, flower not resupinate. Lateral sepals and labellum are inserted at the end of the basal projection of the column. Labellum is articulate on a prominent movable claw. Labellum surface is tuberculate; lamina ovate, no longitudinal groove. Perianth is green or dull red-brown, and up to 8 mm long.

AREA: N.S.W., Qld. and Vic., widespread. TIME: Spring to Summer.

Orchidaceae
Caladenia dilatata

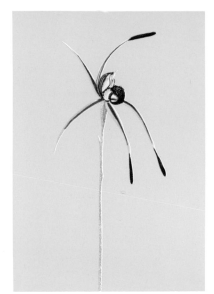

Orchidaceae
Caladenia reticulata

Orchidaceae
Calanthe triplicata

Orchidaceae
Caleana minor

CALOCHILUS CAMPESTRIS

FAMILY: Orchidaceae. COMMON NAME: Copper Bearded Orchid. COLOUR: Yellow-green with red-brown or purple markings. SIZE: Up to 60 cm high.

DESCRIPTION: A glabrous herb, ovoid tubers. Leaf: present, erect, 12 to 30 cm long. There are one to three stem bracts, 5 to 9 cm long. Flowers: two to fifteen, labellum up to 15 mm long, lanceolate or with short glabrous ribbonlike prolongation of the lamina, beset with coppery-red or red-blue hairs. Dark gland on either side at the base of the column, similar to *C. robertsonii*.

AREA: N.S.W., Qld., Vic., S.A. and Tas. TIME: September to December.

CALOCHILUS GRANDIFLORUS

FAMILY: Orchidaceae. COMMON NAME: Bearded Orchid. COLOUR: Golden yellow and purple. SIZE: Up to 60 cm high.

DESCRIPTION: A very slender, glabrous herb with ovoid tubers. Leaf: filiform, erect triangular in section, channelled, green, red at base, 20 to 50 cm long. Stem: two or three bracts with two scarious at base of plant, 4 to 8 cm long. Flowers are solitary or up to ten. Dorsal sepal is erect, cucullate, broadly ovate, acute. Lateral sepal is lanceolate. Petals are ovate-lanceolate and marked with red stripes. Labellum is sessile; lamina is triangular, upper surface covered with long purple-red or red-brown hairs; labellum ends in a ribbonlike appendage.

AREA: South Qld., N.S.W. and north-east Vic. TIME: September to November.

CALOCHILUS ROBERTSONII

FAMILY: Orchidaceae. COMMON NAME: Purple Bearded Orchid. COLOUR: Green with violet-red markings. SIZE: Up to 46 cm high.

DESCRIPTION: Small terrestrial herb, glabrous with ovoid tubers. Leaf: basal, channelled, linear-lanceolate, 20 to 40 cm long; two to four bracts, stem clasping, 7 to 10 cm long. Flowers, one to nine in raceme, petals less than half the length of sepals. Labellum is 2 to 3 cm long; lamina is green, triangular, covered with long violet-red hairs. Column is short with eyelike gland at base of column. Very pale form recorded.

AREA: All states and N.Z., coast and mountains. TIME: September to November.

CORYBAS PRUINOSUS

FAMILY: Orchidaceae. COMMON NAME: Helmet Orchid. COLOUR: Yellow-green with scarlet markings. SIZE: Up to 5 cm high.

DESCRIPTION: Dwarf terrestrial herb, with small globular tuber. Leaf solitary, orbicular-cordate, 15 to 35 cm across. Flower is less than 2 cm long, solitary, almost sessile with very short stalk from base of leaf. Dorsal sepal is narrow, paddle-shaped, concave over the labellum, sparsely blotched along spine. Labellum is contracted towards base with narrow split tube. Lamina is dilated, with fringed margins, pale and dark fimbria. Petals are entire; sepals, erect.

AREA: N.S.W. only, north coast, tablelands and south coast. TIME: April to July.

Orchidaceae
Calochilus campestris

Orchidaceae
Calochilus grandiflorus

Orchidaceae
Calochilus robertsonii

Orchidaceae
Corybas pruinosus

CORYBAS UNGUICULATUS

FAMILY: Orchidaceae. COMMON NAME: Small Helmet Orchid. COLOUR: Red-purple-black. SIZE: Up to 3 cm high.

DESCRIPTION: Small plant. Leaf: ovate-cordate, tending to be three-lobed, prominently ribbed, undersurface purple tinted, 1 to 4 cm long. Flower is solitary, with short pedicle. Dorsal sepal is contracted into narrow claw. Lamina is hooded, orbicular, deeply concave. Lateral sepals are filiform, spreading below labellum. Petals are similar but shorter, spreading each side of labellum. Sepal and petals are marked with red line.

AREA: N.S.W., Vic., Tas., S.A. and south-west W.A., coastal and nearby mountains. TIME: May to October.

CRYPTOSTYLIS HUNTERANA

FAMILY: Orchidaceae. COMMON NAME: Tongue Orchid. COLOUR: Red, green merging into black. SIZE: Up to 45 cm high.

DESCRIPTION: Terrestrial glabrous herb, with fleshy rhizomes, saprophytic. It is leafless with up to eight stem bracts. The two to nine flowers are sessile, reversed. Sepals are 2 cm long; petals are 1 cm long, and yellow. Labellum is undivided pubescent, convex, narrow-oblong, 2 to 3 cm long, green-yellow with red below, with green merging into black on upper portion.

AREA: Rare. N.S.W. and Vic., coastal, sandy and granite soils. Kuring-gai Chase National Park and Gibraltar Range National Park. TIME: December to January.

CRYPTOSTYLIS LEPTOCHILA

FAMILY: Orchidaceae. COMMON NAME: Small Tongue Orchid. COLOUR: Pink. SIZE: Up to 40 cm high.

DESCRIPTION: Erect terrestrial plant, with fleshy rhizomes. Leaves: one to three radical, broad-lanceolate to narrow-lanceolate, 5 to 10 cm long, green uppersurface, red-pink undersurface. Flowers: three to twelve or more, sepals and petals filiform; labellum narrow, dark, pubescent, with margins rolled in, forming thick, linear, channelled lamina; apex recurved.

AREA: N.S.W. to Stanthorpe, Qld., south to Vic. and eastern highlands forests. TIME: December to February.

CRYPTOSTYLIS OVATA

FAMILY: Orchidaceae. COMMON NAME: Slipper Orchid. COLOUR: Red. SIZE: Up to 40 cm long.

DESCRIPTION: Glabrous, terrestrial plant with fleshy rhizomes. Leaves: few, radical, much larger than *C. subulata*, ovate to oblong, 9 to 15 cm long, 3 to 6.5 cm wide, strongly ribbed, green uppersurface; purple-red reverse surface. Petiole is 4 to 8 cm long. Flowers: one to six, very similar to *C. subulata*; labellum similar with wavy margins finely net-veined; lamina differently coloured, surface lightly pubescent.

AREA: Thought to be endemic to W.A., a very recently recorded discovery in the hanging swamps of Dandahra, Gibraltar Range State Forest and National Park, north N.S.W.—New England Tablelands. TIME: October to February.

Orchidaceae
Corybas unguiculata

Orchidaceae
Cryptostylis leptochila

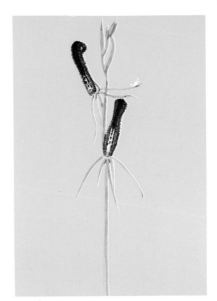

Orchidaceae
Cryptostylis hunterana

Orchidaceae
Cryptostylis ovata

DENDROBIUM GRACILICAULE

FAMILY: Orchidaceae. COMMON NAME: None. COLOUR: Yellow to cream with maroon or red-brown blotches. SIZE: 30 to 90 cm long.

DESCRIPTION: Epiphytic plant. Stems are erect; pseudobulb is narrow and tapering gradually towards the base. Leaves: three to six, lanceolate or narrow-elliptic, slightly sinuate, up to 14 cm long. Flower: five to sixteen in raceme, up to 10 cm long, alternate, perianth yellow, 2 cm across, labellum white to green, petals red-brown or maroon blotches.

AREA: Atherton Tablelands to Alps in N.S.W., also coastal, widespread and rainforests. TIME: July to October.

DENDROBIUM LINGUIFORME VAR. NUGENTII

FAMILY: Orchidaceae. COMMON NAME: Tongue Orchid or Button Orchid. COLOUR: White. SIZE: Creeping on rocks.

DESCRIPTION: Rock plant, with creeping rhizomes and stems. Leaves: short, thick, corrugated above, ovate, obtuse tips 2 to 3 cm long. Perianth is white with faint red or purple markings. Flowers are numerous in dense raceme 6 to 13 cm long; sepals and petals are up to 2 cm long, narrow-linear. Labellum is short; lateral lobes obtuse, prominent, midlobe narrow-ovate, recurved and obtuse. Lamina has three calli. Hardy species which often grows in direct sunlight.

AREA: North Qld. to south N.S.W., coast and nearby mountains. TIME: July to November.

DENDROBIUM MONOPHYLLUM

FAMILY: Orchidaceae. COMMON NAME: Lily of the Valley. COLOUR: Lemon-green. SIZE: Up to 15 cm high.

DESCRIPTION: Erect plant. Pseudobulbs: arising from creeping rhizome, at times numerous, thick narrow-conical, 2.5 to 10 cm high, older bulbs with ribs and furrows. Leaf: solitary, oblong to lanceolate, flat, terminal, 5 to 10 cm long. Raceme is solitary, with terminal as long as leaf. Flowers are small on slender drooping pedicels. Bracts are small; sepals are broad-lanceolate, acute 4 to 6 mm long. Spur is broad, obtuse curved upwards, 3 mm long. Petals are as long as sepals. Labellum lateral lobes are small, midlobe deltoidal to rhomboidal, obtuse. There are one to three calli between the lateral lobes.

AREA: Qld. to north N.S.W., coast and nearby ranges, massed on rocks or trees in full sunlight. TIME: Very irregular, mainly September to October.

DENDROBIUM STRIOLATUM

FAMILY: Orchidaceae. COMMON NAME: Streaked Rock Orchid. COLOUR: Yellow with red stripes. SIZE: Up to 50 cm high.

DESCRIPTION: An upright plant, with slender and branching stems. Rhizomes are extensively creeping and branched, forming mats on rock and cliff face. Leaves: obscurely corrugated, narrow-cylindrical, falcate and pointed. Flowers are solitary or two together, of 2 to 3 cm diameter, and may be yellow-green with brown stripes. Sepals are broad-lanceolate; petals, short and thicker; spur, thick and blunt; labellum, white.

AREA: Reported from Gibraltar Range, Dorrigo, Kempsey area, Barrington Tops, N.S.W. and south to Vic. and north Tas. TIME: September to November.

Orchidaceae
Dendrobium gracilicaule

Orchidaceae
Dendrobium monophyllum

Orchidaceae
Dendrobium linguiforme var. nugentii

Orchidaceae
Dendrobium striolatum

DIURIS CITRINA

FAMILY: Orchidaceae. COMMON NAME: Lemon Diuris. COLOUR: Yellow or pale lemon-yellow. SIZE: Up to 30 cm high.

DESCRIPTION: Finely slender, terrestrial plant. Leaves: two, elongated 12 to 20 cm long, one or two stem bracts. Flowers: three to six in loose raceme, pedicels long, markings very dark brown to almost black. Dorsal sepal is ovate-lanceolate; apex may be recurved or decurved. Lateral sepals are light green, channelled, linear, parallel or crossed, 10 to 12 mm long. Labellum is trilobed, lateral lobes crescent-shaped; midlobe orbicular to sub-orbicular, margin entire.

AREA: Central and north N.S.W., mountains and tablelands. TIME: October to November.

DIURIS PUNCTATA VAR. PUNCTATA (forma blackneyae)

FAMILY: Orchidaceae. COMMON NAME: Purple Doubletails. COLOUR: Generally purple. SIZE: Up to 60 cm high.

DESCRIPTION: Terrestrial, glabrous plant. Leaves: one to four, linear, channelled, 15 to 30 cm long. Flowers: two to ten, lilac to purple, two stem bracts, loose sheathing, subulate. Dorsal sepal is broadly ovate; lateral sepals are 3 to 10 cm long, green to brown, narrow-linear, spreading or parallel or twisted or crossed. A most variable orchid.

AREA: From Atherton Tablelands in Qld. to S.A. in grasslands, open forest along coast or in nearby mountains. TIME: October to December.

DIURIS PUNCTATA VAR. ALBO-VIOLACEA

FAMILY: Orchidaceae. COMMON NAME: Sunshine Diuris or Doubletails. COLOUR: White, white and purple, blotched. SIZE: Up to 60 cm high.

DESCRIPTION: A slender terrestrial, glabrous plant rising from cluster of tubers. This is a most variable orchid. The varietal name refers to the complex colour forms. Thought to be rare outside of Victoria, it is found in profusion in the north-east coastal belt of N.S.W. We have recorded a most complex colour variation from mauve to purple-white, white to sulphur-yellow with pink or red markings. We suggest you send specimens to a herbarium if your project calls for a positive identification.

AREA: N.S.W. to S.A., coastal and in New England Tablelands. TIME: October to December.

EPIDENDRUM X OBRIENIANUM

FAMILY: Orchidaceae. COMMON NAME: Crucifix Orchid. COLOUR: Orange to red. SIZE: Up to 2 metres high.

DESCRIPTION: A scandent, artificial hybrid. Stems are not pseudobulbous, branched near base. Roots are cordlike, branching, numerous, often arising at the leaf and descending to the ground. Leaves ovate-oblong, emarginate, up to 5 cm long. Flowers are numerous in corymbiform raceme, each about 2 to 3 cm in diameter. Sepals and petals are oblong-lanceolate; labellum trilobed, all lobes fringed, midlobe bipartite. This orchid, made in 1890, is a cross between *E. radicans* of Guatemala and *E. evectum* of Colombia.

AREA: Now widespread and naturalised in Qld. scrubs and parts of north N.S.W., commonly cultivated. TIME: Almost continuous throughout the year.

Orchidaceae
Diuris citrina

Orchidaceae
Diuris punctata var. punctata

Orchidaceae
Diuris punctata var. albo-violacea (2 forms)

Orchidaceae
Epidendrum x obrienianum

GALEOLA FOLIATA

FAMILY: Orchidaceae. COMMON NAME: Giant Climbing Orchid. COLOUR: Apricot with red markings. SIZE: Up to 15 metres high.

DESCRIPTION: The tallest growing orchid in the world, growing by means of brownish sucker-like roots, which bite deeply into the bark of forest trees. It has no true leaves, but large bracts 3 to 5 cm long, ovate-lanceolate at the root nodes. Flowers are in extensive panicles, sometimes up to 150 cm long. Sepals and petals are lanceolate; labellum is broadly obovate, the erect part cuneate with raised crimson margined lines along the centre. Lamina is broad; margins white; calli tinted yellow or scarlet. The plant is unmistakable. Very similar to *G. cassythoides*.

AREA: From north Qld. to north N.S.W., coastal and nearby mountains. Becoming rare because of clearing and grazing. TIME: November to January.

GLOSSODIA MAJOR

FAMILY: Orchidaceae. COMMON NAME: Wax-Lip Orchid or Parson-in-the-Pulpit. COLOUR: Vivid mauve. SIZE: Up to 30 cm high.

DESCRIPTION: A slender, hairy plant. Leaf: oblong to oblong-lanceolate, basal, stem-clasping, hairy, 3 to 10 cm long. Flowers: one or two, perianth segments subequal, spreading, elliptic-lanceolate, glandular-hairy, 20 to 25 mm long. Labellum: sessile, ovate-lanceolate, 9 to 12 mm long. Column is erect then incurved, broadly winged, 9 to 12 mm long, scented. Reproduction is by tuber as well as seed.

AREA: South Qld., N.S.W., Vic., Tas. and S.A., coastal and nearby tablelands, open forest and dry soils. TIME: August to November.

LIPARIS COELOGYNOIDES

FAMILY: Orchidaceae. COMMON NAME: None. COLOUR: Flesh apricot or pale green. SIZE: Massed and up to 10 cm high.

DESCRIPTION: Epiphytic or terrestrial plant. Leaves are flaccid and acute, 8 to 12 cm long. Flowers are in racemes, peduncle flat and winged. Labellum is wedge-shaped, 5 to 6 mm long. Sepals are linear, 6 to 7 mm long; petals, linear. Column is erect, incurved, slender, winged.

AREA: North Qld. to north N.S.W., coastal and nearby mountains, on tree trunks in masses. TIME: August to February.

LYPERANTHUS SUAVEOLENS

FAMILY: Orchidaceae. COMMON NAME: Brown Beaks. COLOUR: Yellow to dark brown. SIZE: Up to 45 cm high.

DESCRIPTION: An erect glabrous plant. Tubers are large, globose up to 2 cm diameter, roots fleshy. Leaf: solitary, glabrous, linear to linear-lanceolate, concave, margins incurved, 12 to 20 cm long. Stem bracts are closely sheathing; flowers are in terminal raceme. Dorsal sepal is acuminate broad, tip sometimes recurved; lateral sepals are linear, spreading or recurved. Labellum: erect part broad, incurved margins, lobes rounded, midlobe ovate, obtuse and recurved. Lamina has irregular rows of calli. Column is incurved and winged.

AREA: N.S.W., Vic., Qld. and Tas., coastal and nearby mountains, heathland and open forest in poor soil. TIME: September to November.

Orchidaceae
Galeola foliata

Orchidaceae
Glossodia major

Orchidaceae
Liparis coelogynoides

Orchidaceae
Lyperanthus suaveolens

MICROTIS OBLONGA

FAMILY: Orchidaceae. COMMON NAME: Sweet Onion Orchid. COLOUR: Green.
SIZE: Up to 45 cm high.
DESCRIPTION: Very slender plant. Leaf is solitary, thin, 25 to 50 cm long. Flowers
are small on short pedicels; raceme is 5 to 20 cm long. Dorsal sepal is erect, broad
hood, acute, apex recurved, 3 to 5 mm long; lateral sepals are revolute. Petals erect
or spreading, obtuse, 2 to 3 mm long. Labellum: 2 to 6 mm long, narrow-oblong,
reflexed crenulate margins, two large calli.
AREA: South Qld., N.S.W., Vic., S.A. and Tas., coast and tablelands and
mountains. TIME: October to January.

MICROTIS PARVIFLORA

FAMILY: Orchidaceae. COMMON NAME: Slender Onion Orchid. COLOUR: Green to
gold-green. SIZE: Up to 60 cm high.
DESCRIPTION: Very slender plant. Leaf is solitary, up to 70 cm long. Flowers: very
small, short pedicels, raceme dense, bracteoles long, acuminate. Dorsal sepal:
ovate, recurved point, 1 to 2 mm long. Lateral sepal: variable, oblong, acute,
recurved or revolute. Petals are blunt to oblong-linear. Labellum: oblong to ovate
with rounded, triangular or acuminate tip, recurved reflexed, occasionally inflexed.
AREA: N.S.W., Qld., Vic., S.A., Tas. and south-west of W.A., also Pacific Islands
to China. TIME: October to February.

MICROTIS UNIFOLIA

FAMILY: Orchidaceae. COMMON NAME: Common Onion Orchid. COLOUR: Green.
SIZE: From 10 to 90 cm high.
DESCRIPTION: Extremely variable plant. Leaf is terete, elongated, up to 30 cm
long. Flowers: small, numerous, raceme dense, terminal. Dorsal sepal: short,
acuminate, erect, helmetlike, 2 mm long. Lateral sepals: short, spreading, oblong
recurved. Petals are oblong and erect. Labellum: oblong, sessile, margins irregular,
tip blunt or emarginate.
AREA: All states, N.Z. and as far north as China. TIME: October to January.

PAPILLILABIUM BECKLERI

FAMILY: Orchidaceae. COMMON NAME: None. COLOUR: White and green. SIZE:
Small epiphytic.
DESCRIPTION: A diminutive plant. Roots are flexuose and long. Leaves: two to
four, linear to narrow-lanceolate, 1.5 to 4 cm long, 2 to 4 mm wide. Flowers: three
to six, very fragrant, raceme slender, 3 to 4 cm long. Dorsal sepal: erect, cucullate,
apex recurved; lateral sepals: incurved, 4 to 5 mm long; petals same as sepals;
labellum spur narrow, conical, hollow, 3 to 5 mm long.
AREA: South Qld., north N.S.W., coastal and nearby mountains, on Water Gum
(*Tristania laurina*) and slender branches of trees in moist gullies, close to water.
TIME: September to December.

Orchidaceae
Microtis oblonga

Orchidaceae
Microtis unifolia

Orchidaceae
Microtis parviflora

Orchidaceae
Papillilabium beckleri

PRASOPHYLLUM ARCHERI

FAMILY: Orchidaceae. COMMON NAME: Variable Midge-Orchid. COLOUR: Yellow, green, purple or white with red markings. SIZE: Up to 30 cm high.

DESCRIPTION: A slender plant. Leafless, bracts long, subulate below squat inflorescence. Flowers: two to fifteen, yellow or green with brown, red or purple markings or wholly purple-black. Dorsal sepal: 4 to 6 mm long, labellum only with cilia not dense but conspicuously long. A most variable plant, often described under other names. Specimens reported with fringed margins to the lateral petals.

AREA: South-east Qld., N.S.W., Vic., S.A. and Tas., grasslands, coast and ranges. TIME: November to February.

PRASOPHYLLUM AUREOVIRIDE VAR. ELMAE

FAMILY: Orchidaceae. COMMON NAME: None. COLOUR: Green-gold, gold-yellow. SIZE: Up to 20 cm high.

DESCRIPTION: A robust plant. Leaf bract is under the inflorescence. Flowers: three to twenty, raceme not dense. Lateral sepals are connate, longer than dorsal sepal. Petals: broadly lanceolate, labellum ovate-cuneate, margins entire, calli plate very broad, channelled with crimson marking on perianth segments.

AREA: North Qld. to central N.S.W., coastal and nearby mountains. TIME: March to May.

PRASOPHYLLUM AUSTRALE

FAMILY: Orchidaceae. COMMON NAME: Austral Leek Orchid. COLOUR: Green and white with red and mauve markings. SIZE: From 20 to 80 cm high.

DESCRIPTION: A slender plant with tubers. Leaf is shorter than inflorescence. Flower: sessile, ovaries terete, elongated, flower spike loose. Dorsal sepal: erect or recurved, concave, ovate-lanceolate, 8 mm long. Petals are erect, narrower and shorter than sepals. Labellum: gibbous at base, reflexed at middle, margins undulate.

AREA: N.S.W., Vic., S.A., W.A. and Tas., widespread, coastal and nearby mountains, swamps and moist grassland. TIME: August to January.

PRASOPHYLLUM ELATUM

FAMILY: Orchidaceae. COMMON NAME: Tall Leek Orchid. COLOUR: White and olive-green. SIZE: Up to 130 cm high.

DESCRIPTION: A robust, terrestrial, glabrous herb. It is yellow-green to green or purple-black, with tubers, and short lamina leaf. Flower: large, sessile on narrow, terete, elongate ovary. Dorsal sepal: lanceolate acute, concave, erect or concave, 11 mm long. Petals: narrow, spreading to incurved, falcate-lanceolate. Labellum: not gibbous, sessile, ovate, 8 to 10 mm long, tip red.

AREA: All states, abundant after bush fires, coastal and nearby tablelands. TIME: September to December.

Orchidaceae
Prasophyllum archeri

Orchidaceae
Prasophyllum aureoviride var. elmae

Orchidaceae
Prasophyllum australe

Orchidaceae
Prasophyllum elatum

PRASOPHYLLUM FLAVUM

FAMILY: Orchidaceae. COMMON NAME: Yellow Leek Orchid. COLOUR: Yellow. SIZE: Up to 80 cm high.

DESCRIPTION: Robust, glabrous herb with large rhizomes. Leaf sheath is with short terete lamina. Stem and leaf are purple-black to green-black. Four to forty flower spikes to a raceme. Dorsal sepal is broad-lanceolate; sepals, connate. Petals are narrow, lanceolate. Labellum: sessile, deeply concave, erect or recurved, oblong-lanceolate, 6 to 8 mm long.

AREA: South-east Qld., N.S.W., Vic. and Tas., scattered, coastal and nearby ranges. TIME: July to November.

PRASOPHYLLUM MORRISII

FAMILY: Orchidaceae. COMMON NAME: Bearded Midge-Orchid. COLOUR: Mauve, green and white. SIZE: Up to 35 cm high.

DESCRIPTION: A robust, slender plant. It is leafless except for small subulate bract. Flowers: two to twenty, not crowded, raceme 1 to 5 cm long. Lateral sepals: oblong-lanceolate, falcate, concave, 4 to 5 mm long. Dorsal sepal: broad-ovate, cuculate with acuminate point, margins coloured, 4 to 5 mm long. Petals: deltoid acuminate, fringed with hairs, 4 to 4.5 mm long. Labellum: oblong-ovate, 2 to 3 mm long, margins fringed with long hairs.

AREA: This beautiful species is found in dry sclerophyll forests, central coast of N.S.W. to Vic. and Tas. TIME: December to May.

PRASOPHYLLUM RUFUM

FAMILY: Orchidaceae. COMMON NAME: Red Midge-Orchid. COLOUR: Dark red, red-brown or purple-red. SIZE: Up to 30 cm high.

DESCRIPTION: A most variable slender herb. It is leafless, with stem bracts 1 to 3 cm long. Flowers: very small, few to many, spike 2 to 6 cm long. Dorsal sepal: broad-ovate, cuculate, 2 to 3 mm long. Lateral sepal: broad-lanceolate, diverging often gland-tipped. Petals are lanceolate to triangular. Labellum: deep purple, obovate-cuneate, margins denticulate or serrate, or cilia-like.

AREA: South Qld., N.S.W. and Tas., not Vic., coastal and nearby mountains and tablelands, grasslands or open forest. TIME: January to May.

PTEROSTYLIS ACUMINATA

FAMILY: Orchidaceae. COMMON NAME: Sharp Greenhood. COLOUR: Green. SIZE: Up to 20 cm high.

DESCRIPTION: A glabrous plant. Leaves: basal, rosette, petiolate 1 to 4 cm long, ovate to broad-lanceolate. The one or two stem bracts are small. Flower: solitary, galea 2 to 3 cm long, erect or slightly inclined. Dorsal sepal: erect for half the length then horizontal, apex acuminate; petals also acuminate. Labellum: oblong-linear to linear-lanceolate tapering to recurved acuminate point.

AREA: N.S.W. and Qld., often in abundance in coastal areas. TIME: March to July.

Orchidaceae
Prasophyllum flavum

Orchidaceae
Prasophyllum morrisii

Orchidaceae
Prasophyllum rufum

Orchidaceae
Pterostylis acuminata

PTEROSTYLIS BAPTISTII

FAMILY: Orchidaceae. COMMON NAME: King Greenhood. COLOUR: Green. SIZE: Up to 40 cm high.

DESCRIPTION: A strong plant. Leaves are basal, lanceolate to elliptical, petiolate, 4 to 7 cm long. Stem bracts are 4 to 6 cm long. Flower: solitary, large translucent, galea inflated at base, erect then incurved. Petals are dilated. Lower lip is erect, cuneate, filiform lobes. Labellum is compressed, broad-linear.

AREA: North Qld., N.S.W. and east Vic., coastal and nearby mountains, in dense scrub close to streams and swamps. TIME: August to November.

PTEROSTYLIS BARBATA

FAMILY: Orchidaceae. COMMON NAME: Bird Orchid or Bearded Greenhood. COLOUR: Green. SIZE: Up to 20 cm high.

DESCRIPTION: Unique slender herb. Leaves: imbricate, ovate-lanceolate, acuminate, extending up scape, floral bracts. Flower: solitary, galea erect, with long filiform point; sepals, linear; labellum, 25 mm long, beautiful filiform, beset with long golden lateral hairs, with dark-green or brown clavate knob; basal appendage, oblong-linear. Column upright with filiform point.

AREA: All states except Qld., rare in N.S.W. In W.A. formerly known as *P. turfosa*. TIME: August to November.

PTEROSTYLIS BOORMANII

FAMILY: Orchidaceae. COMMON NAME: None. COLOUR: Red and green. SIZE: Up to 25 cm high.

DESCRIPTION: Slender herb. Leaves: basal, rosette, sessile, elliptical. Stem bracts are closely sheathing. Flowers: three to eight, variable in size, loose raceme. Galea is 12 mm long; apex, a recurved point, 6 to 8 mm long. Lower lip is reflexed; the lobes ovate with filiform point, 10 to 15 mm long. Labellum is thick, fleshy, glandular. A member of the 'rufa' group.

AREA: N.S.W., S.A., Vic. (rare), perhaps Qld. and W.A., tablelands and western N.S.W. in grasslands. TIME: August to November.

PTEROSTYLIS CURTA

FAMILY: Orchidaceae. COMMON NAME: Blunt Greenhood. SIZE: Up to 30 cm high.

DESCRIPTION: A strong, glabrous, common plant. Leaves: two to five, basal, rosette, ovate to oblong-elliptical, 3 to 9 cm long. The two or three stem bracts are loose-sheathing. Flowers: solitary, galea erect, lower lip cuneate. Labellum: movable, obtuse, recurved and protruding through the sinus.

AREA: South Qld., N.S.W., Vic., S.A. and Tas., widespread, coast and tablelands, ranges, temperal woodlands, moist and cool gullies. TIME: July to November.

Orchidaceae
Pterostylis baptistii

Orchidaceae
Pterostylis boormanii

Orchidaceae
Pterostylis barbata

Orchidaceae
Pterostylis curta

PTEROSTYLIS HILDAE

FAMILY: Orchidaceae. COMMON NAME: None. COLOUR: Green. SIZE: Up to 15 cm high.

DESCRIPTION: A slender, glabrous plant. Leaves: two or three, basal, ovate to oblong, long petioles. Two to five stem bracts. Flowers: solitary, apex tinged light brown, galea long and erect with upper part incurved. Sepals: cojoined erect, subulate points embrace the galea. Labellum is oblong, elliptical to spathulate, 9 to 12 mm long, on a movable claw.

AREA: N.S.W. and Qld., coastal and nearby mountains, in or close to subtropical rainforest. TIME: February to October.

PTEROSTYLIS MUTICA

FAMILY: Orchidaceae. COMMON NAME: Midget Greenhood. COLOUR: Green. SIZE: Up to 30 cm high.

DESCRIPTION: A slender, glabrous plant, or may be robust. Leaves: radical, rosette, elliptical to ovate, 1 to 2 cm long, short petioles. Bracts are acute, sheathing. Flowers: two to fifteen, spiral raceme. Galea: gibbous, erect, incurved, obtuse tip. Lower lip is concave with short, broad lobes. Labellum: 3.5 mm long, claw movable with round apex, emarginate.

AREA: South-east Qld. and all states, widespread, coast, mountains and tablelands. TIME: July to January.

PTEROSTYLIS OPHIOGLOSSA

FAMILY: Orchidaceae. COMMON NAME: Snake Tongue Orchid. COLOUR: Green. SIZE: Up to 25 cm high.

DESCRIPTION: Slender, glabrous plant. Leaves: radical, rosette, short petioles, ovate to oblong, obtuse, mucronate, 2 to 4 cm long. Solitary stem bract. Flower is solitary, large; galea 2 to 3 cm long, erect, incurved, acuminate with brown stripes; lower lip, cuneate, two-lobed. Labellum: 12 to 16 mm long on movable claw, oblong-linear, with two narrow lobes extending beyond the sinus of the lower lip.

AREA: N.S.W. and Qld., coast and tablelands. TIME: April to August, at times to September.

PTEROSTYLIS PARVIFLORA

FAMILY: Orchidaceae. COMMON NAME: Tiny Greenhood. COLOUR: Red, green and white. SIZE: Up to 60 cm high.

DESCRIPTION: An erect, slender plant. Leaves are radical but absent at flowering or by one or more at base of scape. Stem leaves are bractlike, acute. Flowers, one to twelve; galea erect, incurved, apex obtuse; petals red at apex. Labellum is oblong to oblong-linear, on movable claw. This species appears in three forms. Its coastal form is a small slender plant with pale flowers. Its tablelands and inland form is tall with many flowers with markings from dark green, yellow-brown to crimson. Its alpine form is short and fleshy, with few flowers, and thought by some to be a distinct variety.

AREA: All states except W.A., widespread. TIME: All the year round depending on altitude and season.

Orchidaceae
Pterostylis hildae

Orchidaceae
Pterostylis mutica

Orchidaceae
Pterostylis ophioglossa

Orchidaceae
Pterostylis parviflora

PTEROSTYLIS PEDUNCULATA

FAMILY: Orchidaceae. COMMON NAME: Maroonhood. COLOUR: Green with deep red markings. SIZE: Up to 30 cm high.

DESCRIPTION: Very slender plant. Leaves: basal rosette, ovate to oblong on long petioles. Stem bracts: one to four, small. Flower is solitary; galea erect for two-thirds, then horizontal with short acute upturned tip. Sepals: cojoined with gibbous sinus, points exceed the galea. Labellum is blunt ovate on movable claw; lamina is with central ridge and channel on underside.

AREA: South-east Qld., N.S.W., Vic. and S.A., coastal, mountains and tablelands in shady gullies, tea-tree scrub. TIME: July to November.

PTEROSTYLIS REVOLUTA

FAMILY: Orchidaceae. COMMON NAME: Autumn Greenhood. COLOUR: Green with white and red markings. SIZE: Up to 25 cm high.

DESCRIPTION: Slender plant. Leaves: radical, rosette separate from stem, ovate to obovate or lanceolate on long petioles. Stem bracts: one to five, small, stem clasping. Flower is solitary and large with dark markings. Galea is erect to inclined, curved, gibbous at base, and arching over lower lip. Dorsal sepals and petals have long filiform points. Lateral sepals are cojoined to form lower lip. Labellum is on movable claw.

AREA: From south-east Qld., N.S.W. to Vic., coast, mountains and tablelands, in dry habitats. TIME: March to July.

PTEROSTYLIS RUFA SSP. ACICULIFORMIS

FAMILY: Orchidaceae. COMMON NAME: Ruddyood. COLOUR: Red and green. SIZE: Up to 20 cm high.

DESCRIPTION: A glabrous plant. Two to five stem bracts, sheathing. Leaves: short petiolate, oblong-lanceolate, basal rosette. Flower: one to ten, long pedicels, glaucous-green with rusty-brown markings. Galea and dorsal sepal: 10 to 15 mm long, compressed, point short and recurved. Lateral sepals are cojoined, reflexed, margins involute. Labellum is fleshy movable, concave.

AREA: Eastern and central N.S.W., Vic. and S.A., widespread over a range of habitats. TIME: September to December.

SARCOCHILUS OLIVACEUS

FAMILY: Orchidaceae. COMMON NAME: Lawyer Orchid. COLOUR: Green-yellow to olive. SIZE: Small epiphyte.

DESCRIPTION: Epiphytic plant with short stems. Leaves: oblong, broad, falcate, flat, thin texture, 8 to 12 cm long. Raceme are several, axillary; peduncle is flexuose. The four to twelve flowers are 2 to 3 cm in diameter. Sepals and petals are narrow-oblong to falcate. Labellum is trilobed, with lateral lobes oblong-falcate and midlobe short and orbicular. Very fragrant orchid.

AREA: South-east Qld. and N.S.W., rainforest and wet sclerophyll, on trees and rocks. TIME: July to November, depending on latitude and altitude.

Orchidaceae
Pterostylis pedunculata

Orchidaceae
Pterostylis revoluta

Orchidaceae
Pterostylis rufa ssp. aciculiformis

Orchidaceae
Sarcochilus olivaceus

SPICULAEA IRRITABILIS

FAMILY: Orchidaceae. COMMON NAME: Leafy Elbow-Orchid. COLOUR: Green with red markings. SIZE: Up to 40 cm high.

DESCRIPTION: Erect, slender plant. Leaves: two to six, basal, ovate-oblong to lanceolate, 3 to 10 cm long, prominent midrib. Flowers: three to ten or more, loose raceme; dorsal sepal erect to incurved, linear only 10 to 15 mm long; lateral sepals deflexed. Petals are filiformlike, deflexed. Labellum is articulate at end of projection of the column; lamina is hammer-shaped, uppersurface covered with long hairs.

AREA: Eastern Qld., to Vic., border, coast and rare on nearby mountains. TIME: December to April.

THELYMITRA ARISTATA

FAMILY: Orchidaceae. COMMON NAME: Scented Sun Orchid. COLOUR: Pink, blue or mauve. SIZE: Up to 90 cm high.

DESCRIPTION: A slender, erect, variable plant. Leaf: sheathing, broad, lanceolate, flat, 12 to 20 cm and more long. Flowers: one to fifteen or more, fragrant; perianth segments elliptical, lanceolate, 1 to 3 cm long, expanding in sunshine. Column is erect and hooded. Habitat: marshy conditions or well drained ridges, in crevices. It has an interesting association with *Dendrobium kingianum*.

AREA: All states, widespread. TIME: August to November.

LINOSPADIX MONOSTACHYUS

FAMILY: Palmae. COMMON NAME: Walking Stick Palm. COLOUR: Cream with red fruit. SIZE: Up to 3 metres high.

DESCRIPTION: A long, slender palm, with closely ringed stems. Leaves are small pinnate fronds. Flower is small, with three segments to the calyx; three petals and six stamens. Inflorescence: a long undivided spike, axil in leaf fronds, up to 70 cm long. Fruit is oval, drupaceous, bright red when mature. Spike of mature fruit resembles strings of red beads.

AREA: N.S.W. and Qld., coast and mountains, and in rainforests. TIME: January to June; seed, June to October.

AOTUS ERICOIDES

FAMILY: Papilionaceae. COMMON NAME: Eggs and Bacon. COLOUR: Yellow with red markings. SIZE: Up to 2 metres high.

DESCRIPTION: Spreading shrub. Leaves are whorled or scattered, linear to narrow-ovate, 6 to 12 mm long, margins revolute, stipules absent. Flowers are solitary or two or three in axillary cluster. Peduncles are short. Bracts are deciduous. Calyx is pubescent, two upper lobes united. Corolla is yellow with red markings; standard twice the calyx. Stamens are free.

CALYX

AREA: South Qld., N.S.W. and Vic., heath and open forests, coastal and nearby mountains. TIME: August to November.

Orchidaceae
biculaea irritabiles

Orchidaceae
Thelymitra aristata

Papilionaceae
Aotus ericoides

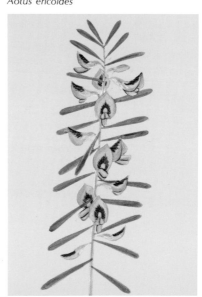

BOSSIAEA NEO-ANGLICA

FAMILY: Papilionaceae. COMMON NAME: None. COLOUR: Red trimmed with yellow. SIZE: Up to a metre high.

DESCRIPTION: A sprawling undershrub. Leaves: small ovate to cordate, pungent pointed, 4 to 6 mm long, stipules prominent. Flower: small, solitary on short peduncle, upper calyx lobes broad and united in tip, lower three calyx lobes small. Standard large, circular to kidney-shaped wings longer than keel; stamens united. Fruit is a flat pod, with thickened margins; seeds are brown strophiolated.

AREA: South-east Qld. and N.S.W., tablelands, coast and mountains, very sandy and rocky soils. TIME: May to November.

CASTANOSPERMUM AUSTRALE

FAMILY: Papilionaceae. COMMON NAME: Black Bean or Morton Bay Chestnut. COLOUR: Yellow-orange. SIZE: Up to 39 metres high.

DESCRIPTION: A fairly large tree. Leaves: large, shiny, pinnate up to 50 cm long, eight to eleven leaflets each 5 to 12 cm long. Flowers: in axillary racemes well down the branch on last year's wood, pea-like 25 mm to 36 mm long. Petals are free; calyx lobes, short and broad; stamens free and protruding beyond the petals. Fruit is large, hard, heavy 15 cm to 25 cm long, elongated, woody pod; it splits to release several large brown seeds with red, soft papery testa. Dark brown timber is easily dressed, polishes well, making excellent cabinet wood.

AREA: Qld. to Bellinger River in N.S.W., in rich coastal soils. TIME: November to January; seed, February to July.

CHORIZEMA ILICIFOLIUM

FAMILY: Papilionaceae. COMMON NAME: Holly Flame-pea or Holly-leaved Chorizema. COLOUR: Red-orange. SIZE: Up to a metre high.

DESCRIPTION: A straggling or spreading decumbent shrub. Branches are slender, glabrous. Leaves are linear-oblong, glabrous, sharply toothed. Flowers are large, in racemes, terminal; calyx lobes short, upper two broader. Standard, circular or kidney-shaped, are longer than wings or keel. Stamens are free. Fruit is a small soft, inflated pod. Seeds are several and brown.

AREA: W.A., south-west, Irwin and Avon districts, grey sands. TIME: July to September.

CROTALARIA MITCHELLII

FAMILY: Papilionaceae. COMMON NAME: Mitchells Bird Flower. COLOUR: Yellow. SIZE: Up to 1.5 metres high.

DESCRIPTION: Silky, pubescent perennial. The single leaflet is ovate-lanceolate or ovate, obtuse or slightly notched, softly pubescent both sides, 1.5 to 4 cm long. Illustrated is the type found along Qld. coast; it is less common in north-east N.S.W., but is recorded from Gloucester. Leaflet has a glabrous uppersurface. Flower is in terminal raceme, calyx pubescent, ovary glabrous.

AREA: N.S.W., Qld., S.A. and central Australia. TIME: July to November.

Papilionaceae
Bossiaea neo-anglica

Papilionaceae
Castanospermum australe

Papilionaceae
Chorizema ilicifolium

Papilionaceae
Crotalaria mitchellii

DAVIESIA ARBOREA

FAMILY: Papilionaceae. COMMON NAME: Weeping Pea. COLOUR: Yellow with red markings. SIZE: Up to 10 metres high.

DESCRIPTION: A small tree or large shrub. Leaves are sessile, linear, alternate up to 15 cm long. Bark is rough with ridges and corky. Inflorescence: pendulous, terminal panicle, 30 cm and more long. Flowers are small; calyx lobes are very short. When in flower this is a most beautiful tree. Branches are long, pendulous, glabrous, willow-like.

AREA: North N.S.W., coastal and mountains, Cangai Forest, Nymboida River, Dorrigo and Gibraltar Range, along the ridges and hill slopes, marginal. TIME: Spring, August to November.

DAVIESIA LATIFOLIA

FAMILY: Papilionaceae. COMMON NAME: Hop Bitter Pea. COLOUR: Yellow with brown markings. SIZE: Up to 3 metres high.

DESCRIPTION: A large, erect or spreading shrub. Leaves are ovate-elliptic to ovate-lanceolate, not spiny. Flowers: 4 to 7 mm long, raceme 2 to 5 cm long, axillary. Calyx lobes are short. Standard broad, emarginate, bracts conspicuous. A most attractive display when in bloom.

AREA: N.S.W., Vic. and Tas., coast, mountains, marginal rainforest and wet sclerophyll forest. TIME: September to November.

DAVIESIA SQUARROSA VAR. SQUARROSA

FAMILY: Papilionaceae. COMMON NAME: Prickly Pea. COLOUR: Yellow with red markings. SIZE: About 1.5 metres high.

DESCRIPTION: An erect, woody, prickly shrub. Branches are angular, long and weak. Leaves are sessile, cordate to narrow-ovate, 6 to 12 mm long, tapering to a sharp pungent point. Flowers, small solitary; peduncles, about 12 mm long; weak filiform.

AREA: N.S.W., coastal and nearby mountains and plateaux. TIME: August to November and later.

Legume fruiting body
of *Goodia latifolia*

Papilionaceae
Daviesia arborea

Papilionaceae
Daviesia latifolia

Papilionaceae
Daviesia squarrosa var. squarrosa

DAVIESIA UMBELLULATA

FAMILY: Papilionaceae. COMMON NAME: Bitter Pea. COLOUR: Yellow. SIZE: Up to a metre high.

DESCRIPTION: A low shrub. Leaves are alternate, linear-elliptic to elliptic to ovate, smooth, stiff, 2 to 3 cm long, protracted into sharp spines. Flowers are small, 8 mm across, in umbel cluster of three to five from leaf axil. Fruit is a small legume.

AREA: Qld., Fraser Island and N.S.W., coastal and nearby mountains, open forests, poor soils. TIME: August to September.

DESMODIUM RHYTIDOPHYLLUM

FAMILY: Papilionaceae. COMMON NAME: None. COLOUR: Pink, mauve or blue. SIZE: Prostrate.

DESCRIPTION: A weak prostrate perennial, trailing or twining slightly. Rusty-villous or tomentose. Leaves three-foliolate; leaflets elliptical to orbicular, ovate to broad-lanceolate, 2 to 6 cm long. Flowers are on filiform peduncles, erect or spread, 1 to 2 cm long. Fruit is deeply indented on lower side. A much coarser plant than *D. varians*.

AREA: N.S.W., coast, mountains and tablelands, widespread in open forests. TIME: Most of the year.

DILLWYNIA HISPIDA

FAMILY: Papilionaceae. COMMON NAME: Red Parrot Pea. COLOUR: Red to crimson. SIZE: Up to 2 metres high.

DESCRIPTION: Slender erect shrub, covered with short hairs to almost glabrous. Leaves are crowded, obtuse, 3 to 15 mm long. Flowers are in cluster in short racemes, short peduncles; subtending leaves very short; calyx is hairy, 6 to 8 mm long; standard 12 to 20 mm long, broad, red and yellow; wings and keel short, keel acuminate. Fruit is a pod, ovoid to globular.

AREA: N.S.W., Vic. and S.A., along roadsides. TIME: August to November.

DILLWYNIA JUNIPERINA

FAMILY: Papilionaceae. COMMON NAME: None. COLOUR: Orange with red markings. SIZE: Up to 2 metres high.

DESCRIPTION: Rigid prickly shrub. Branches divaricate. Leaves rigid, 5 to 15 cm long, spreading, with fine pungent points. Flowers are in terminal cluster; calyx obtuse, u-shaped, 3 to 5 mm long, pubescent, minutely ciliate; upper calyx-lobes connate, short and broad. Standard short; wings flat and spreading; petals persistent. Fruit is surrounded by remains of petals.

AREA: N.S.W., Qld. and Vic., widespread, open forest, dry areas and along roadsides. TIME: August to November.

Papilionaceae
Daviesia umbellulata

Papilionaceae
Desmodium rhytidophyllum

Papilionaceae
Dillwynia hispida

Papilionaceae
Dillwynia juniperina

DILLWYNIA SERICEA

FAMILY: Papilionaceae. COMMON NAME: Showy Parrot Pea. COLOUR: Orange with yellow centre. SIZE: Up to a metre high.

DESCRIPTION: A small shrub, covered with silky, white hairs. Leaves: alternate, terete, channelled uppersurface, straight, glabrous, 7 to 13 mm long. Flower: solitary or pairs, 10 to 13 mm across, calyx hairy to almost glabrous, two upper lobes connate. Plant closely resembles *D. retorta*, at one time classified under same name.

AREA: N.S.W. and Vic., mountains and higher heathlands. TIME: October to December.

GLYCINE CLANDESTINA

FAMILY: Papilionaceae. COMMON NAME: Twining Glycine. COLOUR: Lilac to purple. SIZE: Twining for a metre or more.

DESCRIPTION: A twining herb with perennial rootstock from which arise the slender climbing stems. Leaves are trifoliate; leaflets of upper leaves are lanceolate to linear, acute 1 to 5 cm long; terminal leaflets sessile. Flowers: 5 to 8 mm across, three to twenty in upper axils on slender peduncles, sometimes umbellate; calyx brown and hairy, teeth lanceolate. Fruit is a pod, straight subterete, minutely pubescent, 15 to 25 mm long. A delicate twiner favouring long grass for climbing.

AREA: N.S.W., Qld., Vic., S.A. and W.A., temperate areas, widespread, in many habitats, mountains, Alps, tablelands, dry areas and Coolgardie. TIME: July to November.

GOMPHOLOBIUM GRANDIFLORUM

FAMILY: Papilionaceae. COMMON NAME: Large Wedge Pea. COLOUR: Yellow. SIZE: Up to 2 metres high.

DESCRIPTION: An erect shrub. Three leaflets, digitate, acute with sharp point, revolute, linear, 12 to 25 mm long. Stems are glabrous. Standard 15 to 30 mm long, keel not conspicuously ciliate. Pedicels are short; flowers solitary .or in small racemes.

AREA: Qld., N.S.W., Vic., coast and mountains, plateaux and tablelands, sandy and poor soils, heathlands, and dry sclerophyll forests. TIME: August to November.

GOMPHOLOBIUM MINUS

FAMILY: Papilionaceae. COMMON NAME: None. COLOUR: Yellow. SIZE: Up to 30 cm high.

DESCRIPTION: A low shrub. Branches are pubescent with spreading hairs. Leaflets: three, almost without common petiole, linear to narrow-obovate, revolute margins, glabrous, crowded along branches, 4 to 12 mm long. Flowers are solitary or in pairs; peduncles bibracteate; calyx glabrous, 10 mm long; lobes lanceolate, ciliate; standard obicular; keel obtuse.

AREA: N.S.W., Vic. and S.A., coast, in open forest, sandy soils and heathlands. TIME: September to January.

Papilionaceae
Dillwynia sericea

Papilionaceae
Glycine clandestina

Papilionaceae
Gompholobium grandiflorum

Papilionaceae
Gompholobium minus

GOMPHOLOBIUM PINNATUM

FAMILY: Papilionaceae. COMMON NAME: Poor Man's Gold. COLOUR: Chrome yellow and may have red markings. SIZE: From 30 to 50 cm high.

DESCRIPTION: Low shrub. Leaves: twenty to thirty, pinnately arranged, under 20 mm long, narrow-linear to narrow-elliptic, rhachis 10 to 25 mm long, elongated. Flowers are solitary; calyx 5 to 6 mm long; standard 6 to 10 mm long.

AREA: N.S.W. and Vic., widespread, coast, mountains, sandy soils, heath and dry sclerophyll forest, open forest and cleared land. TIME: July to December.

GOMPHOLOBIUM POLYMORPHUM

FAMILY: Papilionaceae. COMMON NAME: Wedge Pea. COLOUR: Red, crimson, orange-red or orange-yellow. SIZE: Up to a metre high.

DESCRIPTION: A straggling or scandent shrub. Leaflets: three, digitate, linear to cuneate, 1 to 2.5 cm long. Flower is solitary; calyx lobes linear; pedicel much longer than calyx.

AREA: W.A., in stony soil in south-western province, Avon, Darling, Stirling and Irwin districts. TIME: September to November.

HOVEA ACUTIFOLIA

FAMILY: Papilionaceae. COMMON NAME: None. COLOUR: Purple with green centre. SIZE: Up to 2.5 metres high.

DESCRIPTION: A large, bushy, erect shrub. Leaves acuminate, broad, elliptic, 2 to 5 cm long. Underside of leaf is brown-green and softly pubescent. Flowers are usually in clusters of three in leaf axil. Standard is short; wings flat and spreading. The calyx and branches are brown and softly pubescent.

AREA: North N.S.W., Qld., coast and mountains and tablelands, open forests. TIME: August to October.

HOVEA HETEROPHYLLA

FAMILY: Papilionaceae. COMMON NAME: Common Hovea. COLOUR: Lilac to blue. SIZE: Up to 40 cm high.

DESCRIPTION: Small straggling, slender, slightly hairy shrub. Upper leaves are linear—glabrous above and grey, rusty tomentose underneath, 2 to 5 cm long. Lower leaves are almost ovate and slightly tomentose on undersurface. Flowers: solitary or in pairs, axillary; bracteoles linear; calyx lightly tomentose. Fruit is a pod, sessile, globular to ovoid, broad and tomentose.

AREA: N.S.W., Qld., Vic. and S.A., dry sclerophyll forest, coast, mountains and tablelands. TIME: September to December.

Papilionaceae
Gompholobium pinnatum

Papilionaceae
Gompholobium polymorphum

Papilionaceae
Hovea acutifolia

Papilionaceae
Hovea heterophylla

INDIGOFERA AUSTRALIS VAR. AUSTRALIS
FAMILY: Papilionaceae. COMMON NAME: Austral Indigo. COLOUR: Lilac to mauve. SIZE: Up to 3 metres high.

DESCRIPTION: A glabrous, slender shrub. Leaves pinnate, leaflets nine to twenty-one, oblong to oblong-cuneate, 5 to 25 mm long. Flowers: raceme usually as long as the leaves; calyx 2 mm long, teeth equal; standard about 8 mm long; the two wings drop before wilting leaving the narrow, hairy standard.

CALYX

AREA: N.S.W., Qld., Vic., S.A. and W.A., widespread, coast, mountain clearings and open forests. TIME: September to February.

INDIGOFERA AUSTRALIS VAR. SIGNATA
FAMILY: Papilionaceae. COMMON NAME: None. COLOUR: Purple and green. SIZE: Up to 1.5 mm high.

DESCRIPTION: Erect undershrub. Leaves: 3 to 10 cm long, linear, margins crenate, with dark brown markings giving the appearance of bands, with small leaflets. Flowers: long peduncles, five to twelve per raceme, standard erect 10 to 18 mm long with light green blotch. Calyx is 2 mm long, brown, pubescent, teeth unequal. This is a most interesting variety.

AREA: North N.S.W. and south Qld., not widespread. TIME: September to October.

KENNEDIA BECKXIANA
FAMILY: Papilionaceae. COMMON NAME: None. COLOUR: Red. SIZE: Twining up to 3 metres high.

DESCRIPTION: A woody twiner, covered with fine hairs. Leaves: trifoliate; oblong to ovate, wavy, 10 to 20 mm long, margins sinuate or with silky hairs. Flowers: axillary, solitary or pairs, on long peduncles, with connate bracts. This plant is unmistakable. Fruit is a long, flat pod, with grey-brown seeds.

AREA: W.A., coast or moist habitat, Eyre district. TIME: October.

LESPEDEZA JUNCEA
FAMILY: Papilionaceae. COMMON NAME: None. COLOUR: White with mauve markings. SIZE: Up to a metre high.

DESCRIPTION: Erect, slender shrub arising from thick woody root stock. Branches are pubescent. Leaves are trifoliate; leaflets: linear-cuneate, finely mucronate, 10 to 25 mm long. There are two to six flowers in axillary cluster, 4 to 6 mm long. Calyx lobes are acute, rigid. Fruit is an indehiscent legume, sessile, orbicular, 2 to 3 mm diameter.

AREA: N.S.W., coastal strips, nearby mountains, open forest and along roadsides. TIME: February to March.

Papilionaceae
Indigofera australis var. australis

Papilionaceae
Indigofera australis var. signata

Papilionaceae
Kennedia beckxiana

Papilionaceae
Lespedeza juncea

LOTUS AUSTRALIS

FAMILY: Papilionaceae. COMMON NAME: Barwon River Trefoil. COLOUR: Mauve-pink to white. SIZE: Up to 30 cm high.

DESCRIPTION: A low, perennial herb. There are five leaflets—upper three on flat petiole and lower two resembling stipules. Flowers: subsessile, three to eight in umbels, leafy bracts, axillary peduncles. Corolla is 15 mm or longer; calyx is two-lipped, five-lobed.

AREA: N.S.W., Qld., Vic. and S.A., coast and mountains, widespread, grasslands and open forests. TIME: September to March.

MACROPTILIUM ATROPURPUREUM

FAMILY: Papilionaceae. COMMON NAME: Wild Bean. COLOUR: Maroon-black. SIZE: Vine-climber.

DESCRIPTION: Member of climbing bean group and once belonging to the *Phaseolus* genus. Leaves: trifoliate, lanceolate, two lower, lobed, 2 to 5 cm long. Flowers: raceme terminal cluster, two to seven; calyx 10 to 15 mm long, five-lobed. Corolla: twisted, green, wings 15 to 25 mm across. Fruit is a long narrow black bean up to 10 cm long.

AREA: Vigorous growth, found along roadsides, embankments and cuttings. Considered a noxious plant in some shires. N.S.W. and Qld., in warm areas. TIME: All year round, olimax in summer, December to March.

MILLETTIA MEGASPERMA

FAMILY: Papilionaceae. COMMON NAME: Native Wisteria. COLOUR: Mauve. SIZE: Climber to 12 metres high.

DESCRIPTION: A glabrous, woody twiner. Leaves: imparipinnate, nine to thirteen leaflets. Inflorescence: a terminal pendulous spike. Flowers: fifteen to fifty, short peduncles; calyx 3 to 8 mm long, five-lobed. Standard is erect, recurved, 12 to 20 mm long; wings oblong-obovate, longer than keel; keel is spathulate. Tropical and subtropical legume. It is a beautiful display and unmistakable when in bloom.

AREA: North Qld., Mt Elliot National Park, tropical rainforest. TIME: Summer, December to April.

MIRBELIA OXYLOBIOIDES

FAMILY: Papilionaceae. COMMON NAME: Mountain Mirbelia. COLOUR: Orange with red markings. SIZE: Up to 3 metres high.

DESCRIPTION: A wiry, spreading shrub. Leaves ericoid, ternate, oblong to ovate, dark green, 3 to 6 mm long. Branches are also mostly ternate. Flowers are in terminal clusters. Standards: erect, margins tend to incurve, 10 to 12 mm long, keel hidden in wings.

AREA: N.S.W. and Vic., mountains, high country and heathlands. TIME: October to December.

Papilionaceae
Lotus australis

Papilionaceae
Macroptilium atropurpureum

Papilionaceae
Milletia megasperma

Papilionaceae
Mirbelia oxylobioides

MIRBELIA SPECIOSA

FAMILY: Papilionaceae. COMMON NAME: Showy Mirbelia. COLOUR: Red-purple. SIZE: Up to a metre high.

DESCRIPTION: An erect shrub. Branches are glabrous to lightly pubescent. Leaves: ternate but can be displaced, narrow-linear to obtuse to almost pungent, margins closely revolute, 5 to 25 mm long. Flowers: large in comparison to bush, 10 to 15 mm across, sessile in upper axils to form a terminal spike, leafy base. Corolla is brilliant and attractive but pale purple to blue on drying. Fruit is a smooth legume, 0.8 mm long.

AREA: Qld. and N.S.W., coastal and nearby mountains, in heathlands and dry sclerophyll forest on poor soils. TIME: July to September.

OXYLOBIUM ELLIPTICUM VAR. ANGUSTIFOLIUM = ARBORESCENS

FAMILY: Papilionaceae. COMMON NAME: Golden Shaggy Pea. COLOUR: Orange with red markings. SIZE: Up to 2.5 metres high.

DESCRIPTION: A low shrub. Leaves: mucronate at apex with pungent point, elliptical to ovate to narrow-ovate, to linear-lanceolate, margins recurved, more or less pubescent on under surface, 1 to 5 cm long. Flowers are crowded towards end of branches. Standard is 8 to 10 mm long. Fruit: a legume, ovate-acuminate, villous, to 8 mm long.

AREA: N.S.W., Vic. and Tas., high country, mountains, open forests. TIME: September to February.

OXYLOBIUM SCANDENS

FAMILY: Papilionaceae. COMMON NAME: None. COLOUR: Orange with red markings. SIZE: Climber.

DESCRIPTION: Prostrate or climbing shrub. Leaves: usually opposite, entire, elliptic to lanceolate, reticulate, margins not recurved, 2 to 5 cm long. Flowers are in a dense, terminal, umbel-like raceme. Calyx is longer than tube; standard is up to 10 mm long.

AREA: South Qld. and N.S.W., coast and nearby mountains and tablelands in heavier soils. TIME: September to April.

PHYLLOTA PHYLICOIDES

FAMILY: Papilionaceae. COMMON NAME: None. COLOUR: Yellow with red markings. SIZE: Up to 60 cm high.

DESCRIPTION: Erect or ascending shrub. Leaves: numerous, linear, mucronate, 5 to 20 mm long, 1 mm wide. Flowers are up to 10 mm long, with dense, leafy spikes. Bracteoles are lanceolate; calyx has villous hairs. Fruit is a globular legume.

AREA: N.S.W. and Qld., coastal mountains, plateaux and tablelands in higher and dryer areas. TIME: August to November.

Papilionaceae
Mirbelia speciosa

Papilionaceae
Oxylobium scandans

Papilionaceae
Oxylobium ellipticum var. angustifolium
  = arborescens

Papilionaceae
Phyllota phylicoides

PSORALEA PATENS

FAMILY: Papilionaceae. COMMON NAME: Verbine. COLOUR: Pink-purple, blue or white. SIZE: Up to 120 cm high.

DESCRIPTION: Perennial herb. Leaves are pinnately trifoliate; leaflets: ovate-lanceolate, lanceolate to oblong, minutely pubescent to tomentose, obtuse, 1 to 5 cm long, short rigid teeth. Flowers are in axillary spikes or long terminal racemes, with naked part of peduncle hairy and longer than leaf. Calyx: silky-villous, hairs white or black, broad lower tooth; petals are twice as long as calyx. Fruit is a legume pod, pubescent.

AREA: South Qld., western N.S.W., S.A. and south-east of W.A., widespread, western plains and ranges. TIME: Most of the year.

PULTENAEA EUCHILA

FAMILY: Papilionaceae. COMMON NAME: None. COLOUR: Orange. SIZE: Up to 2 metres high.

DESCRIPTION: Erect shrub. Leaves mostly alternate, narrow-obovate to narrow-oblong, obtuse to emarginate; margins are more or less incurved, 1 to 3 cm long. Flowers are axillary 10 to 14 mm long; pedicels 5 to 8 mm long; bracteoles linear.

AREA: N.S.W., Vic., widespread, open forest, along roadsides, medium soils. TIME: August to October.

SESBANIA FORMOSA

FAMILY: Papilionaceae. COMMON NAME: Kimberly Pea Flower. COLOUR: Cream-green. SIZE: Up to 10 metres high.

DESCRIPTION: A small to medium tree. Leaves are pinnate, to 40 cm long; leaflets are ovate to oblong-ovate, glabrous, 2 to 3 cm long. Flowers are large, 6 to 10 cm long, very conspicuous; standard is erect 2 to 5 cm long, margins incurved. Wings form together giving pocket or pouch effect. Loose raceme of three or more, pendulous. The tree flowers in great profusion creating an overwhelming display.

AREA: North and north-west of W.A., Kimberly area, along watercourses. TIME: December to January, May to October.

SPHAEROLOBIUM VIMINEUM

FAMILY: Papilionaceae. COMMON NAME: Leafless Globe Pea. COLOUR: Yellow. SIZE: Up to 50 cm long.

DESCRIPTION: A wiry shrub or semishrub. Branches are soft, glabrous, rushlike, terete, green, barren or with few small scalelike narrow leaves. Flowers are small, numerous, scattered along branches or in terminal spikelike raceme. Calyx: five-lobed, black, imbricate when in bud, two upper united to form large upper lip. Standard is orbicular. Fruit is a pod, globular, stipitate, 3 mm diam.

AREA: Qld., N.S.W., Vic. and S.A., coast and open heathland in ranges, in swampy areas. TIME: September to December.

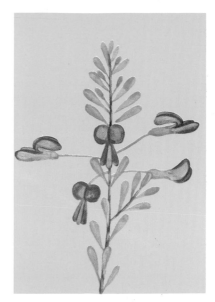

Papilionaceae
Psoralea patens

Papilionaceae
Pultenaea euchila

Papilionaceae
Sesbania formosa

Papilionaceae
Sphaerolobium vimineum

SWAINSONA GALEGIFOLIA VAR. CORONILLIFOLIA

FAMILY: Papilionaceae. COMMON NAME: Darling Pea. COLOUR: Scarlet red. SIZE: Up to 1 metre high.

DESCRIPTION: Erect perennial, glabrous or only sparsely woolly. Leaves are pinnate, 6 to 10 cm long. Leaflets are 12 to 25 mm cuneate, emarginate, concave to channel-shaped. Flowers: twelve to thirty-five in erect racemes; calyx and pedicels are sparsely white-woolly; calyx is 6 to 8 mm long, with teeth more or less deltoid. Standard is up to 2 cm across, oblique calli; keel obtuse; wings longer than keel. Plant is very near *S. greyana*, also near *S. colutoides*. *S. galegifolia* var. *albiflora* (white flower), also reported from west N.S.W. *S. galegifolia* is a very variable species.

AREA: West N.S.W., west Vic., S.A. and south-east Qld., open forests, along roadsides and grasslands, widespread. TIME: August to February.

VICIA ANGUSTIFOLIA

FAMILY: Papilionaceae. COMMON NAME: Narrow-leaf Vetch. COLOUR: Purple or red. SIZE: Up to 40 cm high.

DESCRIPTION: A weak, pubescent, annual herb. Leaves are pinnate, ending in simple or branched tendril. Leaflets: distant, four to seven pairs, 1.5 to 2 cm long, linear to narrow-oblong. Flowers are solitary, rarely two, 10 to 15 mm long. Fruit is a pod 3 to 5 cm long, cylindrical, glabrous, black. *Vicia* sp. is a form, found in S.A., having the broad leaflets of *V. sativa* (Common Vetch) and *V. angustifolia*'s cylindrical black pod. Flowers are sessile; *V. sativa* (Common Vetch) leaflets, 6 to 10 mm wide; *V. angustifolia* (Narrow-leaf Vetch) leaflets, 2 to 4 mm wide. Flowers are in racemes on long peduncles, less than ten in number. *V. hirsuta* (Hairy Vetch) leaflets: six to ten pairs, 5 to 15 mm long. *V. tetrasperma* (Slender Vetch) leaflets: two to five pairs, 5 to 15 mm long, four seed fruit. Flowers in racemes, peduncles of ten up to thirty. *V. villosa* (Russian Vetch) leaflets: five to ten pairs, plant villous-pubescent.

AREA: Qld., N.S.W., Vic. and S.A., cultivated, grasslands. TIME: Spring.

VIMINARIA JUNCEA

FAMILY: Papilionaceae. COMMON NAME: Native Broom. COLOUR: Chrome yellow to orange. SIZE: Up to 5 metres high.

DESCRIPTION: Erect shrub. Branchlets are long, green, wiry, pendulous. Leaves: long, cylindrical, phyllodia, very rarely with one to four leaflets. Flowers are 10 to 15 mm long. Calyx lobes are short; petals to 8 mm long; racemes, long and terminal. Fruit is a legume, small, sessile, ovate.

AREA: N.S.W. and south Qld., coast and nearby mountains and tablelands in moist to wet areas. TIME: September to March (on tablelands).

PASSIFLORA SUBPELTATA

FAMILY: Passifloraceae. COMMON NAME: None. COLOUR: Purple. SIZE: Vine.

DESCRIPTION: Climber with axillary tendrils. Leaves: deeply three-lobed, glabrous, up to 12 cm wide, each lobe up to 8 cm long and 4 cm wide, margins entire. Flowers are bisexual, regular. Petals and calyx-lobes: five and similarly coloured, but calyx-lobes have dark green markings. Petals are longer than calyx lobes; filaments form corona with petals, same colour. Five stamens on long green stalk. Fruit is considered not edible.

AREA: Qld., N.S.W., in and near rainforest, cultivated, introduced. TIME: August to December.

Papilionaceae
Swansiona galegifolia var. coronillifolia

Papilionaceae
Vicia angustifolia

Papilionaceae
Viminaria juncea

Passifloraceae
Passiflora subpeltata

EUSTREPHUS LATIFOLIUS (broad leaf form)
FAMILY: Philesiaceae. COMMON NAME: Wombat Berry or Blackfellows Orange. COLOUR: Pink or White. SIZE: Vine to 3 metres long.

DESCRIPTION: Glabrous, much branched climber. Leaves are usually ovate-lanceolate, 5 to 10 cm long. Flower clusters are axillary in upper leaves. Perianth segments are 4 to 6 mm long, inner segments fringed. Six stamens. Fruit is a berry, orange, globular, 1 to 1.5 cm diameter, seed black.

AREA: Qld., N.S.W. and Vic., widespread, coast, mountains, tablelands, moist areas and wet sclerophyll forests. TIME: September to December.

EUSTREPHUS LATIFOLIUS VAR. ANGUSTIFOLIUS (narrow-leaf form)
FAMILY: Philesiaceae. COMMON NAME: Blackfellows Orange or Wombat Vine or Berry. COLOUR: White or pink. SIZE: Small vine.

DESCRIPTION: Glabrous climber. Leaves are linear, 3 to 8 cm long, otherwise same as broad leaf form. Ovary superior, three locular, axile placentas. Fruit is a berry that splits on ripening; black seeds fall free.

AREA: Same as broad leaf form. TIME: September to December.

GEITONOPLESIUM CYMOSUM
FAMILY: Philesiaceae (syn. Liliaceae). COMMON NAME: Scrambling Lily. COLOUR: Mauve-pink to white. SIZE: Vine.

DESCRIPTION: A glabrous climber, with much tangled branches up to 3 metres long. Leaves: alternate, linear to narrow-ovate, 5 to 8 cm long. Flowers are in paniculate cymes. Six perianth segments, 6 to 8 mm long, inner segments not fringed; filaments free. Fruit is a berry, subglobular, purple-black, 4 to 6 mm diameter; seeds are black.

AREA: N.S.W., Qld. and Vic., coast, mountains, plateaux widespread, moist communities and wet sclerophyll forest. TIME: September to December.

HELMHOLTZIA GLABERRIMA
FAMILY: Philydraceae. COMMON NAME: None. COLOUR: Pale pink. SIZE: About 2 metres high.

DESCRIPTION: A glabrous, perennial, tufted herb. Leaves: distichous, sheathing, keeled at the base, smooth concave, flat distally, up to 2 metres long, 10 to 12 cm wide. Inflorescence is a terminal panicle of flower spikes. Stem is up to 2 metres long, with the lower part barren, glabrous. Panicle is to 60 cm or more long; each flower spike up to 30 cm long, with sessile or very short peduncle. Flowers: bisexual, four petals, floral bracteole, stem bracts.

AREA: Qld., rainforest, along watercourses. TIME: September to December.

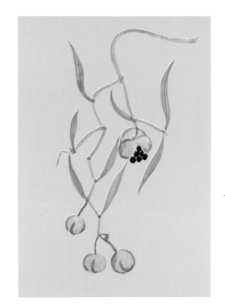

Philesiaceae
Eustrephus latifolius (broad leaf form)

Philesiaceae
Eustrephus latifolius var. angustifolius
(narrow leaf form)

Philesiaceae
Geitonophlesium cymosum

Philydraceae
Helmholtzia glaberrima

BURSARIA SPINOSA

FAMILY: Pittosporaceae. COMMON NAME: Black Thorn or Christmas Bush (in Tasmania). COLOUR: White. SIZE: Up to 3 metres high.

DESCRIPTION: Rigid, spreading shrub. Much branched, branchlets often shortening into spines. Leaves: spathulate, ovate, oblong to cuneate, or emarginate panicles. Five sepals, small-caducous; petals are white, spreading, 4 to 6 mm long. Capsule is flat, thin, brown, truncate, notched, 5 to 10 mm long.

AREA: All states, widespread throughout Australia, tall forests, weed in cultivated land. TIME: October to March.

CHEIRANTHERA CYANEA SYN. C. LINEARIS

FAMILY: Pittosporaceae. COMMON NAME: Finger Flower. COLOUR: Blue-violet. SIZE: About 50 cm high.

DESCRIPTION: A small, erect, graceful, glabrous undershrub or shrub. Leaves: erect, crowded, linear, acute to acute-obtuse, channelled; margins are incurved to revolute, 1.5 to 5 cm long. Flowers are on erect pedicels, solitary or two to five in terminal corymbs or umbels, 2 to 3 cm diameter. Sepals are lanceolate, 4 to 6 mm long; petals are violet or blue, 15 to 20 mm long. There is an anther opening through two confluent terminal pores or short slits. Fruit is a capsule, 12 to 18 mm long. Known as *C. cyanea* in S.A. and *C. linearis* in Vic. and N.S.W.

AREA: N.S.W., Vic., S.A. and Tas., widespread, coast and dry sclerophyll forest and open forests. TIME: October to November.

MARIANTHUS CANDIDUS

FAMILY: Pittosporaceae. COMMON NAME: None. COLOUR: White. SIZE: Up to 4 metres long.

DESCRIPTION: A tall, woody twiner. Leaves: upper and older leaves entire, narrow-elliptical-lanceolate, 6 to 10 cm long; lower and young leaves toothed or lobed. Flowers: four to seven in dense, white, umbel clusters; pedicels short; sepals glabrous or fine silky tomentose, narrow and long; petals spreading, attractively sharply pointed; claws narrow, erect. Style long and subulate.

AREA: W.A., Darling Ranges, clay soil. TIME: October to December.

MARIANTHUS PROCUMBENS

FAMILY: Pittosporaceae. COMMON NAME: None. COLOUR: White, lilac or tinged with red. SIZE: Up to 30 cm high.

DESCRIPTION: Dwarf shrub, glabrous or lightly pubescent—often flowers when a young plant. Leaves: linear to linear-oblong, acute, 5 to 12 mm long. Flowers: solitary or two to four, terminal or close to end of shoots. Petals are 4 to 6 mm long, spreading from middle. Ovary is compressed, coriaceous, 5 to 6 mm diameter.

AREA: N.S.W., south Qld., coast, nearby mountains and tablelands, widespread on heathlands and edge of dry sclerophyll forests. TIME: September to December.

Pittosporaceae
Bursaria spinosa

Pittosporaceae
Cheiranthera cyanea syn. *C. linearis*

Pittosporaceae
Marianthus candidus

Pittosporaceae
Marianthus procumbens

PITTOSPORUM REVOLUTUM

FAMILY: Pittosporaceae. COMMON NAME: Pittosporum. COLOUR: Cream, lemon-yellow. SIZE: Up to 10 metres high.

DESCRIPTION: Small tree. Leaves: rusty-tomentose on undersurface, especially when young, ovate to oblong-elliptic, 4 to 10 cm long; margins slightly revolute. Flowers: bisexual in terminal compound clusters; sepals and petals: five, imbricate; petals, 10 to 15 mm long. Fruit is a large chrome-yellow capsule, 4 to 5 cm long, splits to reveal scarlet berrylike seeds, very sticky, attractive to birds.

AREA: Qld., N.S.W. and Vic., coast, mountains, liking very moist areas. TIME: September to November, seeds April to July.

SOLLYA FUSIFORMIS

FAMILY: Pittosporaceae. COMMON NAME: Australian Bluebell. COLOUR: Blue. SIZE: Twiner up to 2.4 metres.

DESCRIPTION: A trailing twiner with woody base. Leaves: alternate without stiples, elliptic to linear-lanceolate, 2 to 3 cm long. Flowers: four to twelve, bell-shaped, in drooping terminal cymes. Petals: five, small, sharply pointed, spreading. Stamens alternating with petals, free, hypogynous. First discovered in 1791 in gravel and clay of W.A. Introduced to Britain in 1830 to be grown in green houses.

AREA: Near Darling Ranges and south-west W.A. TIME: October to December.

COMESPERMA DEFOLIATUM

FAMILY: Polygalaceae. COMMON NAME: Leafless Milkwort. COLOUR: Blue-mauve. SIZE: Up to 60 cm high.

DESCRIPTION: A delicate, erect, leafless plant. Leaves: minute, linear, reduced to tiny scales. Stems slender and rushlike. Inflorescence racemose. Sepals: five, free, much imbricate, two inner sepals or wings larger and petaloid. Lower three petals connate forming concave keel, enclosing stamens and ovary, two upper petals free. Fruit a capsule, narrowed into a basal stripe.

AREA: N.S.W., Qld. and Vic., coast, mountains, in wet sandy and gravel soils. TIME: October to February.

COMESPERMA VOLUBILE

FAMILY: Polygalaceae. COMMON NAME: Love Creeper. COLOUR: Rich blue-mauve to white. SIZE: Creeper up to 3 metres long.

DESCRIPTION: Glabrous, twining undershrub. Stems furrowed. Leaves distant, oblong-linear to lanceolate, 4 to 30 mm long. Flowers in terminal or axillary racemes. Wings orbicular, larger than outer sepals. Keel not crested, shorter than two posterior petals, which are ciliate and lightly pubescent at base. Fruit capsule not winged, oblong-cuneate, 12 to 14 mm long.

AREA: Qld., N.S.W., Vic., S.A. and south-west W.A., temperate parts of Australian states. TIME: July to October.

Pittosporaceae
Pittosporum revolutum

Pittosporaceae
Sollya fusiformis

Polygalaceae
Comesperma defoliatum

Polygalaceae
Comesperma volubile

MONTIA AUSTRALASICA

FAMILY: Portulacaceae. COMMON NAME: White Purslane. COLOUR: White. SIZE: Creeper.

DESCRIPTION: Prostrate, succulent perennial. Stems creeping, tuberous. Leaves glabrous, thick, linear to oblanceolate, 2 to 8 cm long. Flowers: one to four, long-stalked, in terminal groups 10 to 15 mm across, bisexual, regular. Sepals two; petals five, imbricate. Stamens imbricate. Fruit a capsule. Alpine plant's foliage is more congested and flowers more numerous than lowlands plant.

AREA: Frequent freshwater swamps, and stream sides throughout temperate Australia from sea level to high alps, especially where snow patches linger into summer. TIME: Most of the year.

BANKSIA ERICIFOLIA

FAMILY: Proteaceae. COMMON NAME: Heath Leaved Banksia. COLOUR: Orange to red. SIZE: Up to 6 metres high.

DESCRIPTION: Tall shrub or small tree, glabrous. Leaves alternate, linear, truncate or notched at apex, margins revolute, 10 to 15 mm long. Flower spike up to 15 cm long. Fruit is scarcely protruding from spike.

AREA: N.S.W., Qld. and Vic., widespread, coast, mountains, heath and dry sclerophyll forest. TIME: June to December, and Autumn.

BANKSIA HOOKERIANA

FAMILY: Proteaceae. COMMON NAME: None. COLOUR: Buds pink-white, styles yellow-orange. SIZE: Up to 3 metres high.

DESCRIPTION: Erect shrub. Leaves: linear, narrow, evenly serrate, 10 to 30 cm long, veins inconspicuous. Flower: perianth tube and limb both villous, perianth without long awnlike points. Plant carries a great number of large flowers in relation to its compact, shrubby growth.

AREA: South-west W.A., roadsides. TIME: September to October.

BANKSIA INTEGRIFOLIA

FAMILY: Proteaceae. COMMON NAME: White Honeysuckle or Coast Banksia. COLOUR: Lemon. SIZE: Up to 16 metres and more high.

DESCRIPTION: A tree. Rarely shrubby; only its young branches tomentose. Leaves: mostly entire, rarely toothed, cuneate to oblanceolate, tapering to petiole, 5 to 10 cm long, a white down on underside. Flower: spike oblong or cylindrical, 7 to 14 cm long, 7 cm diameter. Styles are finally straight and spreading. Fruit protrudes from the spike.

AREA: N.S.W., Qld., Vic. and S.A., widespread, coast, mountains, open forests and wet sclerophyll forest. TIME: September to November, but blooms occur all year round.

Portulacaceae
Montia australasica

Proteaceae
Banksia ericifolia

Proteaceae
Banksia hookeriana

Proteaceae
Banksia integrifolia

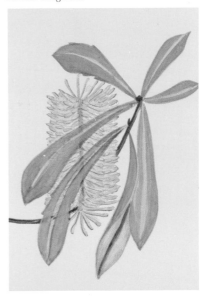

BANKSIA MENZIESII

FAMILY: Proteaceae. COMMON NAME: Firewood Banksia. COLOUR: Deep pink with orange or yellow styles. SIZE: Up to 9 metres high.

DESCRIPTION: Bushy tree, with rough bark. Leaves: alternate, stiff, linear-oblong, margins dentate, 15 to 30 cm long, 2.5 to 4 cm broad, pale green-grey on underside. Midrib rigid and yellow in colour. Flowers: in dense spike, 15 cm long, changing in colour, pink to orange as styles appear, from bottom upwards.

AREA: South-west W.A., coastal plains. TIME: April to June on to September.

BANKSIA SERRATA

FAMILY: Proteaceae. COMMON NAME: Honeysuckle or Saw Banksia. COLOUR: Lemon, buds silver-grey. SIZE: Up to 6 metres high.

DESCRIPTION: Small tree. Leaves: elliptic-oblong to broad-oblong to oblanceolate, dentate, evenly serrate, grey or brown hairs on underside, or glabrous, not white, 8 to 16 cm long, 2 to 4 cm wide, midrib yellow, parallel transverse veins distinct. Flower: spike 8 to 16 cm long, 8 to 10 cm diameter. Perianth dove-grey. Fruit: protruding, tomentose, ovate or round, 3 to 4 cm wide.

AREA: N.S.W., Qld., Vic. and Tas., heathlands of coast and nearby mountains, dry sclerophyll forests, sand dunes, poor soils and granite. TIME: December to March.

CONOSPERMUM CRASSINERVIUM

FAMILY: Proteaceae. COMMON NAME: Smoke Bush. COLOUR: White. SIZE: Up to 50 cm high.

DESCRIPTION: Undershrub. Scapes leafless, stem bracts brown, lanceolate.

ENCLOSING BRACT
FLOWER

Flowers are in large terminal panicle, whole spike very densely villous. Flowers are densely woolly or silky-villous. Perianth: two-lipped, upper lip broad, concave over anthers, lower lip with three narrow lobes. Lips are as long as tube.

AREA: W.A., southern province in sandy valleys. TIME: October to November.

DRYANDRA HEWARDIANA

FAMILY: Proteaceae. COMMON NAME: None. COLOUR: Yellow and brown. SIZE: Up to 3 metres high.

DESCRIPTION: Shrub. Brown, woolly, tomentose. Leaves: pinnatifid, divided almost or quite to midrib, lobes not contiguous, intervening leaf margins not parallel to midrib. Inflorescence is a terminal cluster of flowers. Dryandra's typical leaf structure generally identifies the species.

AREA: Southern province W.A., sandy heath. TIME: September.

Proteaceae
Banksia menziesii

Proteaceae
Banksia serrata

Proteaceae
Conospermum crassinervium

Proteaceae
Dryandra hewardiana

DRYANDRA NIVEA

FAMILY: Proteaceae. COMMON NAME: None. COLOUR: Gold and brown. SIZE: Creeper.

DESCRIPTION: Dwarf shrub. Leaves: pinnatifid, divided almost or quite to midrib, lobes contiguous, flat. Flower is in a terminal head only. Involucral bracts oblong, woolly.

AREA: W.A., in southern provinces generally. TIME: May to August.

DRYANDRA POLYCEPHALA

FAMILY: Proteaceae. COMMON NAME: None. COLOUR: Yellow. SIZE: Up to 3 metres high.

DESCRIPTION: Spreading shrub. Leaves: pinnatifid, divided almost midrib, lobes PERIANTH TUBE contiguous, revolute. Bracts are inner, tapering to long points, and usually plumose. Involucre is less than 1 cm; flower leaves are few, LIMB spreading, 4 to 10 cm long. Perianth tube villous, limb glabrous.

AREA: W.A., southern province generally, gravel areas. TIME: July to September.

GREVILLEA ACANTHIFOLIA

FAMILY: Proteaceae. COMMON NAME: None. COLOUR: Pink to purple and white with red styles. SIZE: Up to 2 metres high.

DESCRIPTION: A spreading shrub. Leaves are pinnate, divided almost to midvein; lobes: cuneate, two to five, each rigid and pungent pointed, green, 2 to 12 mm long. Perianth tube pink to purple, pubescent at base. Inflorescence is a horizontal spike. Styles erect.

AREA: N.S.W., swamps, creeks, coast and mountains in wet areas. TIME: September to December.

Proteaceae
Dryandra nivea

Proteaceae
Dryandra polycephala

Proteaceae
Grevillea acanthifolia

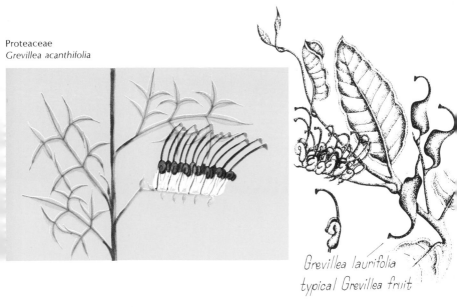

Grevillea laurifolia
typical *Grevillea* fruit

GREVILLEA ALPINA

FAMILY: Proteaceae. COMMON NAME: Goldfields Grevillea. COLOUR: Yellow, red-orange to green-white. SIZE: About a metre high.

DESCRIPTION: A small procumbent or scrambling bush. Leaves: soft, grey-green, ovate to elliptic or oblong to oblanceolate, hairy, 18 to 20 mm long. Perianth tube is hairy, 6 to 9 mm long; lobes hairy. Style is red, hairy. Inflorescence is a terminal spike. Plant procumbent in mountains, grey-downy, narrowly rolled leaves on arching branches on goldfields of Vic.

AREA: N.S.W., Vic. and Tas., in Alps, plains and inland. TIME: September to December.

GREVILLEA AQUIFOLIUM

FAMILY: Proteaceae. COMMON NAME: Holly Grevillea. COLOUR: Green with red styles. SIZE: Up to a metre high.

DESCRIPTION: A variable shrub. Leaves: dull, oblong, margins, undulate, sinuate, with spiny teeth to pungent points. Flowers: small, tube 5 to 8 mm long. Styles are red, 3 cm long. Inflorescences are flowers massed in comb-shape racemes.

AREA: Vic., Grampian Mts., extending to Little Desert. TIME: Spring to Summer.

GREVILLEA INSIGNIS

FAMILY: Proteaceae. COMMON NAME: Native Holly. COLOUR: Red. SIZE: About 3 metres high.

DESCRIPTION: Spreading shrub. Leaves: linear-cuneate to ovate, lobed, margins 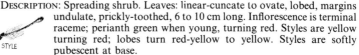 undulate, prickly-toothed, 6 to 10 cm long. Inflorescence is terminal raceme; perianth green when young, turning red. Styles are yellow turning red; lobes turn red-yellow to yellow. Styles are softly pubescent at base.

STYLE

AREA: W.A., southern province in gravel soils. TIME: Spring to Summer.

GREVILLEA JUNCIFOLIA

FAMILY: Proteaceae. COMMON NAME: None. COLOUR: Orange. SIZE: Up to 4 metres high.

DESCRIPTION: Tall shrub. Leaves: erect, linear, rigid, hoary to glabrous, double grooved beneath, pungent, 8 to 25 cm long. Racemes: 8 to 16 cm long, dense panicle; pedicels 10 to 18 mm long, viscid-pubescent. Perianth pubescent, tube 10 mm long; laminae ending in hornlike appendage. Blooms are heavy with nectar and are a prized 'sugar-bag' with Aboriginals. Fruit is hard, acuminate, tomentose 20 to 25 mm long.

AREA: West Qld., west N.S.W., S.A., central Australia, N.T. and W.A., arid, desert soils, favouring red sand, spinifex plains. TIME: August to November.

Proteaceae
Grevillea alpina

Proteaceae
Grevillea aquifolium

Proteaceae
Grevillea insignis

Proteaceae
Grevillea juncifolia

GREVILLEA MUCRONULATA

FAMILY: Proteaceae. COMMON NAME: Green Spider Flower. COLOUR: Green turning blue-purple. SIZE: Up to 2 metres high.

DESCRIPTION: A spreading shrub. Leaves: mucronate, ovate-lanceolate or elliptic, 1 to 2 cm long, pungent point, rusty-hairy on underside. Raceme is a small, loose cluster at end of long stem. Perianth tube 6 mm long, hairy inside, sprinkled outside with oppressed hairs; ovary densely hirsute with brown hairs. *G. mucronulata* and *G. cinerea* form an intergrading complex. *G. cinerea*, perianth densely villous outside, hairs rusty or grey. Leaves are 2 to 3 cm long.

AREA: N.S.W., coast and mountains, widespread. TIME: Most of the year.

GREVILLEA OLEOIDES

FAMILY: Proteaceae. COMMON NAME: Olive Spider Flower. COLOUR: Red. SIZE: Up to 2 metres high.

DESCRIPTION: Erect shrub. Leaves: linear to lanceolate, 5 to 12 cm long, silky-hairy pale green underside, dark green uppersurface. Racemes are sessile, axillary or terminal on very short branches. Perianth tube is 8 to 14 mm long; lobes spread rolled back on to perianth tube, recurved under limb. Ring of hairs encircle inside perianth above the middle. Rich in nectar.

AREA: N.S.W. and Vic., heathlands, dry sclerophyll forest, rocky and sandy river banks. TIME: August to December, often later.

GREVILLEA ROBUSTA

FAMILY: Proteaceae. COMMON NAME: Silky Oak. COLOUR: Golden-orange. SIZE: Up to 30 metres high.

DESCRIPTION: A tall, erect tree. Leaves: bipinnatisect, or much divided, soft, light-green, 15 to 25 cm long. Inflorescence is large, branched, made up of dense erect, long racemes. Flowers are red-yellow; fruit is a boat-shaped follicle; seeds winged.

AREA: Handsome tree native of N.S.W. and Qld., now widely cultivated for ornament. Edge of rainforest, river flats, planted along roadsides. TIME: October to December.

Proteaceae
Grevillea mucronulata

Proteaceae
Grevillea oleoides

Proteaceae
Grevillea robusta

fruit of
Grevillea robusta

GREVILLEA ROSMARINIFOLIA VAR. DIVARICATA

FAMILY: Proteaceae. COMMON NAME: Rosemary Grevillea. COLOUR: Pale pink white or red. SIZE: About 2 metres high.

DESCRIPTION: Very bushy, variable shrub, branching horizontally or nearly so. Leaves: linear, sessile, sharply pointed, margins revolute, 1 to 2 cm long. Raceme loose, terminal; perianth tube recurved under limb. Styles are twice as long as tube. *G. rosmarinifolia* var. *divaricata* is a W.A. form now cultivated in Eastern States. *G. rosmarinifolia* is a very variable bushy species with shorter styles than var. *divaricata*.

AREA: N.S.W. and Vic., coastal strips and nearby mountains, also extensively cultivated. TIME: August to October.

GREVILLEA SERICEA

FAMILY: Proteaceae. COMMON NAME: Silky Spider Flower. COLOUR: Pink. SIZE: Up to 2 metres high.

DESCRIPTION: A small shrub, branches angular when young. Leaves: oblong, narrow-ovate, lanceolate to linear, dark green, glabrous to silky-hairy uppersurface, silky-tomentose undersurface, 1 to 6 cm long. Racemes are dense on short terminal peduncles. Flowers: perianth tube 4 to 8 mm long; lobes separate recurved. Styles are 10 to 20 mm long, at times to 25 mm.

AREA: South Qld., N.S.W., widespread, coast and mountains, plateaux, granite and sandy soils and ridges. TIME: July to December, and most of the year.

GREVILLEA SCORTECHINII

FAMILY: Proteaceae. COMMON NAME: Black Grevillea. COLOUR: Pink with black styles. SIZE: Up to 2 metres high.

DESCRIPTION: A low, glabrous shrub. Branches are glabrous to slightly silky-soft pubescent. Leaves: entire or serrate, lobed, lightly pungent pointed, margins revolute, 4 to 16 cm long; veins distinct, uppersurface green, undersurface pale green, lightly rusty tomentose. Raceme: comb-like, terminal, horizontal; perianth erect, on short peduncles, limb recurved, splitting to release a velvet black erect style, perianth tube 8 to 18 mm long, style 12 to 25 mm and longer.

AREA: Plant becoming rare, Darling Downs in Stanthorpe district, along roadside in isolated areas. TIME: Spring.

GREVILLEA THYMAFOLIA

FAMILY: Proteaceae. COMMON NAME: None. COLOUR: Red. SIZE: Up to 2 metres high.

DESCRIPTION: A slender, spreading, sparsely flowering shrub. Branches are spreading, glabrous, open. Leaves: dark green, oblanceolate to lanceolate, almost sessile on very short petiole, veination distinct, margins wavy, 2 to 10 cm long. Raceme is of three to six flowers, terminal, delicate; perianth pedunculate 10 to 20 mm long, splitting to four spreading lobes, styles one-third the length protruding beyond lobes.

AREA: North N.S.W., creek and river banks in or close to rainforest and wet sclerophyll forest. TIME: August to May.

Proteaceae
Grevillea rosmarinifolia var. divaricata

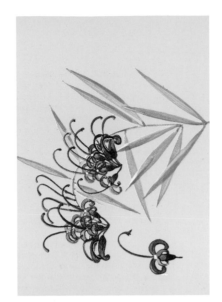

Proteaceae
Grevillea sericea

Proteaceae
Grevillea scortechinii

Proteaceae
Grevillea thymafolia

HAKEA SP. NOVA (undescribed)

FAMILY: Proteaceae. COMMON NAME: None. COLOUR: White. SIZE: Up to 2 metres high.

DESCRIPTION: Erect shrub, glabrous to slightly silky-hairs. Leaves: narrow, linear-terete, pungent pointed, 3 to 10 cm long, dark green. Flowers: three in leaf axil, perianth tube short 6 to 8 mm long, segments free, reflexed. Very common on heathlands in north N.S.W. Very similar to *H. teretifolia*, thought at one time to be a variety.

AREA: North N.S.W., heathlands, Angourie National Park, first collected. TIME: August to October.

HAKEA CONCHJFOLIA

FAMILY: Proteaceae. COMMON NAME: Shell-leaved Hakea. COLOUR: White, lemon or red. SIZE: Up to a metre high.

DESCRIPTION: A low shrub. Leaves: shell-like, more or less heart-shaped, glaucous, edge bordered by short prickly teeth, sinuate, 3 to 5 cm long. Flowers: in axillary cluster, almost enclosed by orbicular, concave leaves. Perianth tube is revolute under the limb, 10 to 18 mm long. Styles are 20 to 25 mm long. Plant has unusual appearance when in bloom.

AREA: W.A. southern province, in sandy heathlands. TIME: May, July to August.

HAKEA ERIANTHA

FAMILY: Proteaceae. COMMON NAME: None. COLOUR: White with green and brown markings. SIZE: Up to 3 metres high and higher.

DESCRIPTION: Erect shrub, with glabrous, smooth bark. Leaves: linear-lanceolate, mucronate, 4 to 10 mm long, tapering at base to very short petiole. Has three to six flowers in axillary cluster. Perianth tube is straight, 2 to 8 mm long. Segments are free. Fruit is a woody follicle, glabrous, 25 to 35 mm long.

AREA: N.S.W., south Qld., coast at mountains and tablelands, common on New England Tablelands. TIME: October to December.

HAKEA TERETIFOLIA

FAMILY: Proteaceae. COMMON NAME: Dagger Hakea. COLOUR: White or lemon. SIZE: Up to 3 metres high.

DESCRIPTION: A straggling, divaricate shrub. Leaves: 2 to 5 cm long, green, stiff, terete with needlelike pungent points. Flowers: axillary clusters, in profusion; perianth 4 to 6 mm long, pubescent. Fruit is acuminate, narrow, 2 to 3 cm long and 10 to 20 mm broad, sharply pointed with angular protuberances, tiny oblique woody crest in the centre.

AREA: N.S.W., Qld., Vic. and Tas., coast, mountains and tablelands in heathlands, widespread. TIME: September to January.

Proteaceae
Hakea sp. nova

Proteaceae
Hakea conchifolia

Proteaceae
Hakea eriantha

Proteaceae
Hakea teretifolia

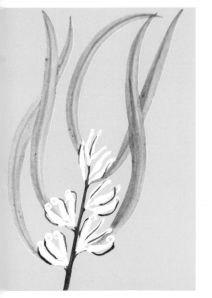

HELICIA YOUNGIANA

FAMILY: Proteaceae. COMMON NAME: None. COLOUR: Pale pink or white. SIZE: Up to 6 metres high.

DESCRIPTION: Shrub to small tree, glabrous. Leaves: coriaceous, oblong to broad-lanceolate to lanceolate, entire to toothed. Flowers: five to twelve, in axillary raceme, 6 to 10 cm long. Perianth is regular, 6 to 8 mm long, split to reveal style, finally separating into four revolute segments. Flowers are 2 to 4 cm long. Fruit is fleshy with hard endocarp.

AREA: North N.S.W. and Qld., rainforest. TIME: September to December.

ISOPOGON LATIFOLIUS

FAMILY: Proteaceae. COMMON NAME: None. COLOUR: Pink-red. SIZE: Up to 3 metres high.

DESCRIPTION: Low shrub. Leaves obovate to elliptic-oblong, flat, 4 to 10 cm long, veins distinct. Flowers are in dense terminal globular spike, sometimes axillary cluster on very short pedicel. Perianth: segments or four lobes, separate, spreading free. Style is brush, lanceolate, with reflexed hairs fusiform.

AREA: W.A., southern provinces. TIME: October to November.

PERSOONIA PINIFOLIA

FAMILY: Proteaceae. COMMON NAME: Pine-leaf Geebung. COLOUR: Yellow. SIZE: Up to 4 metres high.

DESCRIPTION: A shrub. Leaves: floral leaves smaller than foliage leaves, terete, grooved on undersurface, linear-filiform, 2 to 5 cm long. Flowers: almost sessile in axil of floral leaves forming dense terminal raceme 6 to 20 cm long. Perianth segments are lightly pubescent without appendages. Fruit is a drupe, in cluster on drooping ends of branches.

AREA: N.S.W., and south Qld., coast and nearby ranges, plateaux and tablelands, widespread and dry sclerophyll forests. TIME: December to May and throughout most of the year.

PETROPHILA CANESCENS

FAMILY: Proteaceae. COMMON NAME: Conesticks. COLOUR: Lemon-cream. SIZE: Up to a metre high.

DESCRIPTION: Low shrub. Leaves: grey-green, pinnately divided, pinnae again deeply dissected, with cylindrical segments. Flowers are in dense terminal spike (or cone), with each flower sessile within a bract. Perianth tube is short, separating into four linear spreading segments. Old inflorescence resembles a narrow, woody cone.

AREA: N.S.W., sandy soils over granite, tablelands and dry sclerophyll forests. TIME: Spring to Summer, August to December.

Proteaceae
Helicia youngiana

Proteaceae
Persoonia pinifolia

Proteaceae
Isopogon latifolius

Proteaceae
Petrophila canescens

TELOPEA TRUNCATA

FAMILY: Proteaceae. COMMON NAME: Tasmania Waratah. COLOUR: Red or yellow (rare). SIZE: Up to 3 metres high.

DESCRIPTION: Tall shrub, nearly glabrous. Leaves: alternate, hard texture, ovate to oblanceolate, green shiny on uppersurface, pale green undersurface, 5 to 10 cm long. Flowers are pedicellate in pairs arranged in loose terminal head with involucre bracts. Perianth is red, split on lower side; four perianth segments or lobes, ('petals') unilaterally revolute. Styles long, predominant, making showy display. Flower is rich in nectar, providing food for insects, possums and birds alike. Fruit is a long woody follicle containing winged seeds.

AREA: Tas., widespread in mountains and plains. TIME: Spring to Summer, and after into March.

CLEMATIS MICROPHYLLA

FAMILY: Ranunculaceae. COMMON NAME: Small-leaved Clematis or Old Man's Beard. COLOUR: Yellow-cream. SIZE: Climber.

DESCRIPTION: A woody climber. Leaves are on long petioles, trifoliate; leaflets lanceolate-oblong to broad-linear. Flowers: dioecious in short panicles; female flowers with four oblong sepals, 15 to 25 mm long, pubescent outside, four staminodia, abortive anthers, plumose styles. Male flowers have four sepals, twenty to thirty stamens, oblong anthers, petals none. Fruit: clusters of achenes with long feathery plumelike awns, 2 to 4 cm long.

AREA: N.S.W., Qld., Vic., S.A. and Tas., widespread, roadsides, coast, mountains, tablelands and ranges. TIME: August to October.

RANUNCULUS ANEMONEUS

FAMILY: Ranunculaceae. COMMON NAME: Snow Buttercup. COLOUR: White. SIZE: Up to 60 cm high.

DESCRIPTION: Erect herb. Leaves: large luxuriant, divided several times into lanceolate-linear lobes or segments, radical, petioles dilated into scarious sheath. Flowers are solitary, largest of the buttercups, 3 to 6 cm across. Sepals: five imbricate, caducous, petals many, with nectar pit at base, fragile, sparkling white giving appearance of being almost transparent, tips faintly tinted pink underneath.

AREA: N.S.W. and Vic., Alpine habitat, close to snow banks. TIME: Spring to Summer.

POMADERRIS LIGUSTRINA

FAMILY: Rhamnaceae. COMMON NAME: None. COLOUR: Cream. SIZE: Up to 2 metres high.

DESCRIPTION: Erect shrub, with rusty-tomentose young shoots. Leaves: lanceolate, glabrous above, 2 to 8 cm long, densely tomentose underneath. Flowers: in loose terminal panicle, sepals and floral-tube 2 mm long, villous. Five sepals, five petals. Fruit is a capsule, protruding above the disc, separating into three carpels.

AREA: N.S.W., coast, mountains, moist areas, sandstone, granite and shales. TIME: September to October.

Proteaceae
Telopea trunata

Ranunculaceae
Clematis microphylla

Ranunculaceae
Ranunculus anemoneus

Rhamnaceae
Pomaderris ligustrina

FRAGARIA INDICA

FAMILY: Rosaceae. COMMON NAME: Wild Strawberry. COLOUR: Yellow, fruit red. SIZE: Creeper.

DESCRIPTION: A prostrate creeper. Leaves: three-foliate, three leaflets, rarely five, ovate, acute, incised-toothed, green, lightly white tomentose underneath, 1 to 3 cm long. Flowers are solitary in axils, or short terminal panicle. Sepals acuminate; petals almost orbicular. Fruit is globular of many drupes. Introduced from India and Japan and has established itself along roadsides and rainforest area.

AREA: Qld. and north N.S.W., along roadsides and rainforests. TIME: November to December.

RUBUS ELLIPTICUS

FAMILY: Rosaceae. COMMON NAME: Yellow Raspberry. COLOUR: Yellow fruit, white-pink flower. SIZE: Bramble.

DESCRIPTION: Introduced woody, prickly, scrambling climber. Branches: petioles and petiolules covered with numerous, fine, bristlelike, prickles. Leaves: digitate, centre leaflets 3 to 4 cm long and longer, two or three times as long as lateral leaflets, elliptical to obovate, margins dentate, veins distinct. Flower; five petals, obovate, sepals persistent. Fruit is aggregate, yellow cylindrical.

AREA: Qld. and north N.S.W., wet sclerophyll forests. TIME: Spring to Summer.

RUBUS MOOREI

FAMILY: Rosaceae. COMMON NAME: Bush Lawyer. COLOUR: White. SIZE: Climber.

DESCRIPTION: A tall climber. Leaves: digitate, fine leaflets (three at end of branches). Branches: petioles and petiolules covered with numerous, reflexed thorns or prickles. Leaflets: glabrous, elliptic to ovate to lanceolate and often cordate at base, acutely acuminate, dentate toothed, 7 to 12 cm long. Flowers are in loose axillary raceme or panicle. Sepals obtuse, petals obovate. Fruit is an aggregate, dark red.

AREA: Qld., and N.S.W., widespread and rainforest. TIME: Spring to Summer.

BORONIA ANETHIFOLIA

FAMILY: Rutaceae. COMMON NAME: Narrow-leaved Boronia. COLOUR: White or pale pink. SIZE: Up to a metre high.

DESCRIPTION: Erect shrub. Leaves: compound, some leaflets further divided into three entire secondary leaflets, acute, narrow-elliptic to linear, 3 to 10 mm long, oil glands distinct. Flowers: three or more in axillary cymes, the cymes shorter than leaves. Calyx: four-lobed; four petals, spreading.

AREA: N.S.W., mountains and foothills, dry sclerophyll forest, sandstone and granite, shales and heathlands. TIME: August to October.

Rosaceae
Fragaria indica

Rosaceae
Rubus ellipticus

Rosaceae
Rubus moorei

Rutaceae
Boronia anethifolia

BORONIA CAERULESCENS

FAMILY: Rutaceae. COMMON NAME: Blue Boronia. COLOUR: Blue to Mauve. SIZE: Up to a metre high.

DESCRIPTION: Small glabrous to lightly pubescent shrub. Its glands are often very prominent. Leaves are usually erect, thick linear, obtuse, 3 to 7 mm long. Flowers are solitary, axillary; filament flat; margins ciliate.

AREA: South Qld., N.S.W., Vic. and S.A., most of temperate Australia, heathlands. TIME: August to January and often February.

BORONIA FALCIFOLIA

FAMILY: Rutaceae. COMMON NAME: Wallum Boronia. COLOUR: Rose pink. SIZE: Up to 50 cm high.

DESCRIPTION: Erect undershrub with few stems. Leaves: three foliate; leaflets linear, almost terete, 8 to 12 mm long. Flowers are in axillary cymes in upper leaves. Very few flowers in cluster, petals 6 to 10 mm long.

AREA: N.S.W., along coast and nearby foothills and mountains, very common north of the Hunter Valley. TIME: Spring.

BORONIA GRANITICA VAR.

FAMILY: Rutaceae. COMMON NAME: None. COLOUR: Pink. SIZE: Up to 2 metres high.

DESCRIPTION: Compact shrub. Leaves: pinnate; five to nine leaflets, 6 to 8 mm long, glabrous or lightly pubescent, margins ciliate. Flower: 2 to 3 cm across, star-shape; petals 10 to 15 mm long, tips delicately marked with red or mauve spots.

AREA: Qld. and N.S.W., in fissures of granite in granite belts. TIME: August to November.

BORONIA MEGASTIGMA

FAMILY: Rutaceae. COMMON NAME: Brown Boronia or Scented Boronia. COLOUR: Yellow and brown. SIZE: Up to 2 metres high.

DESCRIPTION: Erect shrub, glabrous. Leaves: small, linear, usually in threes, 10 to 13 mm long. Flowers are in leaf axil; petals dark purple to red-brown outside, yellow-green inside. Sepaline anthers are large, black or purple, and quite different to petaline anthers. Blooms have strong perfume. Widely cultivated especially in Melbourne, where it is known as 'Melbourne Boronia'.

AREA: W.A., southern provinces in heathlands and sandy swamps. TIME: August to September.

Rutaceae
Boronia caerulescens

Rutaceae
Boronia falcifolia

Rutaceae
Boronia granitica var. sp.

Rutaceae
Boronia megastigma

BORONIA SERRULATA

FAMILY: Rutaceae. COMMON NAME: Native Rose. COLOUR: Rose pink. SIZE: Up to 150 cm high.

DESCRIPTION: Strong, erect shrub. Leaves: broad-ovate to rhomboidal, serrulate, coriaceous, sessile or nearly so, acute, 8 to 15 mm long. Flowers are solitary in leaf axil, mostly terminal raceme; sepals acute, petals acute, 8 to 12 mm long.

AREA: N.S.W. and Vic., in moist heathlands, coastal and nearby mountains. TIME: August to October.

BORONIA WHITEI

FAMILY: Rutaceae. COMMON NAME: None. COLOUR: Pink-mauve. SIZE: Up to a metre high.

DESCRIPTION: An erect shrub, pubescent. Its young branches are extremely pubescent. Leaves: pinnate, silky hairy. Flowers are star-shaped, one or two in leaf axil, or terminal raceme, few blooms. Sepals are lightly pubescent, light brown, acute. Petals are 8 to 10 mm long, acute. This plant is often confused with *B. granitica.*

AREA: N.S.W., north west slopes, New England Tablelands and not widespread. TIME: September to November.

CORREA BACKHOUSIANA

FAMILY: Rutaceae. COMMON NAME: Native Fuchsia. COLOUR: Pale lemon-green. SIZE: Up to 150 cm and higher.

DESCRIPTION: Tomentose shrub. Stems and branches covered with scalelike hairs. Leaves: orbicular to ovate, obovate to elliptical, thick, 2 to 3 cm long, rusty-woolly tomentose underneath. Calyx: cup-shaped, woolly, 4 to 6 mm long. Corolla: campanulate and star-shape, tube 2 to 3 cm long. Flowers are terminal, one to six together. *C. reflexa* and *C. backhousiana* are now considered separate species.

SCALE-LIKE HAIRS ALONG STEM

AREA: Temperate regions of Australia. TIME: June to October.

CORREA LAWRENCIANA VAR. GLANDULIFERA

FAMILY: Rutaceae. COMMON NAME: Bush Fuchsia. COLOUR: Lemon. SIZE: Up to 4 metres high.

DESCRIPTION: Tall shrub, branches tomentose. Leaves lanceolate, ovate-lanceolate, 4 to 10 cm long, glandular, dark green uppersurface, white tomentose underneath, mid-vein rusty tomentose. Calyx: lobes acute, corolla 2 to 4 cm long, petals acute. Fruit is dehiscent.

Distribution of the species of Correa lawrenciana: var. *lawrenciana*—central and west Vic., north and south Tas., and Canberra district; var. *cordifolia*—south coast N.S.W.; var. *genoensis*—central coast west Tas., Orbust district and King Island; var. *glandulifera*—MacPherson Ranges and Gibraltar Ranges; var. *macrocalyx*—central coast N.S.W.; var. *rosea*—Snowy Mountains, and Alps.

AREA: Vic. and N.S.W. (*See Appendix I*). TIME: May to July.

Rutaceae
Boronia serrulata

Rutaceae
Boronia whitei

Rutaceae
Correa backhousiana

Rutaceae
Correa lawrenciana var. glandulifera

CORREA REFLEXA VAR. CARDINALIS

FAMILY: Rutaceae. COMMON NAME: Native Fuchsia. COLOUR: Red, tips yellow-green. SIZE: About 150 cm high.

DESCRIPTION: Erect shrub, tomentose. Its branches are tomentose. Leaves: coriaceous, spreading or reflexed, ovate-oblong, 2 to 4 cm long, green almost glabrous above; densely white-tomentose underneath, margins lightly recurved. Flowers: one to three, terminating on short axillary branchlets, drooping and almost concealed by two subtending reflexed leaves. Calyx: cup-shape, 6 mm long, white tomentose. Corolla red, 2 to 2.5 cm long; petals green, spreading and recurved.

AREA: Temperate parts of Australia, near coast and nearby mountains. TIME: October to February.

CROWEA SALIGNA

FAMILY: Rutaceae. COMMON NAME: None. COLOUR: Deep pink. SIZE: About a metre high.

DESCRIPTION: Low shrub. Branches are conspicuously angular. Leaves are alternate, thick, narrow-elliptic, 3 to 5 cm long, dark green, shiny above; mid-vein distinct. Flowers are solitary, in leaf axil, 12 to 18 mm long. Calyx is five-lobed; sepals short and broad; petals five, imbricate, pink inside and pink to green outside. Fruit is a schizocarp.

AREA: N.S.W., coastal, mountains and tablelands and south plateaux in sheltered situations. TIME: January to June.

PHEBALIUM SQUAMEUM

FAMILY: Rutaceae. COMMON NAME: Satinwood or Lancewood. COLOUR: White. SIZE: Up to 12 metres high.

DESCRIPTION: An erect shrub to small tree. Branches: undersurface of leaves and inflorescence more or less covered with scurfy (glandular) scales. Leaves: alternate, linear to lanceolate, oblong-lanceolate to elliptic, 2 to 10 cm long, green-white to silvery-white satin underneath. Flowers in axillary corymbs on short, thick scaly peduncles. Petals, five; calyx lobes are very small. Carpels very short beak at fruiting.

AREA: N.S.W., Vic. and Tas., coast, ranges in moist valleys and wet sclerophyll forest. TIME: September to October.

Rutaceae
Correa reflex var. cardinalis

Rutaceae
Crowea saligna

Rutaceae
Phebalium squameum

*fruiting body of
Correa lawrenciana
var. glandulifera*

PHEBALIUM SQUAMULOSUM

FAMILY: Rutaceae. COMMON NAME: Native May. COLOUR: Yellow. SIZE: Up to 4 metres high.

DESCRIPTION: Tall shrub to small tree. Leaves: linear, lanceolate to oblong, 1 to 7 cm long, shiny or may be dull, dark green; uppersurface is pale-green with dark red markings to brown-white; woolly, scaly underneath. Flowers are in terminal raceme; scurfy, sessile umbels or corymbs. Calyx lobes are very short; petals 3 to 4 mm long, yellow inside and scaly outside. Carpels are not beaked at fruiting.

AREA: Qld., N.S.W. and Vic., coastal, mountains, granite and sandstone, widespread in varied situations. TIME: August to October.

PHEBALIUM WOOMBYE

FAMILY: Rutaceae. COMMON NAME: None. COLOUR: White, cream or pink. SIZE: Up to a metre high.

DESCRIPTION: A small shrub. Leaves: linear to elliptic to oblong, 2 to 3 cm long, shiny, green above, pale-green to silvery-green, woody, scaly underneath, margins recurved. Flowers are in terminal corymbs; inflorescence scurfy; calyx is five-toothed, scaly; petals white or cream (a pink form is recorded). Stamens are long.

AREA: Qld., Fraser Island and N.S.W., coastal and dry sclerophyll forest and sandy soils. TIME: August to October. Flowers may be present throughout the year.

PHILOTHECA SALSOLIFOLIA

FAMILY: Rutaceae. COMMON NAME: None. COLOUR: Mauve-pink. SIZE: Up to 1.5 metres high.

DESCRIPTION: Heathlike shrub, glabrous. Its young tips are minutely pubescent. Leaves: narrow-linear to almost terete, crowded, 1 to 4 mm long. Flowers: terminal one to three together; sepals five, broad-deltoid; petals five, imbricate in, bud; stamens ten, similar to *Eriostemon*, but filaments cohering (fused at the base) and without anther appendages.

AREA: Qld. and N.S.W., coastal and nearby ranges, widespread in rocky and sandy soils. TIME: September to December.

CHORETRUM CANDOLLEI (coastal form)

FAMILY: Santalaceae. COMMON NAME: Broom Bush. COLOUR: White. SIZE: Up to 2 metres high.

DESCRIPTION: Erect shrub. Leaves are reduced to minute persistent scales. Branches are green erect and wiry. Flowers are solitary within axil of the minute decurrent bracts. Perianth is five-lobed, surrounded by a number of small bracts. See plate 83 for Granite form.

AREA: Qld. and N.S.W., widespread along coast in sandy soil, along roadsides and dry sclerophyll forest. TIME: Mainly Spring, August to October.

Rutaceae
Phebalium squamulosum

Rutaceae
Phebalium woombye

Rutaceae
Philotheca salsolifolia

Santalaceae
Choretrum canollei (coastal form)

CHORETRUM CANDOLLEI (Granite form)

FAMILY: Santalaceae. COMMON NAME: Broom Bush. COLOUR: White. SIZE: Up to a metre high.

DESCRIPTION: Erect, much branching shrub, with green branchlets. Leaves are reduced to minute persistent scales. Flowers: bisexual, small and numerous, scattered along flowering branchlets. Flowering branch is 1 to 2 mm wide and flowers towards end of branchlet, practically sessile. Perianth is five-lobed, surrounded by number of small bracts. See plate 82 for coastal form.

AREA: N.S.W. and Vic., mountains and ranges in granite areas, dry sclerophyll forests. TIME: October to December.

EXOCARPOS CUPRESSIFORMIS

FAMILY: Santalaceae. COMMON NAME: Native Cherry or Cherry Ballart. COLOUR: Flowers cream, fruit red. SIZE: Up to 7 metres high.

DESCRIPTION: A tall shrub or small tree, parasitic upon roots of other plants. Foliage is light to dark green and gracefully pendulous branches, leafless, angular-terete. Flowers are minute, in short axillary cluster, symmetrical in form (cylindrical spikes 3 to 6 mm long). Flowers dwarfed by colourful fruit. Fruit is a nut supported by a fleshy, berrylike pedicel or stalk. The stalk at first green then yellow then red, is of pleasant flavour.

AREA: N.S.W. and Vic., temperate Australia generally coastal and mountains and ranges. TIME: September to February.

LEPTOMERIA BILLIARDIERI

FAMILY: Santalaceae. COMMON NAME: None. COLOUR: White, fruit red. SIZE: Up to 1.5 metres high.

DESCRIPTION: Erect, tough, leafless shrub. Branches are green, with young shoots with minute scalelike leaves falling off very early. Very short semi-spiny twigs, 15 to 20 mm long. Flowers are bisexual, minute, along the spikes or spiny twigs. Fruit is drupaceous, succulent, red, acid and 5 to 6 mm long.

AREA: N.S.W., in granite; this is a very rare species, but is common on Gibraltar Range and parts of granite belts of south Qld. TIME: September to November.

DODONAEA MEGAZYGA

FAMILY: Sapindaceae. COMMON NAME: Hop Bush. COLOUR: Green turning pink. SIZE: Up to 4 metres high.

DESCRIPTION: Tall shrub or small tree. Leaves: pinnate-compound; leaflets elliptic, acute, margins more or less recurved, 20 to 25 mm long to 4 mm wide, may be opposite or irregularly arranged. Rhachis is winged, glabrous. Flowers are in terminal raceme. Sepals four; petals absent; stamens numerous. Fruit is winged, glabrous capsule, on slender pedicels, 2 to 3 cm long.

AREA: Qld. and N.S.W., ranges, dry sclerophyll forests, marginal to rainforest. TIME: Spring.

Santalaceae
Choretrum candollei (granite form)

Santalaceae
Exocarpos cupressiformis

Santalaceae
Leptomeria billiardieri

Sapindaceae
Dodonaea megazyga

DODONAEA TRUNCATIALIS

FAMILY: Sapindaceae. COMMON NAME: Sticky Hop Bush. COLOUR: Fruit green to pink. SIZE: Up to 3 metres high.

DESCRIPTION: Tall erect shrub, scarcely viscid. Young branches are acutely angled. Leaves: narrow-lanceolate to linear-lanceolate, sinuate-toothed, or entire 3 to 7 cm long. Flowers are apparently axillary on aborted flowering branches, and in small clusters. Wings of capsule wider than long, truncate, 4 to 6 mm wide.

AREA: N.S.W., coastal, foothills, mountains and dry sclerophyll forests. TIME: September to November.

DODONAEA VISCOSA

FAMILY: Sapindaceae. COMMON NAME: Giant or Sticky Hop Bush. COLOUR: Fruit rusty to green. SIZE: Up to 4 metres high.

DESCRIPTION: Viscid shrub, glabrous, with branches more or less angular. Leaves: oblong-cuneate or broadly oblanceolate to narrow oblong or narrow elliptic, 3 to 10 cm long, 6 to 14 mm wide, tapering to short petiole. Flowers are in short panicles or racemes. Sepals four, pubescent; capsule four-winged, may be red or purple, 10 to 18 mm long, and broader than long.

AREA: Qld., N.S.W., Vic. and S.A., throughout Australia and warmer regions of the world. TIME: September to November.

EUPHRASIA GLACIALIS

FAMILY: Scrophulariaceae. COMMON NAME: Glacial Eye Bright. COLOUR: White, pink or purple. SIZE: Up to 30 cm high.

DESCRIPTION: A tufted herb. Leaves: opposite, sessile, elliptic, margins coarsely nine-toothed, light green, 7 to 12 mm long. Calyx four-lobed. Flowers are sessile in terminal spike; corolla is three or four times as long as calyx, tubular at base two-lipped, upper lip recurved two-lobed, lower lip three-lobed. Flower is 10 to 15 mm across, stems usually red-brown. *E. eglandulosa* is a non-glandular species.

AREA: N.S.W., Vic. and A.C.T., Alps, colder climates. TIME: October to February.

EUPHRASIA SPECIOSA

FAMILY: Scrophulariaceae. COMMON NAME: Bright Eyes. COLOUR: Purple.

DESCRIPTION: Erect perennial herb, parasitic on other plant roots. Stems wiry, branching from base. Leaves: opposite sessile, ovate to cuneate, 5 to 15 mm long, margins coarsely toothed. Flowers are sessile in terminal raceme or spike. Calyx four-lobed; corolla tube two or three times as long as calyx; petals form a concave two-lobed upper lip, lower lip spreading in three lobes. Four stamens.

AREA: Temperate Australia, widespread, heathlands, moist soils and along roadsides. TIME: September to November.

Sapindaceae
Dodonaea truncatiales

Sapindeceae
Dodonaea viscosa

Scrophulariceae
Euphrasia glacialis

Scrophulariaceae
Euphrasia speciosa

PARAHEBE SP. NOVA (undescribed)

FAMILY: Scrophulariaceae. COMMON NAME: None. COLOUR: Mauve-purple. SIZE: About 1.5 metres high.

DESCRIPTION: An erect herb with that part of the stem just above the ground. It is woody and perennial. Leaves: deeply serrate, non-stemclasping, light green, 4 to 10 'cm long. Flower is arranged on long terminal raceme, axil in flora leaflets. Calyx is deeply divided; corolla indistinctly tubular; stamens two. Fruit is a compressed capsule. Once thought to be an intermediate between two species, undescribed. Further species reported from various areas in N.S.W.

AREA: N.S.W., Mt Kaputara—Nandiwah Ranges. TIME: Summer and Spring.

VERBASCUM VIRGATUM

FAMILY: Scrophulariaceae. COMMON NAME: Twiggy Mullein. COLOUR: Yellow. SIZE: Up to a metre high.

DESCRIPTION: Erect herb. Leaves rosette of large basal leaves; erect stem with alternate leaves. Cauline leaves are broad-ovate to ovate, with margins decurrent as lines or ridges on the stem. Flowers are several in axil of each bract, arranged up stem in spikelike raceme. Flowers are bisexual; calyx five-lobed; corolla rotate, four-lobed. Fruit is a capsule.

AREA: Qld. and N.S.W., widespread on wastelands and roadsides, introduced. TIME: September to February.

VERONICA DERWENTIA

FAMILY: Scrophulariaceae. COMMON NAME: Derwent Speedwell. COLOUR: White to pallid lilac. SIZE: Up to a metre high.

DESCRIPTION: Small erect undershrub, pubescent on flowering rhachis and pedicels. Leaves: sessile, stem-clasping, broad-lanceolate, acuminate, serrate, glabrous, 4 to 12 cm long. Flowers are in long axillary corymbose raceme; pedicels and calyx, 3 mm long. Corolla lobes are acute. Fruit capsule ovoid.

AREA: N.S.W., Vic., S.A. and Tas., usually near water, moist forest from sea level to sub-Alps. TIME: October to January.

SOLANUM AMBLYMERUM

FAMILY: Solanaceae. COMMON NAME: Nightshade. COLOUR: Purple. SIZE: Up to 3 metres high.

DESCRIPTION: Spreading, spiny shrub. Leaves: entire or with conspicuous basal lobes or leaflets, ovate-lanceolate to narrow-oblong, spiny (long spines along mid vein), 8 to 15 cm long. Flowers: several to many, bisexual, in extra-axillary cymes, in form of raceme or umbels, stellate to broad stellate. Fruit: red to red-black, succulent, 25 mm diameter.

AREA: Qld. and N.S.W., marginal rainforest. TIME: Spring to Summer.

Scrophulariaceae
Parahebe sp. nova (undescribed)

Scrophulariaceae
Verbascum virgatum

Scrophulariaceae
Veronica derwentia

Solanaceae
Solanum amblymerum

SOLANUM AVICULARE

FAMILY: Solanaceae. COMMON NAME: Kangaroo Apple. COLOUR: Blue-purple. SIZE: Up to 3 metres high and higher.

DESCRIPTION: Erect, glabrous, shrubby, perennial, but flowering when young and small. Leaves: petiolate, lanceolate, 8 to 20 cm long, usually entire, earlier leaves with lanceolate lobes near base. Flowers are in loose pedunculate racemelike inflorescence; corolla 2 to 3.5 cm diameter, broad-companulate to rotate, lobes acute. Fruit is a berry, ovoid, orange and edible. *S. laciniatum*, stems are always purple, leaves variable, long linear to palmate, two to six lobes. Flower corolla up to 5 cm diameter, rotate lobes, emarginate and half as long as tube. Fruit is a berry, globular, edible.

LEAF MORE TYPICAL OF S.LACINIATUM THAN S. AVICULARE

AREA: *S. aviculare*, Qld., N.S.W., Vic., S.A. and W.A. *S. laciniatum*, N.S.W., Vic., S.A., W.A. and Tas., widespread, wet sclerophyll forest and rainforest margins. TIME: August to March.

SOLANUM BROWNII SYN. VIOLACEUM

FAMILY: Solanaceae. COMMON NAME: Nightshade. COLOUR: Blue, mauve or rarely white. SIZE: Up to 4 metres high.

DESCRIPTION: A variable tall shrub, having stems covered with fine prickles and long spines along branches. Leaves: oblong to lanceolate or angularly lobed, 8 to 12 cm long, distinctly discolourous, conspicuous spines on upper lamina. Flowers: pedunculate, solitary or two to eight in loose terminal raceme, several to many bisexual. Calyx five-lobed; corolla rotate, stellate; petals emarginate to dentate. Fruit is a berry, green, yellow, to black, 1 to 2 cm diameter. One form of this has been illustrated in *A Field Guide to Wildflowers*, Vol. I, but the above is the most common form found.

AREA: N.S.W. and Vic., marginal rainforest, and wet sclerophyll forest. TIME: September to March.

SOLANUM MAURITIANUM

FAMILY: Solanaceae. COMMON NAME: Wild Tobacco Tree. COLOUR: Purple. SIZE: Up to 6 metres high.

DESCRIPTION: Introduced, large shrub, with branches and leaves having soft dense tomentum of stellate hairs. Leaves: elliptic to ovate to narrow-ovate, acuminate, velvet-like, 8 to 25 cm long. Young axillary leaves are semi-orbicular, recurved and resembling stipules. Flowers in dense pedunculate cymes. Corolla blue or white to purple. Fruit a berry, green turning yellow when mature, 12 to 14 mm diameter.

AREA: Qld., N.S.W. and S.A., roadsides, wasteland and riverbanks. TIME: September to March.

Solanaceae
Solanum aviculare

Solanaceae
Solanum brownii

Solanaceae
Solanum mauritianum

fruiting body of
Solanum mauritianum

SOLANUM PSEUDOCAPSICUM

FAMILY: Solanaceae. COMMON NAME: Madeira Winter Cherry. COLOUR: White. SIZE: Up to 150 cm high.

DESCRIPTION: Introduced, erect shrub. Leaves: lanceolate, 2 to 10 cm long. Flowers: solitary or two or three on short axillary pedicels. Calyx lobes lanceolate, persistent; corolla lobes lanceolate, reflexed, 8 to 10 mm diameter. Hairs, if present, are forked. Fruit a berry, one or two, erect, globular, orange-red when mature, 12 to 15 mm diameter.

AREA: N.S.W., wasteland, wet sclerophyll forest, rainforest margins. TIME: September to March.

SOLANUM STELLIGERUM

FAMILY: Solanaceae. COMMON NAME: Nightshade. COLOUR: Mauve. SIZE: Up to 2 metres high.

DESCRIPTION: Shrub, with prickles on branches only. Leaves: lanceolate to ovate-lanceolate, acute or acuminate, glabrous or almost on uppersurface with one or several prickles; undersurface soft, pale yellow, stellate tomentum, 4 to 10 cm long. Flowers are in lateral cymes; corolla 10 to 12 mm diameter. Fruit a berry, globular, red, 5 to 12 mm diameter.

AREA: N.S.W., widespread, wet sclerophyll forest and rainforest margins. TIME: September to February.

SOLANUM VESCUM

FAMILY: Solanaceae. COMMON NAME: Nightshade. COLOUR: Purple. SIZE: Up to 2 metres high.

DESCRIPTION: A shrub. Leaves: sessile, decurrent, lanceolate to narrow-lanceolate, entire or with few long lobes. Flowers are in loose pedunculate raceme. Corolla is of 3 to 5 cm diameter. Fruit a berry, green-ivory to green-yellow, or purple, ovate to globular, 2 to 4 cm diameter.

AREA: N.S.W., Vic. and Tas., widespread, wet sclerophyll forests and rainforest margins. TIME: October to March.

STACKHOUSIA MONOGYNA

FAMILY: Stackhousiaceae. COMMON NAME: Candles or Creamy Stackhousia. COLOUR: White, cream buds pinkish. SIZE: To 30 cm high.

DESCRIPTION: Slender, erect, glabrous herb. Leaves: linear to lanceolate, rather thick, acute, 1 to 4 cm long, 2 to 6 mm wide. Inflorescence is a dense spike to 12 cm long, elongating at fruiting. Flowers strongly scented; first crowded, then distant in fruit. Calyx 3 mm long; corolla tube 6 to 8 mm long, lobes short obtuse or subacute. Fruitlets are ovoid, 2 to 2.5 mm long.

AREA: Fraser Island, south Qld., N.S.W., Vic. and S.A., widespread, coastal, open forest, clay soils and sand hills. TIME: October to February.

Solanaceae
Solanum pseudocapsicum

Solanaceae
Solanum stelligerum

Solanaceae
Solanum vescum

Stackhousiaceae
Stackhousia monogyna

STACKHOUSIA PULVINARIS

FAMILY: Stackhousiaceae. COMMON NAME: Alpine Stackhousia. COLOUR: Lemon-cream. SIZE: About 5 cm high.

DESCRIPTION: A matted, perennial herb. It is the only prostrate or matted species of this Australian genus. Leaves: green, linear-oblong, 5 to 10 mm long, densely crowded. Flowers are solitary, all other species of this genus having flower spikes. Corolla is of 4 to 5 mm diameter. Scented apparently strongest at night.

AREA: N.S.W., Vic. and Tas., snow mountains, Victoria Alps and Tas. mountains above 1500 metres. TIME: December to February.

STACKHOUSIA VIMINEA

FAMILY: Stackhousiaceae. COMMON NAME: Candles. COLOUR: Lemon-cream. SIZE: Up to 30 cm high.

DESCRIPTION: Very slender, erect, glabrous stem. Leaves: linear-cuneate to obovate or elliptic, 10 to 25 mm long, 1 to 3 mm wide, well developed at base of stem. Spike is the greater part of stem. Flower is solitary distant or distant cluster of two or three. Calyx is 1 to 1.5 mm long, lobes acute. Corolla yellow or green-yellow, tube 4 mm long, lobes acute or acuminate, 2 mm long. Fruitlets are ovoid, 2 to 3 mm long.

AREA: N.S.W., Qld., Vic., S.A. and W.A., sandy soils, open forest, heathland pasture. TIME: July to February.

STYLIDIUM BREVISCAPUM

FAMILY: Stylidiaceae. COMMON NAME: Boomerang Trigger Plant. COLOUR: Orange, yellow, red or white. SIZE: Creeper.

DESCRIPTION: Branched creeper. Old stems develop thickened nodes from which grow black, wiry roots. Leaves: linear to terete, 10 to 15 mm long, clustered or crowded at base of scape. Inflorescence is a terminal cluster. Bracts are 6 to 8 mm long, linear. Calyx 6 to 8 mm toothed, calyx tube 8 to 10 mm long. Corolla deeply five-lobed, lobes imbricate in bud. Style is bent sensitive with triggerlike action.

AREA: W.A., in southern provinces, in gravelly soils. TIME: August to November.

STYLIDIUM CRASSIFOLIUM

FAMILY: Stylidiaceae. COMMON NAME: Thick-leaved Trigger-plant. COLOUR: Pink, variable—white. SIZE: About 60 cm high.

DESCRIPTION: Tufted herb. Leaves are fleshy cluster at base scape, spathulate to narrow-oblanceolate, up to 15 cm long. Inflorescence is a spike up to 25 cm long. Flowers are solitary or two to three in distant cluster. Calyx lobes five, more or less united into two lips. Corolla tubular, deeply five-lobed, lobes imbricate in bud. Column is bent and sensitive, with triggerlike action when touched.

AREA: W.A., southern provinces, sandy heath, swamps, drying creek beds and after bush fires. TIME: November to February.

Stackhousiaceae
Stackhousia pulvinaris

Stackhousiaceae
Stackhousia viminea

Stylidiaceae
Stylidium breviscapum

Stylidiaceae
Stylidium crassifolium

STYLIDIUM SPATHULATUM

FAMILY: Stylidiaceae. COMMON NAME: None. COLOUR: Yellow-lemon. SIZE: About 45 cm high.

DESCRIPTION: Stem herb. Leaves: rosette, spathulate, 15 to 25 mm long, covered with green, yellow or brown hairs. Stems and bracts are glabrous. Inflorescence is a terminal, racemelike spike. Flowers are distant and tending to crowd towards top. Calyx: 8 to 10 mm, calyx lobes five, linear. Corolla tube is 10 to 15 mm long. Trigger plants are so called because of the rapid flick of the column when touched by an insect. The column protrudes in a 'cocked' position between two petals, when insect attempts to take nectar it irritates the sensitive base causing column to straighten instantly, hitting the insect and showering it with pollen.

AREA: W.A., southern provinces, in shady situations. TIME: October.

PIMELEA LIGUSTRINA

FAMILY: Thymelaeaceae. COMMON NAME: Tall Rice Flower. COLOUR: White to pink. SIZE: Up to 2 metres high.

DESCRIPTION: Tall shrub. Leaves: soft, mostly opposite, ovate to oblong to lanceolate, 2 to 8 cm long, thin, flat. Flower: head globular, terminal, 25 mm or more in diameter. Involucral bracts: four, ovate, acute, glabrous outside, pubescent inside; floral tube 10 mm long, lobes only 3 mm long.

AREA: South Qld., N.S.W., Vic., S.A. and Tas., moist situations, near rainforests and stunted form in Alps. TIME: October to February.

PIMELEA LINIFOLIA

FAMILY: Thymelaeaceae. COMMON NAME: Slender Rice Flower or Granny's Bonnet. COLOUR: White. SIZE: Up to a metre high.

DESCRIPTION: Erect or spreading slender plant or shrub. Leaves: narrow-linear to oblong to elliptic, one veined, glabrous, 10 to 25 mm long. Flower head is erect, terminal. Involucral bracts are glabrous inside and outside, although some forms may have hairs on inside, ovate to narrow ovate. Floral tube is villous from base, 8 to 12 mm long. Although illustrated in Vol. I this is a variable plant and this form is most widespread. Possible early reclassification of this genus and species.

AREA: South Qld., N.S.W. and Vic., widespread. TIME: Most of the year.

PIMELEA SUAVEOLENS

FAMILY: Thymelaeaceae. COMMON NAME: Scented Banjine. COLOUR: Lemon. SIZE: About 30 cm high.

DESCRIPTION: Low slender stem shrub, occurring in numerous forms. Leaves: ovate to oblanceolate, mostly opposite, glabrous or almost, 8 to 12 mm long. Flower head is 2 to 5 cm in diameter, terminal. Involucral bracts are large, pubescent. Floral tube is fine, linear, 8 to 15 mm long; lobes spreading; two stamens; petals absent. Heavy scented. Often found in association with white-barked wandoo trees.

AREA: W.A., widespread on midwest coast, south-west and southern inland. TIME: June to November.

Stylidiaceae
Stylidium spathulatum

Thymelaeaceae
Pimelea ligustrina

Thymelaeaceae
Pimelea linifolia

Thymelaeaceae
Pimelea suaveolens

TETRATHECA CILIATA

FAMILY: Tremandraceae. COMMON NAME: Pink Eye. COLOUR: Pink. SIZE: Up to a metre high.

DESCRIPTION: An undershrub. Its branches are slender, and usually pubescent. Leaves: alternate or whorled in three or four, ovate to orbicular, ciliate, acuminate, 8 to 10 mm long. Flowers are on hairy peduncles. Sepals are spreading; petals ovate-oblong, caducous. Seeds are hairy.

AREA: N.S.W., S.A., Vic. and northern Tas. TIME: September to February.

TETRATHECA THYMIFOLIA

FAMILY: Tremandraceae. COMMON NAME: Black-eyed Susan. COLOUR: Pink to mauve. SIZE: Up to a metre high.

DESCRIPTION: Beautiful undershrub, with spreading branches that are terete 30 to 60 cm long. Leaves: dark green alternate in whorls of three or four, narrow-ovate to narrow-lanceolate, 3 to 15 mm long, pubescent to hirsute, margins revolute. Peduncle and sepals have fine hairs. Flowers are solitary, bisexual; petals ovate-oblong. Fruit is a hairy capsule.

AREA: South Qld., N.S.W. and Vic., widespread, coastal and ranges in dry sclerophyll forest and sheltered situations. TIME: August to March.

TRIFOLIUM ARVENSE

TRIBE: Trifolieae. FAMILY: Papilionaceae. COMMON NAME: Hare's Foot Clover. COLOUR: Green-purple or Lavender. SIZE: Up to 30 cm high.

DESCRIPTION: Introduced, erect, slender, pubescent annual. Leaflets: linear-oblong, faintly toothed, 5 to 15 mm long. Flowers are very small in globular-oblong or cylindrical heads, 8 to 12 mm diameter, on long filiform peduncles. Heads give fluffy appearance. Calyx tube is ovoid, villous; the teeth are plumose or bristle-like. Petals are short.

AREA: Qld., N.S.W., Vic and S.A., cleared ground, and roadsides. TIME: October to December.

PLATYSACE ERICOIDES SYN. TRACHYMENE ERICOIDES

FAMILY: Umbelliferae. COMMON NAME: None. SIZE: Up to 30 cm high.

DESCRIPTION: A low shrub. Stems are short, diffuse, glandular pubescent. Leaves are soft and aromatic, linear to subulate, spreading, 5 to 10 mm long. Flowers are small in compact and compound, terminal umbels, calyx teeth small. Petals said to be induplicate-valvate when in bud. *P. linearifolia*, is a shrub 150 cm high. Stems are glabrous, ascending. Leaves narrow-linear, 10 to 25 mm long.

AREA: Qld., N.S.W. and Vic., coast and mountains, in low forest, granite and stone. TIME: Spring.

Tremandraceae
Tetratheca ciliata

Tremandraceae
Tetratheca thymifolia

Trifolieae
Trifolium arvense

Umbelliferae
Platysace ericoides syn. Trachymene ericoides

CHLOANTHES PARVIFLORA

FAMILY: Verbenaceae. COMMON NAME: None. COLOUR: Mauve. SIZE: About a metre high.

DESCRIPTION: Erect shrub. Leaves: opposite, decurrent, lanceolate, bullate, stellate hairs, 1 to 2 cm long. Flowers: solitary, axillary, sessile or almost. Calyx is deeply five-lobed. Corolla is 10 to 15 mm long, blue-mauve to blue-yellow with dark markings, hairs in throat and upper lip. Fruit is a schizocarp.

AREA: Qld. and N.S.W., heathlands, dry sclerophyll forests, coastal and ranges. TIME: Spring and Summer.

LACHNOSTACHYS ALBICANS

FAMILY: Verbenaceae. COMMON NAME: Lamb's Tail. COLOUR: Mauve. SIZE: Up to 90 cm high.

DESCRIPTION: An erect shrub. Leaves: opposite, ovate-lanceolate, decussate, 9 to 12 mm long, hairy with feltlike appearance. Inflorescence is a dense cluster along a long solitary terminal spike on erect branches. Spike is white with silky-wool appearance. Flowers: the corolla and staminal ring are both mauve-violet and encircled in wool-white ball.

AREA: W.A., south western province, in sandy soils. TIME: September to November.

LACHNOSTACHYS VERBASCIFOLIA

FAMILY: Verbenaceae. COMMON NAME: Sheep's Tongue, Lambstails or Blanket Plant. COLOUR: White. SIZE: From 30 to 60 cm high.

DESCRIPTION: A small erect, well developed, densely hairy shrub. Leaves: alternate, stem-clasping, or often cordate at base erect, thick and soft, ovate-lanceolate, margins markedly revolute, densely woolly on both surfaces, 2.5 to 7 cm long. Flowers: densely clustered along terminal spike or spicate-paniculate, or axillary spicate-panicles. Small flower spikes tend to be hidden in woolly felt. Calyx is six to eight partite; corolla, styles and stamens mauve.

AREA: W.A., south province, in sandy soils. TIME: August to September.

VIOLA HEDERACEA

FAMILY: Violaceae. COMMON NAME: Ivy-leaved Violet. COLOUR: White to mauve. SIZE: Up to 15 cm high.

DESCRIPTION: A stemless perennial, with slender stolons. Leaves: dark green, glabrous, reniform to orbicular or sub-orbicular, 1 to 3 cm long, entire or distantly toothed, or crenate. Sepals: lanceolate, 4 to 5 mm long. Petals: 6 to 10 mm long, may be white with purple blotch, lateral one bearded towards base inside. Flower stems are very variable in length.

AREA: Qld., N.S.W., Vic. and S.A., in sheltered moist situations and wet sclerophyll forests. TIME: September to February.

Verbenaceae
Chloanthes parviflora

Verbenaceae
Lachnostachys albicans

Verbenaceae
Lachnostachys verbascifolia

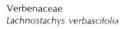

Violaceae
Viola hederacea

CALECTASIA CYANEA

FAMILY: Xanthorrhoeaceae. COMMON NAME: Blue Tinsel Lily. COLOUR: Blue. SIZE: About 50 cm high.

DESCRIPTION: A more or less pubescent shrub. Leaves: erect, crowded, almost pungent, very short. Flower: solitary, terminal on short branches, blue-purple with metallic sheen; perianth funnel-shaped, 7 to 12 mm long; six lobes, lanceolate, radiating from tube, 10 to 15 mm long; anthers yellow, turning red.

Classified in Family: Xanthorrhoeaceae in W.A.; Calectasiaceae in Vic.; Liliaceae in S.A.

AREA: From western Vic., S.A. and W.A., dry sclerophyll forests. TIME: June to October.

LOMANDRA MULTIFLORA

FAMILY: Xanthorrhoeaceae in N.S.W. and W.A.; Liliaceae in S.A. and Vic. COMMON NAME: Many Flowered Mat Rush. COLOUR: Brown and yellow. SIZE: Up to 60 cm high.

DESCRIPTION: A low tussock. Leaves: flat to concave, dark grey-green, rigid, 30 to 60 cm long, 2 to 4 mm wide. Flowers: in cluster along the erect, spreading branches of a rigid panicle, 12 to 30 cm long. Male inflorescence is a spike or panicle, 5 to 30 cm long. Male flowers are 2 to 3 mm long on pedicels 8 to 10 mm long. Female inflorescence is a smaller spike. Flowers are sessile, 3 to 4 mm long. Fruit is a capsule, globular-trigonous, 6 mm diameter, wrinkled.

AREA: N.S.W., Qld., Vic., S.A. and W.A., throughout Australia. TIME: October to November.

HEDYCHIUM FLAVESCENS

FAMILY: Zingiberaceae. COMMON NAME: Wild Ginger. COLOUR: Yellow. SIZE: Up to 2 metres high.

DESCRIPTION: Growing from an edible rhizome system, the plant forms large clumps. Leaves are long and narrow-lanceolate. Raceme is terminal, flowering from bottom as head continues to grow. Flowers: long tube, two staminodes fused to form a two-lobed lip, another two staminodes look like petals. The three petals are relatively inconspicuous narrow appendages. There is one functional stamen, and projecting from a groove in its upper surface, is a style a little longer than the fertile stamen. The nectar is rich and superb perfume of the flowers permeates the surrounding area.

AREA: Qld. and north N.S.W., introduced, in and close to rainforests in rich soils, widely used in domestic gardens throughout Australia. TIME: December to April.

Xanthorrhoeaceae
Calectasia cyanea

Xanthorrhoeaceae
Lomandra multiflora

Zingberaceae
Hedychium flavescens

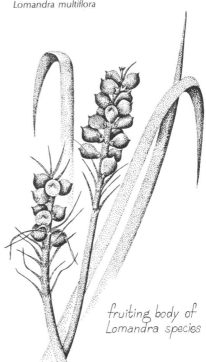

*fruiting body of
Lomandra species*

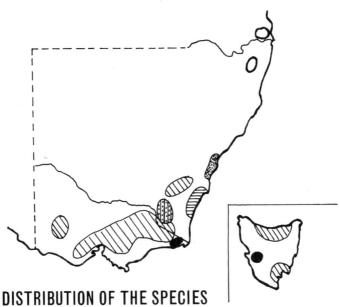

DISTRIBUTION OF THE SPECIES
CORREA LAWRENCIANA IN AUSTRALIA

var. lawrenciana
var. cordifolia
var. genoensis
var. glandulifera
var. macrocalyx
var. rosea

after J. Armstrong

INDEX OF BOTANICAL NAMES

249

INDEX OF COMMON NAMES